K2

Dee Molenaar's drawing of the 1953 accident.

Also by Jim Curran

Trango, the Nameless Tower
K2, Triumph and Tragedy
Suspended Sentences

K2

The Story of the Savage Mountain

Jim Curran

THE
MOUNTAINEERS

ISBN 0-89886-455-0

Copyright © 1995 by Jim Curran

First published in 1995 in Great Britain by
Hodder and Stoughton,
a division of Hodder Headline PLC
338 Euston Road, London NW1 3BH

Published in 1995 in the United States of America by
The Mountaineers, 1011 SW. Klickitat Way, Seattle WA 98134
Published simultaneously in Canada by Douglas & McIntyre Ltd.,
1615 Venables St., Vancouver B.C. V5L 2H1

Typeset by Phoenix Typesetting, Ilkley, West Yorkshire.

Printed and Bound in Great Britain by
Mackays of Chatham PLC.

To Charles Houston
whose two expeditions to K2
remain jewels in the crown
in the annals of Himalayan climbing

Contents

Illustrations

Every effort has been made to trace the photographers whose pictures are used in this book and these have been credited in the captions. Thanks are due to Chris Lister for access to his pictorial archives and to Paul Nunn for access to the archives of *Mountain* magazine. The author and publisher apologise for any errors or omissions of attribution which will be rectified in future editions.

Maps and topographical drawings

The maps on pages 10–11 and 13 were drawn by Rodney Paull. The topographical drawings are by the author.

The Karakoram

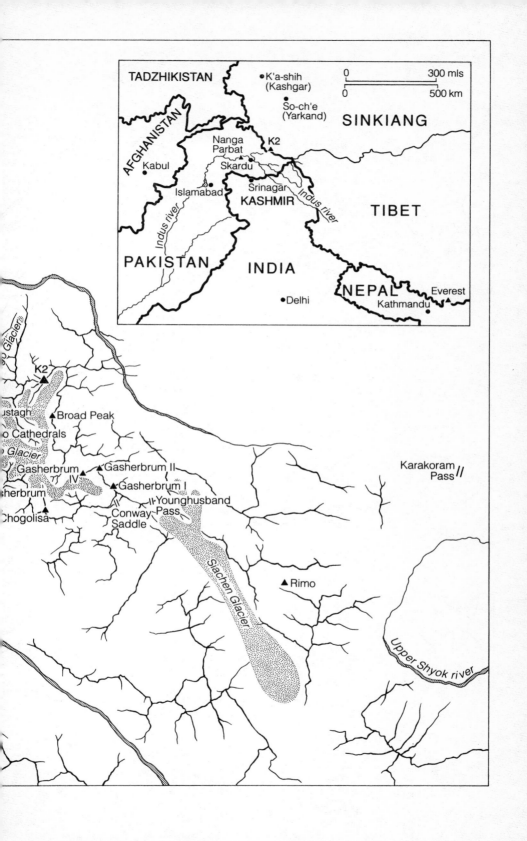

TADZHIKISTAN

K'a-shih
(Kashgar)

So-ch'e
(Yarkand)

SINKIANG

0   300 mls
0   500 km

AFGHANISTAN

Nanga
Parbat   K2

Skardu

Kabul

Islamabad

Srinagar

Indus river

KASHMIR

Indus river

TIBET

PAKISTAN

INDIA

NEPAL   Everest

Kathmandu

Delhi

K2

ustagh

Broad Peak

o Cathedrals

Glacier

Gasherbrum   Gasherbrum II

IV   Gasherbrum I

herbrum   Younghusband
Pass

Chogolisa   Conway
Saddle

Karakoram
Pass

Rimo

Siachen Glacier

Upper Shyok river

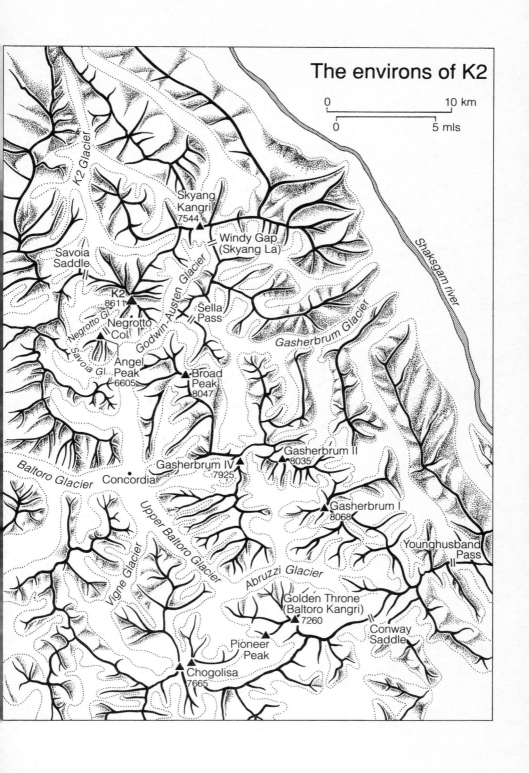

The environs of K2

0   10 km

0   5 mls

Shaksgam river

K2 Glacier

Skyang
Kangri
7544

Windy Gap
(Skyang La)

Savoia
Saddle

Godwin-Austen Glacier

Sella
Pass

Gasherbrum Glacier

K2
8611

Negrotto Gl.

Negrotto
Col

Savoia Gl.

Angel
Peak
6605

Broad
Peak
8047

Gasherbrum II
8035

Baltoro Glacier

Concordia

Gasherbrum IV
7925

Gasherbrum I
8068

Younghusband
Pass

Upper Baltoro Glacier

Abruzzi Glacier

Vigne Glacier

Golden Throne
(Baltoro Kangri)
7260

Conway
Saddle

Pioneer
Peak

Chogolisa
7665

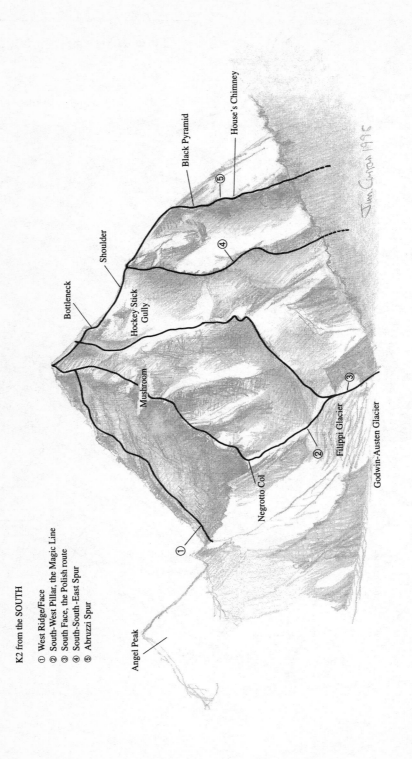

K2 from the SOUTH

① West Ridge/Face
② South-West Pillar, the Magic Line
③ South Face, the Polish route
④ South-South-East Spur
⑤ Abruzzi Spur

Angel Peak

Mushroom

Bottleneck

Shoulder

Hockey Stick Gully

Black Pyramid

House's Chimney

Negrotto Col

Filippi Glacier

Godwin-Austen Glacier

Jim Curran 1995

K2 from the WEST

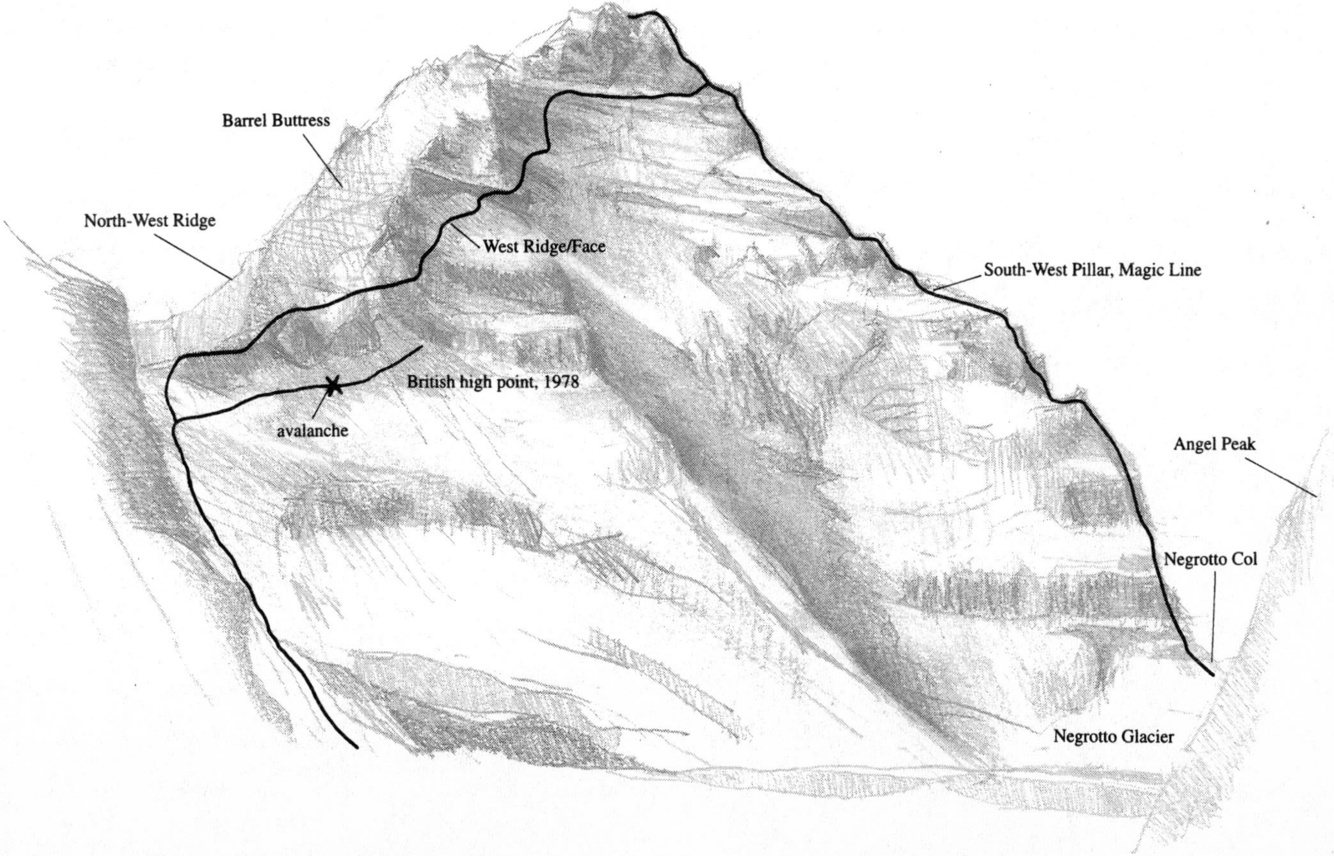

Angel Peak

South-West Pillar, Magic Line

Negrotto Col

Negrotto Glacier

West Ridge/Face

Barrel Buttress

British high point, 1978

avalanche

North-West Ridge

K2 from the NORTH-WEST

West Ridge

Barrel Buttress

North-West Ridge

American Towers

American route

Savoia Glacier

K2 from the NORTH

① North Ridge
② Japanese North-West Face route
③ Junction with North-West Ridge

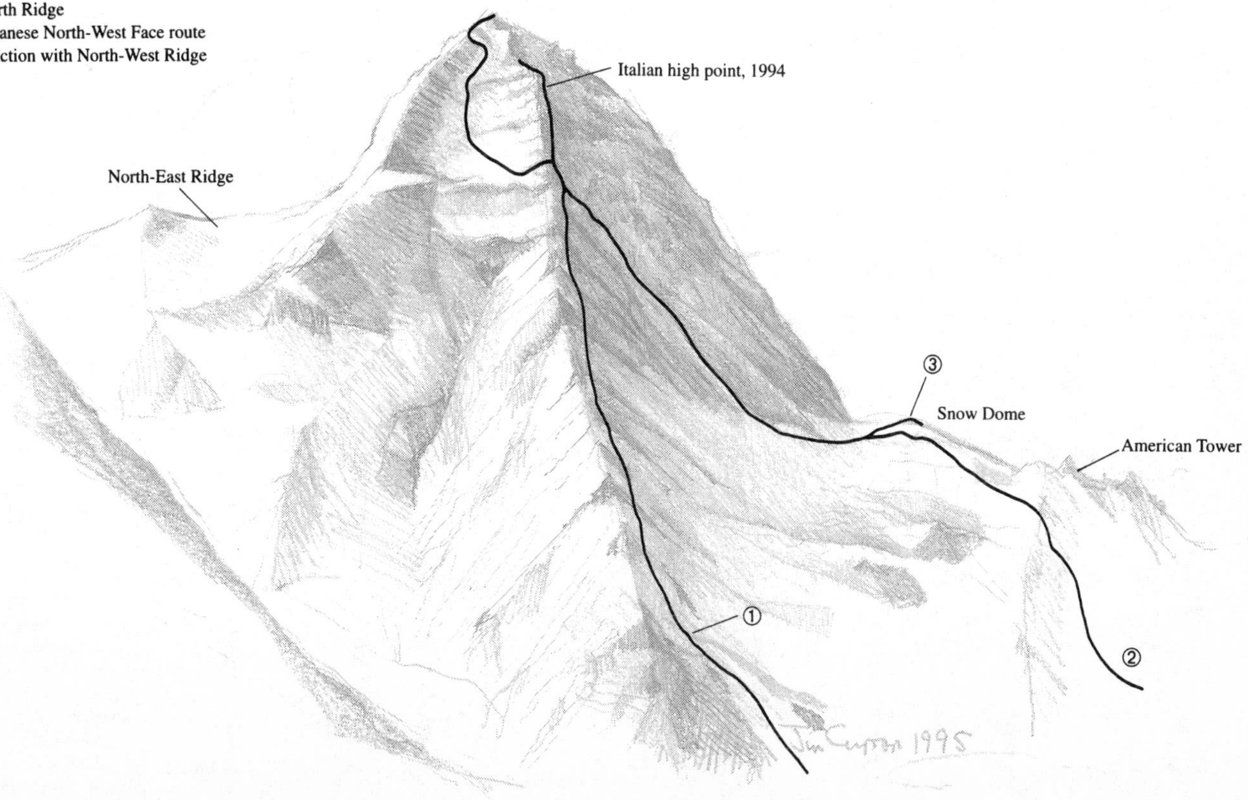

American Tower

Snow Dome

③

Italian high point, 1994

①

②

North-East Ridge

Jim Curran 1995

K2 from the NORTH-EAST

① North-East Ridge
② Knife-edge (foreshortened)
③ Polish attempt, 1976
④ American route to Abruzzi Spur
⑤ Abruzzi Spur
⑥ Bottleneck
⑦ Shoulder
⑧ East Face

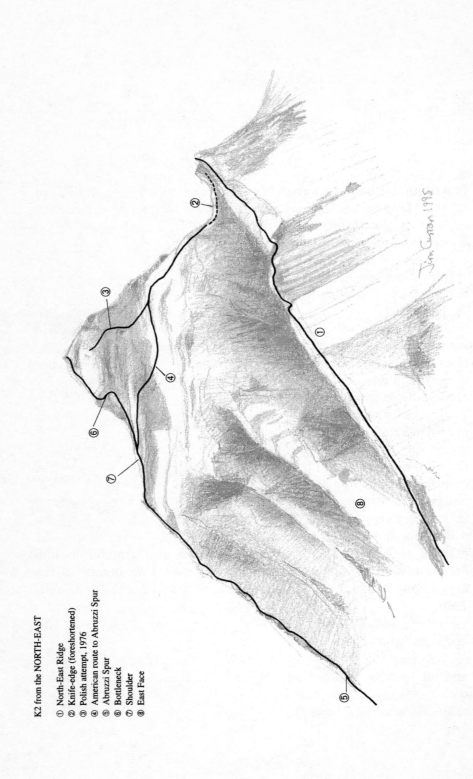

Author's Note

In writing this book I owe a debt to the knowledge and experience of others. Many people have taken the time and trouble to advise, criticise and correct. Without them the book would not exist. To everyone concerned I offer my thanks and, as is the author's prerogative, will embarrass the following by naming them.

In pride of place must come Charles Houston to whom this book is dedicated. Since our first meeting on a filming project at Nanga Parbat Base Camp in 1990, Charlie has cajoled and encouraged me to write the book. His letters have kept me going when I was flagging and his perceptive comments have not been confined to his own expeditions, but have ranged over the whole history of K2 and sometimes entertainingly to other totally unrelated topics. I hope he will enjoy reading the completed work and nervously await the next letter.

Jim Wickwire has generously provided a similar commentary on my interpretation of the more recent American adventures on the mountain; while Greg Child has read the whole manuscript in a far from finished form (an unenviable task) and made very positive contributions. Kurt Diemberger, doyen of the Karakoram and K2, has given me unique insights into the events of 1986, not only during their aftermath, but also on a recent visit to England. It has been a difficult and painful subject for us both, and I am immensely grateful to him for his co-operation. I am also grateful to him for permission to include in my own appendices an update of the expeditions statistics that first appeared in his own book, *The Endless Knot*.

Audrey Salkeld and Xavier Eguskitza have undertaken the updating and I am also grateful to Audrey for bringing her encyclopaedic knowledge of climbing history to bear on the script and for helping me assemble the historical photographs; while my editor, Maggie Body, has for the third time ensured that Curran chaos miraculously turned into Hodder order.

I must thank *Climbing* for supplying invaluable information and *High* for permission to reprint the article in Appendix IV. Lindsay Griffin from Mountain Info at *High* is rapidly becoming an indispensable source of knowledge. The Alpine Club and the Royal Geographical Society Libraries both gave me invaluable assistance also.

I particularly wish to acknowledge those authors whose contributions to the literature of K2 have been important to me while writing the book. I must thank Andy Kauffman for his meticulous research into the events of 1939, and Galen Rowell for the historical perspective of his classic *In the Throne Room of the Mountain Gods*, also Bob Bates, Willi Bauer, Chris Bonington, Greg Child (again), Ardito Desio, Alessandro Gogna, John Keay, Reinhold Messner, Bill Putnam, Rick Ridgeway and Doug Scott. Special thanks go to Hilary Boardman for allowing me access to Peter Boardman's diaries, to Jonathan Pratt for information on his ascent of the West Ridge, to Gill Round for German translation, Geoff Milburn for lending me invaluable source material, Ian Smith for making photographic prints and my daughter Gemma Curran for typing my increasingly illegible handwriting onto an ancient Amstrad; while in Sheffield Geoff Birtles, Paul Nunn and Joe Simpson have all coped admirably with the ups and downs of a neurotic author, providing much needed support and good humour. To all my most sincere thanks.

Jim Curran
Sheffield, February 1995

Introduction

On 15 August, 1986 I walked along the Godwin-Austen Glacier away from K2 Base Camp, traumatised by the harrowing events of that summer and grieving the loss of my friend, Al Rouse, who had died, stormbound, a few days before, alone in a tent on the great Shoulder of K2. It was a brilliant, crystal-clear day and I was mesmerised by the beauty of the mountain that had been the stage for so much drama and tragedy, not just over the last month, but since man had first dared to challenge the lonely eminence of the world's second highest peak.

Later that day I bade K2 a silent farewell from Concordia where three great glaciers meet, and turned away down the Baltoro Glacier, towards home. I realised then with depressing clarity that whatever happened to me in the future, my life would, for better or worse, never be quite the same again.

And so it has proved. As the years passed and the pain of loss became slowly accepted, I realised two things. First, that I was not alone, for over the years events on K2 have left an indelible mark on others. Great names like Charles Houston, Walter Bonatti, Fritz Wiessner, Peter Boardman, Joe Tasker, Doug Scott and Chris Bonington all returned, personally unsuccessful, from the mountain with overwhelming feelings of grief, disappointment and sometimes anger. This I could begin to understand and share even though they were all far more involved as climbers than I could ever hope to be. But the second more gradual realisation was that the story of K2 itself, with all its successes and failures, was one that needed telling in its entirety. True, many books, particularly those by Galen Rowell, Reinhold Messner and Kurt Diemberger, sketch in some of the history, but all of them are understandably centred on the author's own intense experiences during particular expeditions. What I find and continue to find a compulsive fascination is the way so many expeditions have had uncannily similar experiences.

In particular, events on the Abruzzi Spur in 1939, 1953, 1954 and 1986 have become subjects for intense discussion, speculation, disagreement and occasionally lifelong rancour. Circumstances, governed by variables like the weather, human frailty, ambition and misjudgement have produced epics of endurance, suffering and, all too often, stark tragedy. I have tried to set down these events, not to show the presence of any malevolent spirits or imaginary links but simply to see the similarities (and differences) between them.

Whereas the rich and complex history of Everest has been tackled countless times, most recently by Peter Gillman and quite the most comprehensively by Walt Unsworth in his exhaustive reference work, *Everest*, K2 presents a much simpler, yet starker story. First, because it is the second highest point on earth it has never, until recently, attracted the same media fascination nor the obsessive interest of fringe groups or individuals who might have used the mountain for their own ends. Most people attracted to climbing K2 have been at the forefront of mountain exploration of their day. Second, it is recognised as a far harder mountain to climb than Everest. Since its first ascent via the Abruzzi Spur in 1954 K2 has only recently topped the hundred ascents mark, whereas Everest has well over six hundred summiteers. True, more expeditions have been to Everest but when, after the disasters of 1986, *sixteen* successive expeditions failed to climb K2 (most by the Abruzzi) one gets some idea of the relative difficulty of the two peaks. Finally, K2 is one of the most remote of the 8000-metre peaks. Like Everest it borders two countries and has been the victim of political events with one or other side of the mountain out of bounds for long periods. But even now, when access to both mountains is unrestricted, and the mountain travel boom has made K2 a three-week trekkers' trip to Base Camp, it is by far and away the harder mountain to approach, a factor that has undoubtedly contributed to many stressful episodes over the decades. The Chinese side is worse than the Pakistan access, with a serious river crossing and difficult glacier approach that make simply reaching the foot of the mountain a major undertaking. Once there, K2 is truly the Mountain of Mountains.

I have already mentioned Walt Unsworth's great labour of love in which he undertook to describe and assess every expedition to Everest. My approach will be different. I am more interested in reliving the highlights and exploring the shadows of the stories than recording every fact. I make no apology for admitting that some of the expeditions interest me far more than others. Some failures are more compelling than many successes. A complete list of expeditions is provided with other statistics in the Appendices for those who enjoy such things.

Above all, this book exists as a tribute to all those who have set foot on K2, both living and dead. There are many heroes – but few, if any, villains. Just as art sometimes seems to imitate life, so expeditions to K2 have reflected some of the most profound experiences known to man. This then is the story of the Savage Mountain.

The first record of K2 from Montgomerie's angle book, 10 September 1856

1

What's in a Name?

On 10 September, 1856 Lieutenant T. G. Montgomerie of the Great Trigonometric Survey of India arrived at a surveying station situated high on Mount Haramukh, a mountain overlooking the Vale of Kashmir. Encumbered with a big theodolite, the ascent to just under 5000 metres took four days. His reward was a magnificent view to the north, where over 130 miles away the then almost totally unknown Karakoram range stood proud against a clear autumn sky. Montgomerie quickly took bearings on the two most prominent peaks and sketched their outlines in his angle book. He labelled them K (for Karakoram)1 and K2.

K1 with its distinctive double summit was later found to have a local name, Masherbrum, but Montgomerie could never have guessed that the random surveyor's mark he applied to that other distant triangle would not only be retained, but, over the years, become synonymous with difficulty, danger and impersonal savagery. Unwittingly, Montgomerie had named the 'Mountain of Mountains'.

For the modern mountaineer or trekker it is hard to imagine just how mysterious, remote and inaccessible the Himalayan and Karakoram ranges were 140 years ago. They remained so until well after the Second World War, when intercontinental air travel became commonplace. Then in the 1970s and 1980s an explosion of organised mountain travel quite suddenly demystified almost all the high places of the world. To appreciate the achievements of the early explorers one has to think in terms of journeys lasting months or even years, and distances on foot or horseback measured not just in tens but hundreds of miles. Journeys that today seem unremarkable were, in their time, at the sharp end of mountain experience.

By the mid-nineteenth century explorers, map makers and (inevitably) politicians had a rough and ready idea of the scale and extent of the range of mountains that formed the colossal barrier between the Indian sub-continent and the high plateau of Central Asia. Details were few and more attention was paid to exploring the old trade routes over major passes and down valleys than to the countless ice-clad peaks and immense glaciers that hindered access and had little strategic or practical value. Knowledge of what lay beyond the mountains, in Tibet and Chinese Turkestan, in those mysterious lands north of Nepal, the Hindu Kush and Karakoram ranges, was of far more value than the local names and heights of the great mountains that inconveniently raised their snow-clad summits and ridges across the northern limits of the British Raj.

These were the days of the Great Game, the constant jockeying by Russia and Great Britain for power and influence over Central Asia. The long-held expansionist policies of Russia in Turkestan and Afghanistan, grinding inexorably eastwards into China and south-wards towards India, made for a fascinating web of secrecy, intrigue, espionage and duplicity that reached its height in the late nineteenth century. On a practical level the threat of Russian invasion on the North-West Frontier and the possibility of incursions over any of the high mountain passes was real enough to make detailed knowledge of their location and topography a priority.

Nevertheless some of the major peaks, visible from the lowlands, were known, named and measured. Kangchenjunga, 28,208 feet (8598m), so easily seen from Darjeeling, was long thought to be the highest mountain in the world, as on occasion were both Gauri Sankar and Dhaulagiri. But in 1852 Peak XV, which later became known as Mount Everest, was declared at 29,002 feet (8829m) the highest mountain in the world, and in 1858 the height of K2 was computed to be 28,287 feet (8621m), just higher than Kangchenjunga. Despite several minor adjustments and some recent satellite surveys, those original heights were astonishingly accurate[1] and the relationship between the world's first, second and third highest mountains has never changed, though, as will be seen later, it has on occasion been challenged.

Though Everest was known to be the highest, access to it through either Tibet or Nepal was politically impossible, and would remain so until after the First World War. Despite Kangchenjunga's obvious

---

[1] The generally accepted current heights are Everest: 8848m; K2: 8611m; and Kangchenjunga: 8598m.

visible presence it was not until about the end of the nineteenth century that much interest was taken in it or its surroundings. By that time the first explorations of the Karakoram were well under way.

The name Karakoram is given to the great range of mountains that runs for some four hundred kilometres north-west of the Himalaya and north of the River Indus which flows between the two ranges from its source in Tibet down to the Arabian Sea. Geographically and geologically the Karakoram is not strictly part of the Himalaya though it is sometimes assumed to be by mountaineers and trekkers. The term 'Karakoram Himalaya', which might not be geographically correct, yet does make some sense, has been used from very early days. The word Karakoram (or Karakorum) is derived from the Altaic *kara* and *korum*, and seems to mean either black pass or black earth, in either case a strange way of identifying some of the most spectacular mountain scenes in the world. Originally the word may have been used to describe the pass on the ancient trade route connecting India with Central Asia, but the theory is not borne out by the arid scenery which, as in much of the countryside both north and south of the range, is predominantly an all-pervading ochre. There is also a possibility that the name comes by association from Karakorum, which was the ancient centre of Mongolia under Ghengis Khan, the name of the city being gradually transferred to an important pass along a main route leading to it. But in this barren and barely colonised world no derivation rings entirely true.

Within the Karakoram are four of the world's fourteen 8000-metre peaks, over thirty of 7000 metres and literally hundreds of spectacular rock and ice mountains at or above 6000 metres. The range also contains the world's four longest glaciers outside the polar regions – the Siachen (72km), the Hispar (61km), the Biafo (59km) and the Baltoro (57km). These glaciers feed huge volumes of meltwater into the surrounding deserts north of the Himalaya, and, protected from the monsoon, rainfall in the valleys is very low, though the volume of snow that eventually forms the huge glaciers would seem to indicate a higher rainfall than the Himalaya. This is somewhat misleading. The range is significantly further north and thus colder than the Himalaya. Also the average width of the Himalaya is a mere eighty kilometres, whereas the Karakoram is 190 kilometres, so a much greater total volume of precipitation is trapped in the form of snow and ice.

The region is sparsely populated. North of the Karakoram, in what is now Sinkiang (or Xingiang) Province of China, the land is so dry and barren that only a few nomads travel anywhere near the mountains, which consequently have remained almost completely unexplored and unnamed until comparatively recently. On the southern (Pakistan) slopes the Balti and Hunza tribesmen inhabit every valley and side valley that can support a meagre livelihood. Ingenious irrigation channels divert glacier meltwater for miles around rocky hillsides to cultivate lush green oases of barley, poplar and apricot groves.

The Baltis speak an ancient Tibetan dialect and there are still a few remnants of Buddhist culture in what has become known as Baltistan or Little Tibet. One obvious example is a huge carved Buddha on a rock near Skardu. The Baltis themselves were converted to Islam at the turn of the fourteenth and fifteenth centuries. Originally Baltistan must have been under the rule of Tibet when trade routes across the Mustagh and Karakoram Passes were open, though the Balti people are fundamentally of Indo-European origin. Over the centuries cross strains have produced a bewildering variety of Asian, Mongol and even Negroid features. Long since cut off from their Buddhist roots, economic, social and religious, the Baltis still retain echoes of Tibet in things like their salted tea, the hairstyles of their women, items of jewellery and the way of carrying babies on the shoulder. The Balti language is not a written one and details of Balti history are scanty. What is certain is that until the middle of the twentieth century, with the advent of the aeroplane, the helicopter and modern roads (more or less arriving in that order), the Baltis were effectively isolated from almost all outside culture: far more than the Sherpas in Nepal, whose traditions of trading and travel have been maintained to the present day. A graphic comparison is seen within the bazaars of Skardu and Kathmandu. In the latter it is possible to equip an Everest expedition fully from scratch. In 1986 on my last visit to Skardu, it was difficult to buy a single secondhand sleeping-bag for our Base Camp cook.

It is easy to dismiss Balti culture as simply backward or primitive; it is certainly static and self-contained. Thus it has become and remains a source of much perplexity, wonder and irritation to the Western mind. The culture clash of East and West is heightened in Baltistan, and has made for increased stress and pressure affecting expeditions to the area. Some indeed have never even reached their objective through failing to adjust to the realities of Balti existence.

Before the Great Trigonometric Survey of India laboriously and methodically mapped its way north through India, few people, Balti or European, had any knowledge of the highest Karakoram peaks. Some had names, but many more were apparently of little significance to the local population. The nomenclature of the peaks surrounding the Baltoro Glacier for example is fairly typical of much of the Karakoram, with names that are sometimes obvious, sometimes obscure, occasionally controversial, and often non-existent. At the snout of the great glacier on the north flanks are the spectacular Trango Towers, focus of much high-standard rock-climbing since the mid 1970s. Trango is probably derived from *tramga*, or sheep pen, and there are certainly remnants of enclosures on the lateral moraines of the glacier that drains the side valley under the Towers. Further up are the Baltoro Cathedrals, great triangular wedges with obvious similarities to Gothic architecture and self-evidently named by Western expeditions. On the south side of the Baltoro is Masherbrum, a name that could be derived from an apparent resemblance of its twin summits to a muzzle loading gun or *mashadar* (*brum* means mountain). But Masherbrum is also visible from the south from the village of Kaphalu where people say that *masha* means queen or lady, which is perhaps more plausible. Similarly, at the head of the Baltoro rises Gasherbrum IV. Gasherbrum could mean 'Shining Wall' or, more likely, it is derived from *rgasha* – beautiful. Both meanings are certainly true descriptions of the imposing Gasherbrum IV, but now no less than five mountains are called Gasherbrum, which seems rather unimaginative, not to mention confusing.

From the great confluence of glaciers at the head of the Baltoro, the two great giants of the Karakoram come into view. There is little evidence that Broad Peak or K2 itself have local names. In the case of K2 this gave rise to a rumbling controversy which has never really been completely resolved.

Despite fashionable sniping at the imperialistic British for insensitively imposing European names on anything and everything in their path, the GTS was actually painstaking in seeking out local names. The big exception to this was Mount Everest, named in honour of the Surveyor General of India, from 1833–43, Sir George Everest. There is good evidence to suppose that the Tibetan name 'Chomolungma' was known but ignored in order to pay tribute to the man who was most responsible for the Survey. Everest himself was not keen on the precedent and it was not until the turn of the century that the name was generally accepted. Today, with increased interest in Buddhism and respect for the plight of Tibet, Chomolungma is often rather self-consciously used, but it is inconceivable that the name Everest will ever disappear from general use.

But K2, the surveyor's symbol, is an altogether different case. Montgomerie himself wrote, 'Every endeavour will be made to find a local name if it has one.' But the mountain's remoteness made this unlikely. It is not visible from Askole, the last village before the desolation of the Baltoro, and only fleetingly glimpsed from Paiju campsite at the snout of the glacier. From there, and from one of two other vantage points on the Baltoro, it has no great significance. Few Baltis would have gone far enough for the first real view of the mountain and though 'Chogori' has sometimes been put forward as its original name, there is little or no reason to justify this. Chogori simply means 'Great Mountain' and is likely to have been the sort of bemused answer given to the question 'What's that called?' Even the name K2 is now quite often applied to other mountains and I remember being baffled after our successful ascent of the Trango Tower in 1976 when asked by a porter in Askole if we had climbed our *kaitu*. From the north it must be open to question whether K2 had ever registered as a peak worthy of a name, for the nearest habitation is much further away than Askole. Other local names for K2 have been offered – Dapsang, Lamba Pahar, Akhbar, Shinmarg, Chiring, Babur, Laufafahad – their very number contributing to the impression that as the mountain lacks a common name it would be quite arbitrary to settle for one rather than another. Better perhaps the impersonal surveyor's notation.

There were however some attempts to follow the Everest precedent and commemorate a famous personage, Mount Albert, Mount Waugh, Montgomerie and Godwin-Austen all being mooted at various times. None, mercifully, was taken seriously except the name of Godwin-Austen whose exploration of the Karakoram is the subject of the next chapter. But the name, which was rejected by the Royal Geographical Society, found its way on to some maps and literature which persisted until comparatively recently, and survives in the name of the glacier below the mountain's South-East Face.

It was an Italian expedition that first succeeded in climbing the mountain in 1954 and in 1959 another Italian, Fosco Maraini, in his authoritative book *Karakoram – the ascent of Gasherbrum IV* makes the case most eloquently for keeping the name K2 and must have the last word on the subject:

. . . K2 may owe its origin to chance, but it is a name in itself, and one of striking originality. Sybilline, magical, with a slight touch of fantasy. A short name but one that is pure and peremptory, so charged with evocation that it threatens to break through its bleak syllabic bonds. And at the same time a name instinct with mystery and suggestion: a name that scraps race, religion, history and past. No country claims it, no latitudes and longitudes and geography, no dictionary words. No, just the bare bones of a name, all rock and ice and storm and abyss. It makes no attempt to sound human. It is atoms and stars. It has the nakedness of the world before the first man – or of the cindered planet after the last.

2

The First Intruders

Though Montgomerie had sighted K2 in 1856 and was awarded the Gold Medal of the Royal Geographical Society in 1865 for his work on the GTS, he was never to get any nearer the elusive giant. But the Karakoram range was not entirely unknown or unvisited by Europeans. Twenty years earlier Baltistan had been visited by the British explorer Godfrey Thomas Vigne. Because of his surname it is often assumed that Vigne was French. Vigne was actually the archetypal nineteenth-century British gentleman, Harrow-educated, a good amateur sportsman (he played cricket for the MCC), a keen shot and a talented artist. He practised law until 1830, then abruptly gave it up for a life of exploration and adventure. After a visit to Persia in 1833 he carried on to India and, on a whim, decided to 'run up at once to the cool air of the Himalaya'. It was a whim that lasted five years, during which time Vigne travelled extensively in Baltistan, Kashmir and Ladakh, making friends (and a few enemies) wherever he went. He was a compulsive yet casual wanderer. No comprehensive record of his extensive travels exists and what does is as confusing as his travels often were. It is certain that for some time he was based in Skardu having befriended Ahmed Shah, the Raja of Baltistan. From here Vigne made at least four journeys into the Karakoram, including a journey to the snout of the Chogo Lungma Glacier at the head of the Basho Valley and an unsuccessful attempt to reach the New Mustagh Pass. His pioneering travels were rewarded by having a glacier named after him, the Vigne Glacier, which flows from the north-west flanks of Chogolisa into the Upper Baltoro Glacier.

Other early visitors to the Karakoram were the German brothers Hermann and Robert Schlagintweit who were the first Europeans to cross the whole breadth of mountains between India and Turkestan, and discovered that the Karakoram and Kun Lun mountains to the north were quite distinct ranges. With Germanic thoroughness they recorded every fact, however trivial, of their journeys and unfortunately succeeded so well in this task that their considerable achievements are overshadowed by the tedium of their exhaustive, pedantic records.

Neither Hermann nor Robert Schlagintweit penetrated the heart of the Karakoram, but in 1856, the year Montgomerie sighted K2, a third brother, Adolph, did reach the New Mustagh Pass at the head of the Chiring Glacier which connects with the Panmah Glacier. Adolph repeated his brothers' journey, reaching Yarkand and even further north to Kashgar where he became involved in a civil uprising and was murdered. The three German brothers were given scant recognition by the British and the New Mustagh Pass remained a mysterious riddle, though it did not take long for an attempt to solve it. The following year (the year of the Indian Mutiny) Lieutenant Henry Haversham Godwin-Austen joined the Kashmir Survey to serve under Montgomerie. In 1861 he was sent to Baltistan to explore the New Mustagh Pass, the Baltoro Glacier and to find out exactly where K2 was in relation to the Karakoram watershed and Chinese Turkestan.

Godwin-Austen seemed destined for success. Son of a geologist and grandson of a general, he was small, tough, determined, and an extremely talented draughtsman. Sandhurst-educated and taught topographical drawing 'of the old French school', he had a sound understanding of the geological structure underlying the appearance of the spectacular mountains of the Karakoram. He and Montgomerie did not hit it off. Godwin-Austen suspected his superior was claiming too much credit for others' efforts and rather unfairly disparaged his lack of hard-won experience in the field. Montgomerie was impressed by Godwin-Austen's artistic flair and was perhaps jealous of a talent greater than his own. Sending him to explore the innermost secrets of the remote Karakoram (perhaps to keep him out of harm's way, for he was not an easy man to work with) was an inspired choice, for Godwin-Austen's enthusiasm, energy and endurance were to be given a stern test by the task in front of him.

He was not a mountaineer in the technical sense, but thought nothing of racing up steep hillsides for hundreds of metres to check angles, map, and make sketches. His first objective was to find the New Mustagh Pass on the disused trade route north to Yarkand on the edge of the great Taklamakan Desert. Privately, Godwin-Austen hoped to cross the pass and explore the valleys and glaciers beyond the frontier. The route from the last village, initially, follows the same path as one follows to the Baltoro: across the snout of the Biafo Glacier, which leads west towards the Latok and Ogre peaks, and then up the west banks of the Dumordo river to the Panmah Glacier. Godwin-Austen and his team of some sixty porters, guides and assistants walked up and on to the glacier and struggled up the moraines for two days before camping in poor visibility. After a freezing night on the glacier he pressed on with just eight porters in an attempt to reach the pass. As the glacier became heavily crevassed and snow covered they roped themselves together looking 'like a long chain of criminals'. They turned back a mile from the col and beat an epic retreat in a blizzard. Rather curiously, as he had failed to reach it, Godwin-Austen remained convinced that the pass was a feasible route for pack animals! Retracing their steps the party resumed their progress up the Braldu valley towards the snout of the Baltoro Glacier. No Europeans had ever set foot on it and the route to the Old Mustagh Pass, which follows the Baltoro for a couple of days, was all but forgotten, so that few, if any, porters would know where, or how far, they were going. It seemed that glacial movement had, over the years, caused both passes to fall into disuse.

Godwin-Austen and his men were about to step into one of the great sanctuaries of high mountains in the world. It is hard to imagine how exciting and frightening this must have been. They were right out on a limb: about three hundred miles of harsh walking had brought them this far, they were physically and spiritually a long way from home and completely without support if anything went wrong. Even today with radio communication and the possibility of helicopter rescue, the first impressions of the Baltoro are quite overwhelming. A vast sea of ice-covered rubble stretches endlessly away and though the glacier is two miles wide, one feels dwarfed by the monumental spires and buttresses of orange granite that tower above the north side like the nave of some vast cathedral. Awe at the view is soon tempered by the tedium of endlessly flogging up and down and around the huge waves and bulges of gravel-covered ice, or grinding along the unstable lateral moraines.

Godwin-Austen pushed up the glacier for about fifteen miles, until he was level with Masherbrum to the south and the Mustagh Glacier to the north leading to the Old Mustagh Pass. He could see the stunning West Face of Gasherbrum IV still sixteen miles away, but no obvious end to the glacier, and no sight of K2. The position of that peak remained elusive. He decided that his party had come far enough. Every day forward meant their dwindling supplies would be stretched for the return. Askole was now over thirty miles away and the nearest source of any replenishment. But before he started the long journey back, Godwin-Austen did what he had so often done before.

He started ascending the first long stony hillside, itself just an outlying subsidiary foothill of Masherbrum, in the forlorn hope of seeing over the tangle of peaks and spurs of the northern flanks of the Baltoro. After six hundred metres he was rewarded by a glimpse of a higher point beyond the intervening ridges. 'After another sharp push up to a point from which it was impossible to mount further, there no longer remained a doubt about it. There, with not a particle of cloud to hide it, was the great peak K2.'

What Godwin-Austen was actually looking at was the upper part of the West Ridge, the West Face, the South-West Ridge and the South-East Ridge of K2. From this angle, it is predominantly a rock peak with characteristic bands of snow and ice cutting across the top of the West Face. It must have seemed from his vantage point some sixteen miles away, utterly impregnable. What was almost certain was that K2 was actually on the Karakoram watershed and that the glaciers from the southern base did flow directly to the Baltoro. It was therefore still in India, and part of the British Empire. Though the frontier was unresolved in detail, there was no doubt that K2 either defined it or was entirely within Indian territory. He could return satisfied.

Godwin-Austen spent two more years working in eastern Ladakh before being sent to the other end of the Himalaya to survey the country around Darjeeling. He became ill with fever and had to retire early. On his return to England he recovered and spent the rest of his life working on many branches of the natural sciences as well as combining his interest in painting and geology. He was elected to the Royal Society and awarded the Founders Medal of the Royal Geographical Society. He died aged eighty-nine in 1924. Although the RGS never recognised the name Mount Godwin-Austen, the glacier (which he never saw) that runs from the foot of K2 to the Baltoro still bears his name. Few would quibble with that.

After Godwin-Austen's foray up the Baltoro in 1861, twenty-six years were to pass before the area was visited again by a European.

Francis Edward Younghusband was born on 31 May, 1863. Educated at Clifton College and Sandhurst he joined the King's Dragoon Guards at Meerut in 1882. It was a smart regiment and Younghusband lacked the money to keep up the endless social round of officers' mess and polo field. Attracted to the cavalry by his independent, pushing character, he found the heat and boredom of the Indian plains a disappointment.

After two years he was given the chance to break loose. He was sent to reconnoitre the Kohat frontier near Peshawar, then perceived as a possible place for the threatened Russian invasion. Younghusband quickly became a pawn in the Great Game and the King's Dragoon Guards saw little more of him.

In 1886 and still only twenty-three years old, Younghusband was given six months' leave to go to Manchuria and traverse much of the vulnerable Chinese frontier threatened by the Russian army. From Peking he then made a quite incredible journey in 1887. Managing to ignore or avoid his recall to India by sea, he set out to cross the Gobi Desert through Inner Mongolia to Sinkiang, Kashgar and Yarkand, travelling alone, mostly on horseback and by night. This must have been an epic adventure, yet it pales into insignificance compared with the last leg of his journey 'home' to India.

When Younghusband arrived in Yarkand he was handed a letter from a Colonel Mark Bell, VC, Head of the Intelligence Department in India. Bell had met Younghusband in Peking and also travelled across China, though not by such an adventurous journey. Bell suggested that Younghusband crown his travels by exploring the Shaksgam valley and Mustagh Pass instead of the 'normal' crossing of the Karakoram Pass to the east of the high mountains. Younghusband knew it had not been crossed for many years but

> I was thrilled with the prospect of such an exploration. I had no mountaineering experience. I had no mountaineering appliances. I had not even enough money, and the only pair of boots I had left was a nailless pair of 'town' boots bought in a store in Peking. Still, I never doubted that I would get through somehow or other – 'muddle through' as we like to call it in England.

He was lucky to find a guide, Wali, who originally came from Askole and had actually crossed the pass twenty-five years before. Wali

initially distrusted Younghusband, saying that he would not show
him the way because he knew the English used maps and ignored
the advice of guides. Younghusband riposted that as there was no
map for him to use he would just have to trust him, and the two
quickly established a rapport.

Together with four Balti porters, several Ladakhis and thirteen
ponies, the little caravan left Yarkand, crossed the Kun Lun mountains and followed the Yarkand river into the Aghil range where
Wali promptly admitted he had forgotten the way. Younghusband
himself reconnoitred a route through a maze of minor gorges and
boulder-filled stream beds that the ponies could only just manage. At
last they emerged on to open ground. Ahead was the first subsidiary
pass to be crossed the following day.

> Now! – now at last – I was to see all that I had dreamed of . . .
> Now I was on the verge of the very inmost core of the Himalaya
> . . . The strain of the great adventure was sensibly tightening on
> me. And as it came I braced myself to meet it. And real life
> began to tingle through my veins.

The next day Wali and Younghusband marched ahead of the caravan.
Wali did not exude confidence: 'He knew we should have to turn
sharply either to the right or to the left, but which it was he couldn't
say for certain.' But soon a wide valley opened on the left which he
immediately recognised. It was easy and Younghusband, bursting
with enthusiasm and impatience, struck out for the pass, finding that
it receded as he advanced. At last he breasted the last rise.

> Beyond was the fulfilment of every dream . . . What I had so ar-
> dently longed to see was now spread out before me. Where I had
> reached, no white man had ever reached before. And there before
> me were peaks of 26,000 feet, and in one case 28,000 in height
> rising above a valley bottom only 12,000 feet above sea level . . .

They descended the pass into the 'Oprang' or Shaksgam valley as it
later became known and found a comfortable bivouac in what proved
to be the last traces of willow jungle with plenty of firewood before
the great struggle for the Mustagh Pass itself. The next day started
with a surprise.

*   *   *

Ever since I had begun to think about the Himalaya I had wanted to see at quite close quarters some stupendous snowy peak. Now, all of a sudden, as we rounded a corner, I saw, up a side valley on the left, a real monarch which threw utterly in the shade my uncle's picture of 'A Peak in the Kuen-Lun'. It towered thousands of feet above me and quite close by; and it was one of those sights which make you literally gasp as you suddenly see them . . . I kept saying to myself, 'How simply splendid! How splendid!'

It was of course the north side of K2 itself, no more than twelve miles away. The view from the north is possibly the most impressive of all with the arrow-like North Ridge seen head on, and the North-East and North-West Ridges forming a near perfect cone. It was a sight that was to intrigue mountaineers for decades to come, for it was not until 1982 that an attempt would be made to climb it.

Younghusband was soon to be introduced to both the fascinations and tribulations of glacier travel as this was the first time he had ever set foot on one, and for three days they advanced up the Sarpo Laggo Glacier towards their goal. Then, a setback; two porters reconnoitred the way over the New Mustagh Pass and down to the Panmah Glacier. They reported that it was quite impractical for ponies, possibly even for men. Wali said the only thing to do was to try the Old Mustagh Pass leading down to the Baltoro Glacier. Full of foreboding, yet still totally convinced it would somehow all come good in the end, Younghusband and his team slept on the glacier with the night cold gripping tighter all around. Early next morning they set off for the pass itself, leaving behind the ponies and some of the men. They carried just enough food to see them to Askole, hopefully only three or four days' march. The idea was to send provisions back over the pass for the rearguard who would then retreat with the ponies and go right round by the distant Karakoram Pass to Leh. It was a fragile plan, and failure did not bear thinking about for either party.

It took six hours to reach the top. The climb was 'only severe on account of the difficulty of breathing . . . and keen as I was to see the top of the pass there was no possibility of pushing on as I had at the Aghil Pass; I could only drag wearily along with the rest.'

At midday they reached the 5420-metre col and found to their horror that the far side was an almost sheer drop. Younghusband was appalled: 'But I did not say so. For I wanted to know what the men thought of it . . . this might be something not much out of the ordinary which no true mountaineer would think a great deal of . . .' Wali, aware now that his reputation was on the line, proved resolute. His honour was at stake and, after all, success was within sight.

Younghusband had read that mountaineers roped themselves together, and using spare ropes from the ponies and even turbans and waistbands tied together, they improvised one. Using a pick axe Wali cut steps in the steep ice wall below them. Younghusband soon realised that without a belay the security of the 'rope' was largely illusory. His boots were worn smooth and he tied handkerchiefs around them in an attempt to create more friction. Nervously they started down. Halfway a Balti slipped and was held. Wali shouted and swore at him which somehow made him pull himself together and gave everyone some confidence. Descending from one rock island to another they gradually lost height and by sunset the slope eased off and they could walk together without cutting steps. The gamble had paid off. They had indeed 'muddled through'.

Now in India, Younghusband had achieved his objective but his journey was far from over. He descended to the Baltoro Glacier, waxing eloquent over the terrific granite architecture of the Trango Towers and the Baltoro Cathedrals, and three days later arrived in Askole where he was given a mixed reception. Food, in the shape of a greasy mutton curry, was welcome but the inhabitants were appalled that Wali should have betrayed the secrets of the Mustagh Pass to an Englishman. If he could cross, so could others. Wali dared not stay in his own village and carried on with Younghusband to Kashmir.

One would have thought that by now Younghusband might have had enough, but he returned to the Panmah Glacier and explored the New Mustagh Pass, finding the approach from the south as impractical as from the north. With relief at the end of his exploratory duties he returned and made his way down to Srinagar, still another couple of hundred miles away. On his arrival he realised that he was bearded, filthy and dressed in 'native' clothes, so he quickly purchased a European jacket, waistcoat and knickerbockers and spent two hours washing and shaving before meeting Captain Ramsey, the political agent in Srinagar: 'It was very trying therefore that Ramsey immediately after shaking hands said, "Wouldn't you like to have a wash?"'

Younghusband returned to Yarkand in 1889 with six Gurkhas to explore the Saltoro and Shimshal Passes. During his travels he met what was in effect his 'opponent' in the Great Game, Captain B. Grombczewski, an agent of the Tsar who was in the area with a small group of Cossack soldiers. Grombczewski was in fact a Pole, and the first in a line of those hard and intrepid explorers which has continued to the present day. It was quite clear that he was engaged in the same work as Younghusband. He too visited the Shaksgam valley and saw K2 from the north, as well as exploring the mountains around Kashgar. He told Younghusband that before he had left St Petersburg he had marked down the areas of the frontier region unknown to Europeans and now he had met an Englishman who already knew the whole ground! Grombczewski also informed him, rather chillingly, that if the English didn't believe the Russians would actually invade India, the officers of the Russian army thought of nothing else. Nevertheless they parted on friendly terms – one of the few occasions when Russians and English actually met on the frontiers of India.

Younghusband's career was to take him all over the Himalaya – notably in 1903 when he led the ill-advised mission to Lhasa – and until his death in 1942 aged seventy-eight he was a keen follower of Himalayan climbing, and instrumental in setting up the early Everest expeditions. He was to become decidedly eccentric, a religious and sexual freethinker whose undoubted sincerity caused him to support many curious societies and causes, as the physical adventures of his youth gave way to mental explorations that were even more bizarre. Though he was not really a mountaineer, Younghusband's epic journey in 1887 was conducted in the spirit of true exploratory adventure and his crossing of the Mustagh Pass with Wali was as risky as many Alpine climbs of the day.

3

Conway – Connoisseur or Con Man?

Most climbing historians credit Sir Martin Conway with the first recognisable mountaineering expedition to the Karakoram in 1892. Certainly it is generally assumed that he was the first European to reach the head of the Baltoro Glacier and to get a clear view of K2. The history books may or may not be correct in the first assumption, but are certainly wrong in the second. Two years earlier a little-known Italian had travelled to the foot of K2 and might possibly have been the first person to set foot on the mountain. Roberto Lerco was born in Gressoney in the Aosta valley but lived in Vienna. In 1887 Lerco had made two notable ascents in the Caucasus: the second ascent of Kasbek and the third of Elbruz, the highest peak in Europe. Like Vigne before him, Lerco was motivated by adventure pure and simple. He had no interest in publicising his activities and very little is known of them. It is certain however that he travelled around the valleys at the foot of Nanga Parbat and that he ventured up the Baltoro to the foot of K2. This is confirmed by remarks he made on his return which could only have resulted from firsthand knowledge. A particularly intriguing comment concerns the South-East Spur of K2 and the observation that an obstacle on it would stop an ascent. Could this be a reference to House's Chimney? This is the technical crux of the ridge, a steep crack through a buttress at 6600 metres that was not climbed until 1938. How could Lerco have spotted this? From the moraines on the Godwin-Austen Glacier, the site of present-day Base Camps, the South-East Spur of K2 is seen in its lower half as a broken rocky spine. True, the buttress of House's Chimney is visible as a break or step in the ridge – but no inference can be made from such a distance as to its difficulty. From the foot of the spur – the site of present-day Advance Base Camps – a grossly foreshortened view of myriad disconnected outcrops separated by snow slopes at around forty-five degrees gives little idea of how easy or difficult any one section might be. House's Chimney *is* visible but looks as though it could be avoided on its eastern flank. It is hard to see how Lerco could have known that the Chimney (if indeed it was this to which he was referring) would prove to be so hard to climb without actually getting a lot closer to it, perhaps even to its base. Could this have happened in 1890? It is a wonderful thought that an unknown climber could ascend the bottom 1000 metres of the Abruzzi Spur with no fuss or publicity and leave no evidence of his passing. I have to confess that I rather hope he did. Whatever the truth, the activities of this self-effacing man around the foot of K2 present an intriguing little mystery that will probably never be solved.

The next visitors to the Baltoro marked the dawn of the 'expedition' era. William Martin Conway was an art historian and a professor at Liverpool University. A member of the Alpine Club and later its president, Conway epitomised the romantic Victorian explorer-mountaineer. A genuine lover of mountains and of mountain travel, Conway stood for what was already coming to be seen as the traditional wing of the Alpine Club, and one that was at odds with a newer breed of climbers like Alfred Mummery and Oscar Eckenstein who were more interested in seeking out difficulty for its own sake.

In 1892 Conway set out on his most ambitious journey, to explore the Hispar, Biafo and Baltoro Glaciers. He was accompanied by Matthias Zurbriggen, one of the great Alpine guides, A. D. McCormick, an artist, J. H. Roudebush, four Gurkhas and Oscar Eckenstein. Conway had considered inviting Mummery but, though he personally liked him, their climbing objectives and motivation were very different. Mummery later told Conway that if he had accompanied him to the Karakoram, Conway would not have achieved half as much. All the more curious then to invite Eckenstein. Born in London in 1859 of a German father and English mother, Eckenstein studied chemistry, first at London University, then in his father's home town of Bonn. His scientific mind sought practical solutions to mechanical problems and he was the first person to understand that balance rather than brute strength was the key to rock climbing. In Britain he devised the art of bouldering – there is still an Eckenstein boulder below the Pen y Pass Youth Hostel in North Wales. He also invented what was the prototype modern crampon and designed a short ice-axe that could be used with one hand on steep ground. His ideas were far-reaching but his newfangled crampons and ice-axe found little immediate acceptance. Eckenstein was a blunt abrasive man with little respect for the Alpine Club. Conway, with his long Alpenstock and love of mountain travel must have stood for everything that Eckenstein resented. Unsurprisingly, their friendship did not blossom in the harsh environment they were about to visit.

Conway produced a large volume, *Climbing and Exploring in the Karakoram Himalaya*, that is often cited as the earliest example of the modern expedition book. (Whether that is a derogatory comment or not depends on your view of expedition books.) It is an exhaustive work describing, virtually day by day, the minutiae of what was after all a monumental undertaking. Some of the writing is laboured and has not stood the test of time, but for the persevering reader there is much to enjoy and occasionally even laugh at, for Conway was a surprisingly good observer of daily life. The book was also a remarkable pictorial record. In an age when photography was rapidly replacing engraving A. D. McCormick made a defiant last stand for the artist in the field. Three hundred black and white illustrations adorn the book, and they brilliantly portray the time-less grandeur of the mountain landscape and the almost unchanged way of Balti life. They manage to be informative, evocative and imaginative at the same time.

Conway's party set out from England in February 1892 and would not return until December. They travelled on the steamship *Ocampo* to Karachi, by train to Abbottabad, then by *ekka*, a horse-drawn two-wheeled carriage, to Srinagar in the Vale of Kashmir, the starting point for all subsequent Karakoram expeditions in the pre-Partition days before the creation of Pakistan in 1947. By now their number had risen to seven, for in Abbottabad they were joined by one Lieutenant C. G. Bruce of the Fifth Gurkha Rifles. This was the Hon. Charles Granville Bruce – later leader of two early British Everest expeditions – a larger-than-life character much loved by his men. 'Bruiser' Bruce, bursting with energy and enthusiasm, was described by Conway as 'a steam engine plus goods train'.

The party left Srinagar on 13 April, at first by boat on the Dal Lake, singing 'Ta-ra-ra-boom-de-ay and I know not what other ribald ditties'; Parbir Thapa, one of the Gurkhas, did rather better with his rendition of 'Two Lovely Black Eyes'. One can almost sense the relief of an expedition actually getting under way at last.

They reached Gilgit via the Burzil Pass with spectacular views of Nanga Parbat on 5 May. Conway describes their arrival in town in a way that will strike a chord with all Himalayan travellers on their last legs:

> 'Where does the Colonel Sahib live?'
> 'That way.'
> 'How far off?'
> 'Not far. A little way.'
> 'A mile?'
> 'Yes, a mile.'
> 'Perhaps two miles?'
> 'Yes, two miles.'
> 'Out with it, man! How many miles?'
> 'As many as the sahib pleases.'

An early lesson in trekking lore – always ask how long, not how far, and take the answer with a pinch of salt!

From Gilgit, Conway's main objective was to traverse the Hispar and Biafo Glacier systems. Soon they had to cross the Gilgit river and encountered their first *jhula*, or *jola*. These frail and alarming rope bridges feature in virtually every subsequent expedition account, and some are still in use today. The three twisted birch-twig cables form a V, two parallel ones providing hand rails, connected by a twig lattice to a lower footway. Conway's description of crossing the swollen glacial rivers by these contraptions could be written by any visitor to the Karakoram.

> The natives let them get into a rotten condition before they mend them and the reader will readily perceive that a rotten, swaying, giddy *jhula* with one or two of the cables broken, no cross ties and very few Vs is about as nasty a thing for a landsman to cross as may well be imagined . . . At the best they remind me of the loathsome sea and they always make me giddy.

Conway's long and complex explorations led him up the Hispar Glacier to the Hispar Pass which brought him to Snow Lake, the great basin at the head of the Sim Kang and Biafo Glaciers. He passed by the Ogre and the Latok Peaks. Conway originally named a prominent rocky spire the Ogre and its satellite needles the Ogre's Fingers. I have never understood how or why this peak is now called Conway's Ogre and the 'real' Ogre transferred to the highest summit of the group whose local name is Baintha Brakk. Such are the vagaries of naming mountains that it has even been said that Conway was mistaken in his original name – as if the 'real' Ogre had somehow always possessed sole rights to the European title and Conway had perversely stolen it. In fact even Conway's Ogre has a local name, Uzum Brakk, and today local names prevail. However, Conway's title for the Latok peaks – the Five Virgins – sounds like something out of a rugby club song and has thankfully never been adopted.

Descending from the snout of the Biafo, Conway briefly visited the nearby village of Askole, where he spent four days reprovisioning, sorting out new porters – and getting rid of Eckenstein. In his book Conway dismisses what happened in three short sentences: 'Eckenstein had never been well since reaching Gilgit. It was evidently useless for him to come further with us so I decided he had better return to England. The winding up of arrangements with him delayed us an extra day.'

Eckenstein, who wrote his own book about the expedition, managed to cut the incident down to just two sentences. They are however rather more illuminating. He and Conway 'had a sort of general meeting at which it was arranged that I should leave the expedition. There had been a good deal of friction.' It is tempting, even one hundred years later, to take sides in what was obviously a much deeper rift than the two accounts reveal. Eckenstein may have been unwell, but even so, he had crossed the Nushik Pass and descended the Chogo Lungma Glacier with Bruce before travelling via Skardu, Shigar and the Skoro La to meet the main party. He must have been frustrated both by his own lack of achievement and by Conway's remorseless progress through the most spectacular mountain scenery without any attempt to climb anything significant. It is easy to imagine, after six months, an active climber bridling against an expedition leader forever listing the variety of moss, lichen and butterflies he had observed that day. Conway for his part must have been equally irritated by the tactless and critical Eckenstein, particularly if he suspected that he wasn't pulling his weight as a team member. Their parting was perhaps inevitable. It was to have repercussions ten years later, and became the source of much speculation.

There is a curious little postscript to the parting of the ways that takes the form of a letter written by Conway to the Secretary of the

Royal Geographical Society from Abbottabad on 2 November, 1892 on his way home:

> After we left Askoley for the Baltoro Glacier, Mr Eckenstein, who remained behind, found a man who drew for him on the sand a rough map of that glacier and its surrounding mountains. He put in both the Mustagh Passes, the Mustagh Peak, K2, Gusherbrum [sic], and Masherbrum, all in their right places. He stated that Skinmang is the local name for the great Mustagh Peak, and Chirling the name for K2. I have recently noticed that though the great Mustagh Peak is scarcely, if at all, indicated on the Government map, it is quite clearly marked on the map that illustrated Colonel Godwin-Austen's paper in the 'Proceedings' of the Royal Geographical Society.

This significant piece of information never found its way into Conway's book and it is not clear why he wrote the letter in the first place – unless Eckenstein was already casting doubt as to who had first been to Concordia. But the intriguing thing is of course how the man knew about the relative positions so clearly. Could he have accompanied the elusive Roberto Lerco? Or did the Baltis know far more about the area than they were prepared to let on? Was there a deep suspicion of letting any foreigner know too much about the lie of the land which they actually knew very well? Or was he a Balti with an inquisitive nature who had explored the Baltoro to find new grazing grounds? Whatever the answer Conway can have been none too pleased to find out that someone had been there first.

On 31 July he set out again from Askole and retraced his steps across the terminal moraines of the Biafo Glacier. Ahead lay the Baltoro and the last and most important part of his long journey. Bad weather set in once they got on to the glacier, on which Conway found the going much harder than either the Hispar or the Biafo. Then the weather cleared and on 10 August they arrived at the confluence of three great glaciers. It is worth quoting Conway at length.

> . . . We could look up the various side glaciers to the south, and discover the order and arrangement of the peaks at their heads, but it was not these that startled our interest and made us halt this early in the cold morning. A far more important object was in sight fifteen miles to the south-east.

The great Baltoro Glacier is formed by the union at the west foot of Gusherbrum of three affluents, I named them Godwin-Austen Glacier, Throne Glacier and Vigne Glacier. The Godwin-Austen descends from K2. The Vigne Glacier comes in from the south and is fed by the Chogolisa peaks. The Throne Glacier divides about eight miles above the great crossing or 'Place de la Concorde' (as a similar place at the head of the Aletsch Glacier is called) and between them rises a rounded mountain mass. To it I gave the name Golden Throne (23,600 feet) for it is throne-like in form and there are traces of gold in its volcanic substance.

It was then, the most brilliant of all the mountains we saw, that had been rising into view with our ascent and now in the dim dawn smote upon our delighted eyes when we turned round. With one consent we cried out, 'That is the peak for us; we will go that way and no other.'

With these three paragraphs Conway's book changes from being, by and large, an objective account to a highly personal – even prejudiced – one. How could he of all people, an art historian, make such a peculiar aesthetic judgement? For on arrival at Concordia what hits you right between the eyeballs is the first overwhelming view of K2 itself. Even at twelve miles distant it simply dominates everything else including Broad Peak. Only the West Face of Gasherbrum competes with it (though even this is better viewed from further down the Baltoro). To the south Chogolisa is the mountain that stands out. By contrast the Golden Throne (called Baltoro Kangri today) is quite insignificant. (I have to confess that when I arrived at Concordia in 1986 I can't remember seeing it at all!) I'm afraid that Conway's misplaced accolade was caused by the realisation that it was one of the very few big peaks he had seen in the Karakoram that seemed to offer him any chance of scaling, certainly the only one in the Baltoro region.

From this point in the book Conway loses no opportunity to sing the praises of the Golden Throne and make disparaging comment about K2. Climbing a ridge on the north side of the Baltoro, Conway and McCormick find the expected view almost blocked by an unexpected snow ridge: '. . . Above the ridge there rose into the air an ugly mass of rock, without nobility of form or grandeur of mass . . . McCormick with his bag of blocks and colours cried out in disgust, "What have I brought these here for?"' Later on near the foot of the Golden Throne Conway again sees K2: '. . . Under almost any circumstances of light and weather Gusherbrum is a finer mountain from this side than his loftier neighbour. The North Face of K2 appears to be its best front.' (This last comment must have been based on Younghusband's account, for Conway could only guess what it might look like.)

Finally when McCormick paints the classic view of K2 from the south Conway comments, 'K2 showed himself from time to time, but not in a picturesque fashion.' One cannot help but feel a distinct suspicion of sour grapes. Whether or not Conway really thought K2 a disappointment is not entirely clear. He put forward the name the 'Watchtower' for K2 in the preface to his book, which implies some sense of awe even if it is totally inappropriate, as the length of the Baltoro is positively cluttered with towers, which K2 certainly isn't. For someone who at times thought up some very good names – Mitre Peak, Concordia, Crystal Peak, the Golden Throne, even Bride Peak (Chogolisa) – he also had his fair share of awful ones, which luckily have never caught on.

Conway's fascination with the Golden Throne knew no bounds, and page after page is devoted to describing it under every variety of light and shade. I fear there is a misplaced attempt to give the mountain more than its due, and to exaggerate the importance of Conway's ascent of one of its satellite summits which he called Pioneer Peak. This was really just a point on a ridge. Conway, Zurbriggen, Bruce and two Gurkhas, Parbir and Harkbir, reached the top on 25 August – complete with compass, clinometer and plane table. The barometer recorded an altitude of 22,600 feet which Conway, by some complex wishful thinking, rounded up to over 23,000. He also claimed a world altitude record which is highly dubious. The Atacama Indians in South America went to similar heights hundreds of years before, and Conway's Peak has since been measured as only 21,332 feet (6500m). The ascent was still the high point, both literally and metaphorically, of the expedition, though their journey was far from over. They returned to Skardu, then followed the Indus to Karghil and Leh in Ladakh, returning to Srinagar on 11 October. Conway sailed from Bombay on 27 November: '. . . I reached London on December 20th, just in time for the Annual Dinner of the Alpine Club.'

Conway's accounts of his adventures, through lectures and, of course, the book, earned him high praise at the time. His exaggerated mountaineering claims have since tended to obscure the importance of his exhaustive explorations. There is also a feeling that Conway was simply a product of British imperial arrogance, that such 'exploration' merely reveals the depths of the explorer's own ignorance. For are not the valleys inhabited, the passes and glaciers explored and known by the local inhabitants? To which the only answer must be that the thirst for knowledge, the recording of information and above all the desire 'to see round the next corner' is so ingrained into Western culture that, without it, no Himalayan peak would ever have been climbed, no trek to a Base Camp ever undertaken, and no photographs, paintings, or films ever made. Conway's journey of discovery in 1892 was, for better or worse, the prototype on which so many of the big twentieth-century expeditions were based. In particular the first expeditions to Everest after the First World War owed much to Conway.

Martin Conway went on to be President of the Alpine Club and later Lord Conway of Allington. He climbed Illimani in the Bolivian Andes and made the third ascent of Aconcagua. He died in 1937. Charles Bruce was to become General Bruce and lead the 1922 Everest Expedition. But Matthias Zurbriggen, the great Swiss guide who continued to make first ascents in New Zealand and South America, including Aconcagua (solo), was not so fortunate. He ended up an alcoholic, destitute, and hanged himself in Geneva in 1917.

4

The Great Beast 666

While Conway reaped the plaudits after his return from India, Eckenstein was ignored, returning to North Wales to climb on his beloved Lliwedd, and quietly develop his theories of balance and technique. His suspicions of the Alpine Club and all it stood for had been proved all too true.

Then in 1898 he met the man who was to become an unlikely and quite bizarre cult figure of the twentieth century. Climber, mystic, charlatan, magician, Satanist, 'sex fiend', Aleister Crowley was all of these and more. He was born in 1875 in Leamington, Warwickshire. His father, a brewer, was an active member of the Plymouth Brethren, a sect that believed they were the only true Christians, took the Bible as the literal truth and thought that the Second Coming was imminent.

Possibly as a result of extreme indoctrination, Crowley by the age of eleven decided that the Devil was a far more interesting alternative and from then on devoted most of his life to worshipping 'the Beast 666'. But Crowley was no fool. Clever, articulate and widely read, he was educated at Malvern and Tonbridge and then Cambridge University. He clearly suffered or entertained delusions of grandeur from an early age, leaving Cambridge without a degree and taking a flat in London under the name of Count Vladimir Svaref and undertaking a 'career' of magic in the Outer Order of the Great White Brotherhood.

It would be tedious to delve too deeply here into Crowley's strange obsessions: suffice to say he gives them an extensive airing in what he called 'an autohagiography' – *The Confessions of Aleister Crowley*. They are best summarised by his own Law of Mankind – 'Do What Thou Wilt Shall Be the Whole of the Law.' It has often been said that with this exhortation to 'do your own thing', and his obsessions with sex, drugs and Eastern philosophy, Crowley would have passed unnoticed in the Californian hippy scene or in the flower-power streets of London, and his brooding face actually appears on the Beatles' *Sergeant Pepper* album, the cult icon of the 'sixties. I am not so sure. Crowley was an arrogant and devious character who fell out with almost everyone he met – an extraordinary figure in any age, and not a particularly likeable one. Almost the only person he didn't end up despising was Oscar Eckenstein to whom his *Confessions* are dedicated along with, amongst others, the explorer Richard Burton and the artist Augustus John.

One of Crowley's few redeeming features was his love of climbing and mountains generally. He was, in the words of Tom Longstaff, the great Himalayan pioneer, 'a fine climber, if an unconventional one'. He started climbing on the chalk cliffs of Beachy Head, which must have given him a refined eye for the safest line up what is still considered suicidally dangerous ground – only recently have any of the sea cliffs of the south of England been explored using ice-climbing gear in the soft rock.

He climbed in the Lakes and the Alps – again unconventionally. Longstaff saw him solo the dangerous and difficult true right side of the Mer de Glace icefall below the Géant, a horribly risky and ill-advised escapade by any standards. Crowley despised guided climbing and it was this that probably attracted him to Eckenstein – and vice versa. In one scathing passage in *Confessions* he sums up his feelings for the climbing establishment of the late 1890s:

> Mountaineering differs from other sports in one important aspect. A man cannot obtain a reputation at cricket or football by hiring professionals to play for him. His achievements are checked by averages. But hardly anyone in England at that time knew anything about mountaineering. Various old fogeys who could not have climbed the simplest rocks in Cumberland or led across an easy Alpine pass, had been personally conducted by peasants up a few mountains and written themselves into fame.

In some ways Crowley was indeed a climber ahead of his time, in attitude if not achievement. Hatred of guides, pitons and fixed ropes (which were already in use in the Alps) would strike chords with generations of climbers to come. But compared with the great British names of his day – Mummery, Collie, Raeburn and Eckenstein himself – Crowley was an erratic and occasional performer who, had it not been for the notoriety of his private and public life, would probably have only been a footnote in the history of Victorian climbing.

In 1901 he and Eckenstein joined forces for the first time and climbed together in Mexico. Eckenstein had his own typically forthright views on Crowley's obsessions with magic: 'He openly jeered at me for wasting my time on such rubbish . . . he said, "Give up your Magick with all its romantic fascinations and deceitful thoughts. Promise to do this for a time and I will teach you how to master your mind."' Yet somehow their unlikely friendship survived. They climbed Ixtaccihuatl, 'the most beautiful mountain in Mexico', several times and Popocatapetl, Crowley claiming, incidentally, to have broken 'several world records'. On their return to civilisation they were gently made aware of the terrible news that Queen Victoria was dead, at which they (or perhaps just Crowley?) broke into 'shouts of joy and an impromptu war dance'. The successful expedition was a preparation for the following year, for Eckenstein had invited Crowley to go with him to the Karakoram to climb Chogo Ri, as Crowley invariably refers to K2.

The 1902 K2 expedition has the distinction of being the first actually to declare its intention to climb the mountain. Led by Eckenstein with Crowley his deputy, it included one other Englishman, Guy Knowles, a twenty-two-year-old from Trinity College, Cambridge; two Austrians, Heinrich Pfannl and Victor Wesseley; and a Swiss doctor, Jules Jacot-Guillarmod. The Austrians were reputed to be the best rock climbers in their country, but neither Knowles nor Guillarmod had much mountain experience. It was not, therefore, a very strong team that met in Rawalpindi at the end of March.

They had drawn up formal conditions for the expedition, agreeing that each should contribute the then huge sum of £1000. Guy Knowles later told John Symonds, author of *The Great Beast*, the biography of Crowley, that Crowley contributed nothing and he, Knowles, put up most of the money for the expedition. This would seem a likely scenario and would certainly explain his presence in the party. Other key passages in the contract stipulated absolute obedience to the leader, unless to obey an order meant the loss of life, permission to be obtained from Eckenstein before the purchase of anything, an order not to interfere in the beliefs and customs of the natives and to 'leave the women alone'.

No sooner had they set out than there occurred an incident that has been the source of conjecture and rumour ever since. A telegram arrived from the Governor of Rawalpindi recalling Eckenstein and forbidding him to enter Kashmir. The reason for this is far from clear. Crowley was convinced that Sir Martin Conway, by now President of the Alpine Club, had somehow managed to use his influence with Curzon, the Viceroy of India, to attempt to sabotage the expedition, inspired by jealousy and as revenge for his quarrel with Eckenstein in 1892. Guy Knowles seems to have agreed that this was the explanation but there is no other evidence to support it. Could Conway have perpetrated this rather squalid little plot? And to what purpose? True he could have been worried that his achievements on the Golden Throne and Pioneer Peak might be reassessed, and even eclipsed by Eckenstein's team, but he must have realised that sooner or later someone would return and that any record was there for the taking. Would he have risked his own reputation on such meagre grounds? Exposure would surely have been a humiliation he dare not risk. Yet pride does take strange forms and there remains a small unanswered question mark over Conway's conduct. This argument can of course be crudely countered by the fact that as Crowley himself was the one to make the allegation against Conway it may well have been a fabrication designed to show the Alpine Club and its president in the worst possible light.

There are at least two other possible explanations. One quite likely scenario is that Eckenstein, with his German-Jewish name, was thought to be a Prussian spy. This, given the state of paranoia over the intentions of Russia, cannot be dismissed lightly. Any rumours surfacing from the presence of an expedition composed of (seemingly) a majority of 'foreigners' would have to be investigated and the incident could simply have been the knee-jerk reaction of a nervous official.

The other possibility is equally plausible. Louis Baume in his authoritative book *Sivalaya – the 8000-metre peaks of the Himalaya* reveals that a brief article appeared in the *Friend of India* on 1 May reporting that Eckenstein's expedition was to climb Mount Everest! Though this is erroneous to the point of absurdity (Rawalpindi being about eight hundred miles away from the mountain in any case), it is possible that unfounded rumours of an illicit journey into Tibet or Nepal could have reached the ear of Curzon who was at the time involved in the first diplomatic moves to mount an official British expedition to Everest. Eckenstein's recall to explain himself would clearly be necessary before he could continue.

Whether by conspiracy or cock-up, Eckenstein was delayed for three weeks before persuading Curzon himself that his motives were innocent. He managed to catch up with the others at Srinagar. Writing of the affair, Crowley makes a wholehearted defence of his friend from real or imaginary injustice: 'Eckenstein was the noblest man that I have ever known. His integrity was absolute and his sympathetic understanding of the native character supreme.'

After this first setback the expedition proceeded reasonably smoothly to Askole, arriving on 26 May. Before they got there they had their first introduction to a rope bridge, which gave Crowley an excuse for a gratuitously snide dig at Conway: 'They are a little terrifying at first sight, it is only fair to admit, but one cannot help thinking that Sir Martin Conway was almost too considerate of the nervousness of others when he insisted on roping Zurbriggen on one side of him and Bruce on the other before pirouetting lightly across.'

At Askole Crowley and Eckenstein had a brief but unpleasant altercation over how many books Crowley should be allowed to take in his personal gear limit of forty pounds. Crowley threatened to leave the expedition if he couldn't take 'Milton and the rest' and eventually won the argument claiming he would rather risk physical than intellectual starvation. (Though I have never risked either, I do recall Alan Rouse in Skardu in 1986 also getting quite upset at the number of paperbacks I thought necessary to last our own K2 expedition. Like Crowley, I too got my own way, but even so the books ran out long before my return.)

Before they left Askole the two Austrians, Wesseley and Pfannl, asked for permission to take three days' provisions in their rucksacks and go off and climb K2! Crowley was astonished that after so much travelling they were still incapable of grasping the scale and distances involved in climbing the Karakoram mountains. Whether their intentions were serious or a try-on is debatable, for Crowley himself admits that they all found Eckenstein's discipline difficult to accept. In any case they were refused and, like so many expeditions to come, the team began developing the irreconcilable differences that would make any remote chance of success on the mountain even slimmer. Crowley in particular lost no opportunity to disparage the Austrians and his comments are unpleasantly xenophobic.

Slowly they made their way up the Baltoro, finding as do most
trekkers today that 'the journey is morally tedious and physically
wearisome beyond belief. The compensation is the majesty of the
surrounding mountains.' Urdokas, the last grassy oasis on the true
left or southern bank of the Baltoro, and commanding superb views
of the Trango Towers and Cathedrals, was 'a veritable Beulah . . . the
atmosphere of restfulness is paramount. There was here quite a lot of
grass: even some flowers.' Sadly, this is not the case today. Urdokas
is now almost bare of vegetation and horribly polluted.

Three days later Crowley arrived at the head of the Baltoro Glacier,
and with astounding cheek observed, 'I was irresistibly reminded of
Concordia Platz in the Oberland and named the plateau in affec-
tionate remembrance.' Conway had not only named Concordia in
1892 but recorded the fact in his book published in 1894! Crowley
continues with a description of the view from Concordia that is
first accurate, if incomplete, and then vitriolic and bordering on
defamatory:

> Once again the astounding variety of nature in this district
> impressed itself upon my mind. One would have said that it
> was theoretically impossible to combine so many different types
> of mountain. The only exception to the otherwise invariable
> rule of practical inaccessibility was the Golden Throne, a minor
> point of which Conway claims to have climbed. I was very
> disgusted at the bad taste of some of the coolies who had
> been with him in saying that he had never been on the moun-
> tain at all, but turned back at the foot of the icefall. How
> could such common creatures presume to decide such a delicate
> scientific question of this sort?

Ironically, Crowley was so keen to put the boot into Conway that
he never really gave K2 the description it deserved. His memory,
too, seems to be a little at fault in his account of his approach to
K2. On 16 June he left ahead of the others to reconnoitre the best
route and walked up the Godwin-Austen Glacier ('where man had
never yet trodden'). He camped at roughly 'the first of a subsidiary
spur descending from the ridge of which Chogo Ri is the climax', in
other words the site of all future Base Camps. Here he observed the
mountain 'all day and night', coming to the conclusion that 'while
the South Face, perhaps possible theoretically, meant a complicated

climb with no halfway house, there should be no difficulty in walking up the snow slopes on the east-south-east to the snowy shoulder below the final rock pyramid'. In order to see these slopes Crowley must have first viewed them from Concordia, for here, so close to the mountain, they are blocked by the rocky silhouette of the South-East Spur. It is true that from Concordia it does look as though it might be possible to climb to the Shoulder almost entirely on snow (though 'walking up' is surely a tongue-in-cheek understatement), but this is, of course, an illusion, as history would prove.

Here it is appropriate to understand the layout of at least the south side of K2 as seen from Concordia by Conway's and Eckenstein's expeditions. From here K2 appears to be a not quite perfect four-sided pyramid – a classic yet erroneous illusion that would take a long time to dispel. The far left skyline ridge is the West Ridge; nearer, the South-West Ridge runs towards an obvious col joining K2 to an elegant satellite, the Angelus or Angel Peak, at the foot of which base camps are normally placed on the Godwin-Austen Glacier. Between the West and the South-West Ridges is the foreshortened and rocky West Face. To the right of the South-West Ridge is the vast amphitheatre of the South Face seen head on with its own hanging glacier, spurs, séracs and retaining walls. It is bounded by the South-East Ridge which forms the right profile. The South-East Spur drops from the Shoulder of K2 to the Godwin-Austen Glacier. The true South-East Ridge as such doesn't really exist below the Shoulder, as it consists of huge snowfields and various ribs that stretch to the North-East Ridge, out of sight from Concordia. The Godwin-Austen Glacier runs at first due north then north-east, around the base of the mountain to a wide basin and horseshoe of smaller peaks, of which Skyang Kangri (Staircase Peak) is the largest.

Crowley's assessment of the South Face is almost as wildly optimistic as Pfannl and Wesseley's intention of climbing K2 in three days from Askole, and it is questionable whether any credit given to him in being the first person to spot the feasibility of the South-East Spur is really justified, with or without the competing claim of Robert Lerco. He didn't appear to notice the barrier that would come to be known as House's Chimney and totally ignored the presence of the Black Pyramid, the large broken buttress below the Shoulder. As for the difficulties *above* it, over thirty years would elapse before anyone even realised that the last six hundred metres of the South-East Ridge would prove to be as hard, or harder, a way to the top, as any of the

8000-metre peaks. But however unaware of the true problems posed by the Spur, Crowley did recognise that it was the most likely weakness, and this must be acknowledged.

He pushed on through the small and relatively innocuous icefall on the Godwin-Austen Glacier and camped below the South-East Spur. When Eckenstein caught him up he immediately poured cold water on Crowley's proposed route and his choice of camp, ignoring the latter's assertions that they would be unlikely '. . . to meet any conditions which would make Camp X other than a desirable country residence for a gentleman in failing health'. Despite his misgivings, Crowley accepted Eckenstein's decision to send back the porters and abandon the South-East Spur. Yet 'It was so obviously right to take them up the slopes to the shoulder and establish the camp at a point whence Chogo Ri could have been reached without question in one fine day.' If only it was that simple! The porters were much relieved, for they had been convinced that Crowley had been planning to lead them to their deaths over a non-existent pass to Yarkand. (But did they *know* that there was no pass?) 'Their delight at being reprieved was pathetically charming.' Crowley, unlike many of his successors, did seem genuinely fond of the Balti people and treated them well and sympathetically throughout. (Or at least he claims to have done.)

On 19 and 20 July Pfannl, Wesseley, Knowles and Guillarmod arrived. So, too, did a blizzard a couple of days later, which pinned them down for three further days. Then it was decided to reconnoitre the long and complex North-East Ridge and also go up to what Crowley called Windy Gap, the col at the very end of the Godwin-Austen Glacier.

Here, with hindsight that is all too easy, Eckenstein would have been wise to change his objectives. Skyang Kangri (or Staircase Peak) might *just* have been within their abilities to climb. At 24,750 feet (7544m), it would have been a truly remarkable ascent for its time – a height record that would stand for many years. But it is easy to see that at this very early stage of Himalayan climbing almost every decision was made in ignorance of scale, technical difficulty and, above all, altitude. Here lack of knowledge was almost total. No one knew whether it was possible to live for any length of time above 6000 metres, and the mechanics of acclimatisation were a closed book. Even so, Crowley, by luck or good judgement (or Satanic intervention?), stumbled upon an important insight when he asserted that the only way of getting up the really high mountains was to 'lay in a stock of energy, get rid of all your fat at the exact moment when you have a chance to climb a mountain, and jump back out of its reach, so to speak, before it can take its revenge'. This is an almost exact description of the alpine-style tactics developed and promulgated seventy years later by Reinhold Messner and others, but occasionally demonstrated earlier, notably by Tom Longstaff's ascent of Trisul (7120m), when he climbed the last 2000 metres in just ten hours. Crowley, never losing a chance to criticise the Alpine Club, later poured scorn on the siege mentality of acclimatisation shown in the early Everest expeditions.

Eckenstein's decision to attempt the North-East Ridge was a strange one. It is very long and complex and quite obviously difficult. Presumably he chose it because it looked to be at an easier angle than the South-East Spur, and possibly because he thought it might prove to be safer. But the classic view from Windy Gap shows an interminable knife-edged ridge leading the featureless upper slopes of the mountain and a final steepening in the summit cone. The ridge was not to succumb until 1978 when it was climbed by a very strong American expedition who nevertheless took over two months to reach the summit. In 1902 Eckenstein's little team didn't stand a chance.

At first Pfannl and Wesseley made some progress and reached a high of around 21,000 feet (6400m). Then Pfannl fell ill and a protracted rescue had to be undertaken, Crowley almost casually explaining that Pfannl had oedema of both lungs and had to lose height to recover. Whether the diagnosis was Crowley's or Guillarmod's is irrelevant: one of them made an astoundingly accurate observation, and prescribed the only successful action to be taken. Both high-altitude pulmonary and cerebral oedema have only comparatively recently begun to be understood and remedies developed to counteract their potentially fatal results. Amazingly Crowley appeared to know and understand the problem years before it was accepted that the illness wasn't simply pneumonia. Even the deaths on K2 in 1954 of the Italian Mario Puchoz, and on Masherbrum in 1957 of Bob Downes, were both misdiagnosed as pneumonia.

Pfannl's illness and complicated evacuation to Urdokas effectively put an end to any concerted attempt on the mountain. Both Eckenstein and Crowley fell ill, Crowley with a bout of malaria and, semi-delirious, he threatened Guy Knowles with a revolver. Knowles disarmed him with a blow to the stomach. Returning to

Urdokas they found Pfannl much recovered. Wesseley had earlier irritated Crowley with his eating habits.

> In order to eat he would bend his head over his plate, and, using his knife and fork like the blades of a paddle wheel, would churn the food into his mouth with a rapid rotatory motion. There was always some going up and some going down . . . It was the most disgusting sight I have ever seen . . . I admit my human weakness. All forms of genius should be admired and studied and Wesseley was a world champion.

Now they found Wesseley had 'stolen' the bulk of the emergency rations. He was expelled from the expedition and Pfannl went with him.

And so for the first but certainly not the last time, a K2 expedition ended in disarray and petty feuding, a circumstance not unique in the annals of Himalayan climbing, but there does seem to be something in the very remoteness and savagery of K2 and its surroundings that undermines the unity of so many expeditions. The relentless strain of just living there is much greater than, for example, the Everest Base Camp, which has easy access to civilisation in the form of tea houses, villages, and varied company.

Eckenstein's expedition was studiously ignored by the British establishment and there is no mention of it in the *Alpine Journal* of the time. Younghusband, whose book *Epic of Mount Everest* starts with a brief resumé of Himalayan exploration in general only mentions that, 'The Swiss, Dr Jacot-Guillarmod, explored in the same region,' which is not even damning with faint praise!

Given the result of the 1902 expedition it is almost unbelievable that any two members of it should ever contemplate another joint project, but in 1905 Crowley and Guillarmod teamed up for an attempt on Kangchenjunga. Eckenstein and Knowles wisely declined to accompany them and the expedition ended disastrously with the death of a Swiss climber, Alexis Pache, and three porters. Crowley was not directly involved but his behaviour throughout the expedition and particularly after the accident was irresponsible and callous in the extreme. Crowley was emphatically disowned by the Alpine Club who pointed out in the *Alpine Journal* of 1906 that Crowley had never had any connection with the Club. From then on Crowley lost interest in climbing, and his life degenerated into the self-indulgent, self-deluding shambles that lasted until his death in 1947.

But it is hard not to feel sorry for Eckenstein. Two visits to the Karakoram had both ended in disappointment and though he doubtless didn't help his own cause by his own attitude, he must have felt he deserved a lot more credit, both for his explorations of K2 and his undoubted contribution to the techniques of climbing. Eckenstein died in 1921 a rather isolated eccentric. The man whom Longstaff described as a 'rough diamond' would doubtless be amazed to see, seventy years later, the technical revolution of ice climbing with short, dropped head axes, rigid clip-on crampons, and plastic boots. Had he been born one hundred years later, he might have made a fortune designing, manufacturing and marketing his inventions.

5

The First Italian Campaign

Before K2 was visited again brief mention must be made of two eccentric middle-aged American explorers, Dr William Hunter Workman and his wife Fanny Bullock Workman. On a bicycle tour of India in 1898, they decided to visit the Himalaya and, with no mountain experience behind them, got to Ladakh, and probably the Karakoram Pass. From then on they were hooked and, bicycles abandoned, they spent most of the next twelve years on seven extensive visits to the Karakoram. Strangely they never set foot on the Baltoro or got near K2. During their explorations they climbed several minor peaks around Snow Lake and the Hispar and Biafo Glaciers but much of the ground they covered was already known. It is tempting to see them as the forerunners of the archetypal tourist: impatient, critical, often at odds with their porters and local inhabitants, self-important and at times unscrupulous. Nevertheless they wrote extensively and their books are lavishly illustrated, though their maps contained many errors and false assumptions, and for many years their findings were the source of much controversy while at the same time stimulating further exploration. But spending so long in the area and covering so much ground must have brought its own rewards. Their last exploration in 1912 was to survey the great Siachen Glacier to the south-east of K2. It was possibly their most valuable contribution to Karakoram exploration, even though the Siachen had already been visited by Tom Longstaff.

After a seven-year lull, an expedition once again toiled up the Baltoro Glacier en route for K2. On 26 March, 1909, Luigi Amedeo di Savoia, Duke of the Abruzzi, had set sail from Marseilles with a large, carefully selected and well-equipped party. The Duke of the Abruzzi was no dilettante, he was Italy's leading explorer who had, in 1899, come within two hundred miles of the North Pole.

Two years earlier he had organised an expedition to Nanga Parbat which had been called off due to an outbreak of bubonic plague. Instead he climbed Mount St Elias (5500m) on the borders of Canada and Alaska. In 1906 he led a brilliant expedition to the Ruwenzori Range (the Mountains of the Moon) in Africa during which all the major peaks were climbed.

Many of the Duke's team had proved themselves before and included the biologist and doctor Filippo de Filippi (who later wrote the expedition book, a classic work), Federico Negrotto the surveyor, and seven guides from Courmayeur – Henri, Alexis and Emil Brocherel, Joseph and Laurent Petigax, Albert Savoye and Ernest Barux. Last but certainly not least was the mountain photographer, Vittorio Sella.

Sella is still remembered as possibly the greatest ever mountain photographer. His name is synonymous with technical perfection and aesthetic refinement. Using a cumbersome plate camera he achieved the major successes of his life when he produced the definitive record of the Baltoro mountains. The pictures were to inspire climbers and photographers for generations to come. But by some strange quirk of fate neither of the two most famous photographs brought back by the expedition were quite what they seemed. The first was Sella's wonderful telephoto shot of the Mustagh Tower seen from the Upper Baltoro Glacier. From this point, due south-east of the mountain, both summits of the peak are in line and the mountain appears as a slender tooth, the epitome of the impossible. It was a stunning photograph that, fifty years later, would be the trigger for both British and French teams to compete for the first ascent. In reality, however, the Mustagh Tower, while undoubtedly spectacular, proved to be not as impregnable as it had seemed. Both expeditions succeeded in climbing two ridges that were not nearly as steep as Sella's full-frontal view suggested.

The second is probably the most famous image of the expedition and one of the great mountain photographs of all time – K2 seen from Windy Gap, a magnificent study of light, shade, texture and form, one of the few photos that in its abstract simplicity gives a clue as to the incredible size of the mountain. With plumes of snow blowing over the summit ridges the mountain is transformed into the ethereal symbol of 'the Savage Mountain'. But this photo was actually taken by the Duke himself and has been constantly miscredited to Sella ever since. Perhaps it is not such a major error, for Sella's expertise and advice were largely responsible for a uniformly high standard of photography throughout the expedition.

When the Duke and his team arrived in India they wasted no time. Helped by Sir Francis Younghusband, now resident in Kashmir, the expedition took only three weeks to reach Askole and by 24 May it had reached Concordia. The Duke made Urdokas his Base Camp and the network of flattened terraces for tent platforms is still in use today. The whole expedition was ruthlessly efficient and well led, with supplies organised and replenished at Urdokas to be ferried up the glacier to the Advance Base at the foot of K2.

On reaching Concordia, de Filippi describes the first overwhelming sight of the mountain. One cannot help comparing it to Conway's impressions of the same view.

Suddenly and without warning, as if a veil had been lifted from our eyes, the wide Godwin-Austen valley lay before us in its own whole length. Down at the end, alone, detached from all the other mountains soared up K2, the indisputable sovereign of the region, gigantic and solitary, hidden from human sight in innumerable ranges, jealously defended by a vast throng of vassal peaks, protected from invasion by miles and miles of glaciers. Even to get within sight of it demands so much contrivance, so much marching, such a sum of labour.

It fills the whole end of the valley, with nothing to draw the attention from it. All the lines of the landscape seem to meet and converge in it. The mountains group themselves about it, yet without any intrusion upon it, or interference with its extraordinary upward effort. Its lines are ideally proportioned and perfectly balanced, its architectural design is powerful, adequate to the majesty of the peak without being heavy; the steepness of its sides, its ridges and its glaciers is appalling; its rocky wall is 12,000 feet high.

Curiously de Filippi also describes K2 as a pyramid, with four ridges. Even allowing for the fact that the North Ridge is not visible from the Baltoro side of the mountain, the North-West, West, South-West, South-East and North-East Ridges are, and de Filippi in the course of the expedition must have been aware that from almost any view-point three different ridges can be seen. Perhaps subconsciously he wanted the mountain to conform to a geometric norm.

At the foot of the mountain the Duke did what Eckenstein and Crowley had failed to do, which was to reconnoitre (as far as practicable) the whole base of the mountain and all its ridges. A quick foray to the Upper Godwin-Austen resulted in a summary dismissal of the North-East Ridge. Retreating, he turned left to explore the glacier that runs under the West Face of the mountain and joins the Godwin-Austen below Angel Peak. The Duke named this the Savoia Glacier, after the family estates in Italy. He saw a high col at the end of the glacier that seemed to lead on to the North-West Ridge, but this too was quickly rejected as being too steep for porters.

Instead, the Duke elected to make his first attempt on the South-East Spur. Spur is the technically accurate designation as it is a subsidiary ridge that doesn't actually go to the summit, meeting the Shoulder of K2 at around 7500 metres. Like so much of K2, the Abruzzi Spur seems from a distance to be such a cleancut feature, yet it proves at close quarters to be much more broken and complex. In this respect K2 is not dissimilar to the Matterhorn, whose familiar outlines disappear into a mass of shattered buttresses, ribs and gullies the nearer one gets. The Duke's plan was simple and in a letter from Base Camp de Filippi describes it.

> . . . His Highness set out the day before yesterday after the light camp had been carried from here to the Ridge. The guides have been busy yesterday and again today on preparing the route as far as some red rocks about 1000 metres further up. The idea is to take the camp to this point tomorrow. Then two or three days will be spent overcoming the next 1000 metres as far as a large snowclad shoulder 800 or 900 metres below the summit. A single Mummery [tent] and the sleeping-bags of His Highness' three guides is all that is being taken up to the Shoulder. When the porters have brought these up they will come back and sleep at the red rocks. His Highness and the guides should then be able to reach the summit the following day.

It was only a marginally more realistic plan than Aleister Crowley's 'walk to the Shoulder' had been, and stood no chance of success. In the event it was soon discovered that the Spur was too steep and featureless for laden porters, and the attempt petered out at around 6250 metres. But in setting foot on the Spur he named the Abruzzi, the Duke made the first recorded inroad on what would eventually become the line of the first ascent.

The Duke then resumed his explorations of the Savoia and Upper Godwin-Austen Glaciers. On the West Side of the mountain Sella photographed the superb view known as 'panorama E'. Taken from high on the Savoia Glacier, it shows the Savoia Saddle and the North-West Ridge in profile with its characteristic tilting strata. Apparently wedged between the North-West and the West Ridge is a colossal, black, barrel-shaped buttress. It must be the single most impressive rock formation on K2 and is even today a futuristic project that seems most unlikely to be climbed before the twenty-first century. The West Ridge of K2 is also seen in profile running all the way down to the glacier. This photograph was one that would inspire an American expedition to attempt the North-West Ridge in 1975. The Duke himself was convinced that the favourably angled strata of this ridge would make for easier climbing and provide good campsites, which were both noticeably absent on the Abruzzi, and he tried again to reach the Savoia Saddle. It took his three guides twelve hours of step-cutting up the long final ice slope, where disappointment awaited them. On the north side of the pass a large cornice blocked the view across to the North Face and a succession of pinnacles and towers prevented any further progression up the ridge. Across the col the slope dropped steeply away to the K2 Glacier far below and prevented any access to the north side. Wearily the Duke and his guides retraced their steps down to the Savoia Glacier where they were met by porters with lanterns and hot drinks. It had been a sixteen-hour day.

Concluding that any other routes from the western flanks were completely beyond the pale, the Duke once more moved up to the North-East Ridge, where from the slopes of Skyang Kangri he took his famous photograph. Even after a detailed survey of the approaches to the ridge the Duke's team could find no readily accessible route. Like Eckenstein before them, they passed up the chance to make a determined attempt on Skyang Kangri and, discouraged by lack of significant progress, turned their attentions to Chogolisa (Bride Peak). The Duke's view was that K2 would never be climbed. It was the considered opinion of a serious and responsible expedition leader who, while not achieving a great deal in terms of altitude, had undoubted success in surveying, mapping and photography. His reputation and stature were doubtless factors in deterring anyone else from attempting the mountain for almost thirty years.

Chogolisa proved to be a far more amenable proposition. With a bit more luck with the weather the Duke would surely have climbed it, but only some 150 metres from the top, on the last long snow ridge, thick cloud made further progress too dangerous. Aware of the possibility of walking over the edge of the corniced ridge his party retreated. Their height record of 7500 metres would stand for thirty years.

Though de Filippi returned to the eastern Karakoram in 1913 for a comprehensive and detailed exploration of the Siachen and Rimo Glaciers and the head of the Shaksgam valley, K2 was not on the agenda. Neither was it in 1929 when yet another Italian expedition set sail. Originally planned for 1928 to mark the tenth anniversary of the end of the First World War, the expedition was also to coincide with one to the North Pole. K2 and/or Broad Peak were to be the objectives but internal strife caused the grandiose project to be modified, and then postponed for a year. In the end it became lamely designated the 'Italian Geographical Expedition to the Karakoram', with no mountaineering objectives at all. Led by Aimone di Savoia-Aosta, Duke of Spoleto, the geological and geographical research was left in the more than capable hands of Ardito Desio, for whom the Karakoram was to become the focus of a lifetime's work and research and who would play a crucial part in the first ascent of K2 twenty-five years later.

Amongst its other achievements the expedition explored the Sarpo Laggo Glacier and the Shaksgam valley, and Desio himself took the first photograph of K2 from the north with its appalling hanging glaciers and North Ridge seen head on.

In 1937 a small British expedition was active in the same region. Eric Shipton and Bill Tilman were undoubtedly the two leading British explorer-mountaineers of the 1930s, with insatiable appetites for lightweight forays into unknown areas. They were both motivated by curiosity and the desire to see round the next corner. To give their expedition the scientific respectability that would induce financial backing they were accompanied by the surveyor Michael Spender and John Auden of the Geological Survey of India; by coincidence both brothers of distinguished poets, Stephen Spender and W. H. Auden.

The expedition was the subject of what many consider to be the finest of Eric Shipton's many books, *Blank on the Map*, which has inspired later generations of climbers, including Peter Boardman and Joe Tasker. Its accounts of the months spent exploring the

Shaksgam, Biafo Glacier, Snow Lake, Panmah and Hispar Glaciers is a celebration of the freedom to wander at will with only the most basic logistical restrictions. On Shipton's own admission '. . . no experience of mine has been fuller, no undertaking more richly rewarded than those few months among the unknown mountains beyond the crest of the Karakoram.'

Like Ardito Desio, Shipton saw and photographed the North Face of K2 and wrote eloquently of the experience:

> The afternoon was fine and nothing interrupted my view of the great amphitheatre about me. The cliffs and ridges of K2 rose out of the glacier in one stupendous sweep to the summit of the mountain 12,000 feet above. The sight was beyond my comprehension, and I sat gazing at it, with a kind of timid fascination, watching wreaths of mist creep in and out of corries utterly remote. I saw ice avalanches, weighing perhaps hundreds of tons, break off from a hanging glacier, nearly two miles above my head: the ice was ground to a fine powder and drifted away in the breeze long before it reached the foot of the glacier, nor did any sound reach my ears.

These words were to have a profound influence on the Austrian climber Kurt Diemberger, and in the years before China opened up the northern approach to K2, many climbers found that Shipton's text and the black and white photography that accompanied it epitomised all that was inaccessible and therefore most desirable in Himalayan mountaineering.

But it is one of the minor mysteries of Karakoram history that between 1909 and 1938 no expedition attempted to climb K2 and none (apart from the aborted 1929 Italian débâcle) was even planned. Given the developments in both the Alps and the Himalaya in the 1920s and 1930s it seems almost unbelievable in retrospect. True, Everest occupied almost all the thoughts of the British, while Kangchenjunga and Nanga Parbat were almost exclusively the preserves of German climbers. Could it be that K2 was already suffering the 'second highest, second best' syndrome that would dog expeditions, publicity and sponsorship in the 'seventies and 'eighties? Was there an almost subconscious fear that even achieving success on K2 would attract little credit? Or was it simply that the sleeping giant was so remote and impersonal that it had just been forgotten? Whatever the reason, K2 was long overdue for an attempt. Even as Shipton and Tilman were exploring the glaciers at the foot of the North Face, 11,000 miles away in Boston, USA, the first steps were already under way to challenge the mountain.

6

Cowboys on K2

If a realistic attempt to climb K2 needed a fresh approach, what could be more appropriate than that it should come from the New World, though the driving force behind the American 1938 K2 expedition was in fact a German *émigré* from Dresden. Fritz Wiessner had lived in the States since 1929 and was an American citizen. He joined the American Alpine Club in 1932 and the same year was a member of a combined German–American–Austrian expedition to Nanga Parbat. An excellent rock climber (brought up on the spectacular sandstone cliffs of the Elbe Valley), he had an impressive track record in the Alps, America and Canada, including the first ascent of Mount Waddington. In early 1937 Wiessner, with the President of the AAC, made a formal application to climb K2, but it was not until November that permission arrived for 1938. Should this attempt be unsuccessful the permit would be renewed for 1939.

Faced with the pressure of organising a major expedition in a very short time, and having his own business commitments to cope with as well, Wiessner pulled out of the first attempt, while making it clear he wished to lead the 1939 expedition. Andy Kauffman and Bill Putnam in their excellent account *K2, the 1939 Tragedy* surmised that Wiessner may well have done this in order to let others make a first try; then in the event of failure he could take advantage of their experience. He had done this successfully before, both in Europe and on Mount Waddington. (It is perhaps also worth noting that the 1932 Nanga Parbat expedition was also the first attempt on that mountain since Mummery's ill-fated expedition in 1895. It failed, possibly reinforcing Wiessner's reluctance to do the same in 1938.) Whether a deliberate ploy or not, Wiessner recommended that the leadership should be given to Charles Houston, and with his appointment the first of the truly great climbers to be forever linked with K2 took the centre stage.

Charlie Houston was then a medical student aged twenty-five. He had started his climbing career at the age of twelve in the Alps with his father. Houston admired the British climbing traditions and didn't have much use for artificial aids. He had made a number of good climbs in the Alps and had been with Washburn on Mount Crillon, Alaska. In 1934 he made the first ascent of Mount Foraker and two years later, though cruelly robbed of the summit itself through food poisoning, he was in the party which achieved the first ascent of Nanda Devi in 1936. Both these climbs had been made by small, cohesive groups of close friends and in excellent style. On Nanda Devi, Houston had the temerity to invite Bill Tilman and Noel Odell of Everest fame, both well known and at the height of their powers. He was delighted that they agreed to accompany a group of almost unknown young Americans. The expedition was a model of democratic decision-making. So much so that they even planned not to release the names of any successful summiteers. In the event this proved a practical impossibility, but it did show the depth of harmony and friendship that prevailed in the team. These qualities were to be the foundation of both the 1938 expedition and again in 1953 when Houston returned to K2.

When Charlie Houston accepted the leadership from Wiessner he had not much time to pick a team and organise the expedition. His brief from the American Alpine Club was twofold, to make a complete reconnaissance of the mountain and only then attempt to climb it. Houston had no hesitation in choosing Robert H. Bates. Bob Bates was also twenty-eight, a teacher, and had been on several major expeditions to Alaska. Perhaps his most impressive effort was with Bradford Washburn: the epic traverse of the unclimbed Mount Lucania and Mount Steele ending with a 125 mile walk out during which each man lost twenty pounds in weight. Like Houston, Bob Bates espoused the self-supporting 'small is beautiful' ethos long before it became fashionable. Bill House at twenty-five was a major force in Yale Mountaineering Club and a past President. He had climbed the Devils Tower in Wyoming and Mount Waddington, both with Fritz Wiessner. W. F. Loomis who had been on Nanda Devi with Houston could not join the party but recommended Teton guide Paul Petzoldt, who amongst other hard climbs had been involved in a bizarre rescue of a publicity-seeking parachutist marooned on the top of Devils Tower. Petzoldt cunningly bought fifty pitons in Europe on his way to India, which were all used.

Dick Burdsall was forty-two. In 1932 he had climbed Minya Konka, a mountain actually in China but on the edge of the Tibetan Plateau. It was one of those peaks once rumoured to be the highest mountain on earth at 30,000 feet but in fact proved to be only 24,900 (7590m). The final team member was Captain Norman Streatfeild, a Scot based in India in the Bengal Mountain Artillery, who was to be transport officer and had already been up the Baltoro Glacier to perform the same job on Gasherbrum I (Hidden Peak) with the 1936 French expedition.

Bill Tilman, who was on his way to lead an Everest expedition, chose six experienced Sherpas to travel across India from Darjeeling to join Houston. Their sirdar, or head man, was Pasang Kikuli who had been Houston's personal Sherpa on Nanda Devi and had been several times to Kangchenjunga, as well as Nanga Parbat and Everest, thus amassing more Himalayan experience than the rest of the expedition put together!

It was a happy, relaxed and efficient party that set off from Srinagar on the 300-mile approach to K2. Bob Bates, who with Charlie Houston wrote the expedition book, described with awe and humility every new vista, every novel experience and their sense of anticipation as they slowly approached the mountain. Bates also recalls early during the walk-in seeing some initials carved on water-worn rock on the banks of the Dras river: 'H.H.G.A. 1861–2–3'. Henry Haversham Godwin-Austen had obviously not been above producing his own bit of minor vandalism!

When the team reached Askole, Paul Petzoldt came down with a high fever and delirium. Houston, as the expedition doctor, stayed with him while the rest carried on. In his words, 'I hadn't a clue what was wrong . . . It was agreed that if he recovered we would try to join them; if he died, I would bury him and join them! It was scary because he was in fact very sick for three days. When we got home my consultants felt he had developed sandfly or Dengue fever.' Petzoldt did recover and he and Houston caught up the rest of the team at Urdokas.

Despite a porter strike beyond Askole, which was quickly defeated by the assurance that the climbers would simply carry their own gear and not pay the porters anything at all, the expedition reached Base Camp on 12 June. Awed by the immensity of the mountain, they decided to split up to reconnoitre the three obvious possibilities previously investigated by the Duke of the Abruzzi: the North-West Ridge, North-East Ridge and the Abruzzi Spur. The North-East Ridge was quickly dismissed. The mile-long knife-edged ridge looked out of the question. But, like the Duke before them, Bill House was convinced that the North-West Ridge with its favourable strata would be the best bet.

Although climbing standards had improved almost beyond recognition since 1908 and the American team had a wealth of varied experience, the slopes to the Savoia Saddle climbed by the Duke's guides in twelve hours defeated them three times, not because of any intrinsic difficulty but because of the impossibility of carrying loads up to the Saddle. They surmised that snow conditions had changed dramatically over the years, which was quite possible as they were moving on pure green ice. By the late 'thirties ten-point crampons were becoming generally accepted (with the notable exception of in Scotland!) but twelve-point 'lobster claw' crampons had not yet been invented. Kicking steps on snow, or step-cutting, was to remain the standard practice for many years to come. Cutting long lines of steps on hard ice was dreaded as time consuming and dangerous. Today, given the right consistency, such ice climbing is almost relished for its speed and safety. Also porters were rarely, if ever, issued with crampons and preferred to stick to rock wherever possible, however loose and unreliable. The result was that the lines of routes in both the Alps and Himalaya were often chosen for very different reasons than they are today.

Two of the three possible routes on K2 had now been eliminated and the reconnaissance party on the Abruzzi Spur were not encouraged. Though they had not been stopped by any insurmountable difficulties, they had found it insecure and lacking safe campsites. Houston had actually found a few pieces of weathered wood on the remnants of a tent platform, marking one of the Duke of the Abruzzi's camps.

These reconnaissances had used up valuable time. It was not until 1 July that the whole team assembled at the foot of the Abruzzi Spur and committed themselves to an all-out attempt. Later they were criticised for spending so long going over old ground. Oscar Dyhrenfurth in particular questioned their judgement quite sharply. But it was part of their brief to explore and it was certainly possible that thirty years of technical advances may well have invalidated the Duke of the Abruzzi's assessments. Ironically it proved to be the

Abruzzi Spur itself, dismissed in 1909 for its steepness and lack of campsites, that was to prove the key.

Supplies were by now running low. Worse, a three-gallon drum of gasoline had been crushed by a boulder. Streatfeild and two porters trekked across to the old French Base Camp at the foot of Gasherbrum I, where he knew that a cache of fuel had been left. But it had long since been removed by porters from Askole who had returned after the expedition to loot anything of value (a tradition that continues to the present day).

The first 1000 metres of the Spur was dominated by the need to find safe campsites. They spent several days puzzling an intricate line through tottering rock towers and little gullies before they came upon a perfect site for Camp II in a little hollow. Above this finding a good safe site became increasingly difficult. Rotten rock and frequent stonefall made progress alarming. In particular there was an ever-present danger of the leading climbers knocking rock on those below. Camp III was particularly vulnerable and two tents scored direct hits; fortunately no one was hurt. Eventually Streatfeild and Burdsall decided to descend with three Sherpas and continue the reconnaissance, mapping and photographing. Houston, Bates, House, Petzoldt and three Sherpas continued climbing upwards. In fact of the Sherpas only Pasang Kikuli ever climbed above Camp III.

The diminished team pressed on. Petzoldt led a hard, steep pitch up an overhang. Above, easier ground led to the base of a formidable barrier, a vertical band of red rock fifty metres high. Camp IV was pitched at its foot and to Bill House and Bob Bates fell the task of climbing this, the crux of the Abruzzi Spur.

Bill House was the best rock climber of the expedition and he set off up a wide chimney that narrowed to an awkward ice-filled crack. It took him four hours of desperate effort to climb twenty-five metres. It was almost completely unprotected, with only occasional resting places. At 6700 metres it was a superb lead. In 1980 Peter Boardman, arguably Britain's best Himalayan climber at that time, climbed House's Chimney and was impressed and surprised at its technical difficulty. He thought that when it was first climbed it must have been the hardest pitch in the Himalaya. Certainly it was far harder than anything climbed on Everest in the 1920s and 1930s. Camp V was placed at the top of the Chimney only a couple of rope lengths above Camp IV.

Above Camp V lurked the Black Pyramid, a complex area of steep weathered slabs and icy gullies. While the climbing was not as hard as House's Chimney it was sustained and serious, good ledges and belays were hard to find. It took a further camp halfway up which was literally hacked out of rock and rubble, before at last on 19 July only an icy traverse barred the way to Camp VII, at 7700 metres, just 200 metres below the great snowy Shoulder of K2.[1]

At this point the four climbers paused for thought. Their position could be seen in two ways. Optimistically they were poised for a real chance of a summit attempt. They had ten days' food left and with one more camp high on the Shoulder and three days of fine weather K2 could be theirs. And yet . . . and yet . . . The weather, which had been brilliant, surely couldn't last much longer? Away to the south the monsoon clouds could be seen building up on the horizon. Should they risk being trapped so high on the mountain? Could they manage to get down in a storm?

Two factors undoubtedly influenced their decision. Houston and his team were brought up in a tradition that valued safety and caution as a priority. Gambling with your life was not on. They were climbing for fun, not for fame and glory. The second factor was the original brief: to reconnoitre the mountain and, if possible, make an attempt on the summit. Psychologically it would have been hard for them suddenly to adopt the ruthless determination needed to climb K2 when they had already fulfilled most of their hopes and expectations. At its simplest, they were probably not quite psyched up enough to go for it. In the end they opted for something of a compromise. Houston and Petzoldt (chosen, as on Nanda Devi, by a majority vote) would climb as high as they could on the Shoulder and examine the final summit slopes. Surely there must have been a lurking hope that, just possibly, they might achieve a bit more than that . . .

All four climbers, plus the indomitable Pasang Kikuli, helped establish Camp VII and on the morning of 20 July the five made it to the site just below the Shoulder. Petzoldt and Houston were left to dig out a campsite and prepare for their final effort. Then suddenly a major problem presented itself. They had somehow forgotten to bring any matches with them. Unable to melt snow, so essential for survival,

[1] All the heights of campsites on the Abruzzi Spur are approximate. No two expeditions seem to give exactly the same heights for their camps and on the Shoulder in particular it is impossible to be precise about where each expedition put its tents. The foot of the Shoulder is generally considered to be at about 7800 metres and the top of the Bottleneck Couloir at about 8200 metres.

their attempt would fail before it had begun. A frantic search revealed nine matches in Houston's pockets. All were unreliable and three were used to light the stove. Six were left to last the next day and following morning. They had melted enough snow to reheat in the cold light of dawn and three more matches went to make breakfast. Then, unladen with camping gear, they set off.

The Shoulder of K2 is one of the very few easy-angled areas on the whole mountain. At its lowest point it is almost flat, steepening gently before butting up against a band of rock above which a huge sérac is poised like a frozen wave about to break. Avalanche debris often litters the upper part of the Shoulder and photos of the sérac band taken over the years show marked differences as massive chunks break off. But these collapses are mercifully infrequent and although it is possible that some climbers missing on the upper slopes in later years might have been struck, there is no evidence to prove it. Nevertheless the upper area of the Shoulder is still a dangerous place because of its altitude, and the danger of storms.

On 21 July, 1938, Petzoldt and Houston became the first to tread the snows of the Shoulder, ploughing through waist-deep powder and making slow progress. They pressed on up its crest until just under 8000 metres Houston had had enough. Petzoldt carried on for about fifty metres until he could see that there was a real chance of forcing through the rock band above him and there was what seemed to be a good, safe campsite below it. Petzoldt was now only some 600 metres from the summit which from the Shoulder seemed tantalisingly close.

Meanwhile Houston sat looking out towards Concordia about 3500 metres below him. It was a profound moment: 'I felt that all my previous life had reached a climax in these last hours of intense struggle against nature and yet nature had been very indulgent . . . I believe in those minutes at 26,000 feet on K2 I reached depths of feeling which I can never reach again.'

Petzoldt joined him and soon the two men descended to Camp VII in the twilight. Parched and exhausted they carefully prepared the stove and, with the very last match, it lit. Hot tea was brewed, but a cold breakfast was inevitable. In the morning a big ring around the sun and high clouds approaching confirmed their decision to go down, though the expected storm did not arrive.

The expedition retreated safely and methodically. By any standards it had done exceptionally well, certainly achieving a lot more than most of the British Everest expeditions in the 1930s, and yet there were people who felt it should have done even better. Oscar Dyhrenfurth even suggested that had Fritz Wiessner been present the mountain might well have been climbed; a contentious argument as will be seen from the next chapter. It seems just as likely that the expedition might have torn itself apart. *Cowboys on K2*, as Charlie Houston wryly nicknames their expedition book, *Five Miles High*, remains as a superb reminder of all that is best on a harmonious expedition. Tolerance, good humour and democratic decisions have been none too common on so many subsequent K2 expeditions. *Five Miles High* should be compulsory reading for anyone contemplating going to K2, and perhaps even more so for many who have returned from the mountain at odds with themselves or their companions.

7

Neither Saint nor Sinner

The tragic events of 1939, the recriminations and endless feuds, remain a tender scar in the annals of American climbing. So much has been written, analysed and dissected that the events of 1939 have become to Americans what Whymper and the Matterhorn were to the British, the Frêney Pillar disaster to the Italians or the 1934 Nanga Parbat tragedy to the Germans. Now, fifty-five years later, it seems pointless and cruel to try and load all the blame for what happened on any one person: a chain of events unfolded, in which several people played key roles – the interaction between them produced a terrible result.

Fritz Hermann Ernst Wiessner was thirty-nine, a stocky, immensely powerful man, whose commitment to lead and make the first ascent of K2 was absolute. Once Houston's expedition returned with the welcome news that a reasonable way had been found up the mountain, Wiessner set about organising the second attempt. It is easy to see in retrospect how the seeds of disaster were sown, almost from the outset, for a variety of reasons. Money or lack of it came high on the list. None of the 1938 team could afford to return so soon, and none was invited, with the exception of Bill House whose wealthy Pittsburgh family might have footed the bill. House had the talent and the experience to be high on Wiessner's list of candidates. He had also climbed with Wiessner frequently and it was this that caused him to pull out. For Wiessner was, by every account, a difficult man to spend any length of time with.

With America still fighting depression, Wiessner was forced from an early stage to invite people who could help pay for the expedition. Given that the initial pool of experienced climbers in the States was so small, and the four climbers from 1938 already discounted, his team was never a strong one and over the months leading to departure his first-choice climbers all dropped out. Sterling Hendricks, Alfred Lindley, Bestor Robinson and Roger Witney were all experienced climbers. Each withdrew with compelling excuses but underneath there was a feeling that Wiessner's personality was a common problem.

It is hard to discuss this without bringing up his German background, and all too easy to fall into the trap of racial stereotyping. Undoubtedly Wiessner was a rigid, single-minded, humourless and authoritarian figure. But these are by no means exclusively Teutonic characteristics – it is not hard to think of British, French and Italian climbers who have over the years displayed the same qualities and earned themselves huge accolades in the process. Many superstar climbers are impatient, intolerant, and totally unable to empathise with lesser mortals. This was at the heart of Fritz Wiessner's problem. The very qualities he displayed that might enable him to climb K2 could also be the undoing of the whole expedition, particularly an American one, with its own culture of democratic discussion and joint decision-making.

In the end Wiessner's team was both unbalanced and weak, so much so that even before it set out, questions were being asked about its chances of success. Maybe any other leader than Fritz Wiessner would have called the expedition off. But any other leader than Fritz Wiessner might not have ended up with such a curious collection of personalities, whose commitment to success varied widely and whose comprehension of what they were letting themselves in for was blinkered by Wiessner's own tunnel vision.

The team finally consisted of Wiessner himself leading, as always, from the front. His deputy leader was Tony Cromwell, a man whose main interest was mountaineering but not at a high level, and invariably in the company of guides. His private income was doubtless a factor in his selection, but he was also an efficient expedition treasurer. His climbing inadequacies were overlooked: he had after all amassed a lot of mountain experience. Chappel Cranmer and George Sheldon were both twenty and students at Dartmouth College. Both were promising but inexperienced climbers being thrown in at the deep end. The oddest choice was undoubtedly Dudley Wolfe. He was seriously rich, described by his nephew as 'being like something out of Scott Fitzgerald's The Great Gatsby'. He had all the playboy toys: power boats, yachts, fast cars. He had taken to skiing, then mountaineering at which he was enthusiastic but almost totally without ability. It frequently took two guides to haul his ungainly bulk up easy climbs. Worse, he was incapable of descending even easy ground without constant supervision and encouragement. But he was fit, strong and determined, and totally under the spell of Fritz Wiessner, who had obviously selected him for his money. Dudley Wolfe was desperate to prove himself and find meaning in a life that had often lacked direction. It was this combination of blind devotion, misplaced ambition and lack of skill and experience that would prove to be a fatal brew.

The last member to join up (or possibly be press-ganged) was twenty-seven-year-old pre-medical student at Dartmouth, Jack Durrance. When Bestor Robinson dropped out at the last moment with Wiessner already in Europe buying equipment, Durrance was drafted in with anonymous financial backing from members of the American Alpine Club. In the summers Durrance was a mountain guide in the Tetons with an excellent record of technical rock climbs. He certainly was quite good enough to join the team, but he had not met Wiessner, nor had he been chosen by him. Their first encounter sowed the seeds of a resentment that would last a lifetime.

Jack Durrance sailed for Europe. At Genoa he boarded the ship for India before the rest of the team and bumped into an elderly Italian gentleman looking for expedition members. It was the eighty-year-old photographer Vittorio Sella, anxious to meet the men returning to his beloved Karakoram. Five minutes later Wiessner arrived, intending, as leader, to be the one to welcome Sella. Instead he found him in conversation with a stranger. Durrance introduced himself and explained that Bestor Robinson was not coming. 'Can't quite forget Fritz's look of disappointment at finding insignificant Jack filling Bestor Robinson's boots,' Durrance wrote in his diary.

Despite his cold welcome the expedition quickly settled down and the voyage to Bombay was a pleasant interlude with its fair share of shipboard romance. The party travelled by train up to Srinagar in Kashmir where they picked up their English transport officer, Joe Trench, and nine Darjeeling Sherpas including, once again, Pasang Kikuli as sirdar. Four of the others had also been on Houston's expedition and, on paper at least, they seemed to be one part of Wiessner's expedition that was well up to scratch.

On 2 May, having found time for two weeks' skiing above Srinagar, the team set out following the by now well-known 300-mile approach march to Base Camp. This passed off uneventfully, apart from the almost mandatory porter strike at Urdokas, until on 30 May, just below Concordia, a tarpaulin was lost in a crevasse. Chappel Cranmer spent an age on the end of a rope searching for it before being hauled back to the surface. This immersion at 4500 metres must have been cold and exhausting and almost certainly precipitated a far more serious problem when two days later, on arrival at Base Camp, Cranmer developed what would now be quickly diagnosed as pulmonary oedema. Jack Durrance, despite an almost complete lack of medical experience, had been appointed expedition doctor on the strength of his future as a medical student, and was faced with a major crisis.

Cranmer sank into delirium, coughing up evil, bubbly fluid and developing diarrhoea as well. Interviewed years later, Durrance recalled, 'I never knew anyone could be so sick and stay alive . . . from the day I entered medical school until now at seventy-five, I've never had a worse patient than my first.' He did everything he could to keep his patient warm, dry and clean. 'In those days I wasn't very good at that sort of thing but I did what I could, everything I thought would be of help.' Durrance without doubt saved his life. After two days the crisis passed. Chappel would live but was already a non-starter for K2 itself. The team was down to five Americans, though Wiessner himself was always reluctant to accept that Chappel had been so ill.

Work started on the Abruzzi Spur on 8 June. Wiessner, out in front most, if not all, of the time, quickly found out that he was the only person able to make any progress on the mountain. Unlike in 1938 the weather was poor (perhaps 'typical' is a better word), with strong winds, frequent short storms, and between 21 and 29 June, a big storm that had the effect of dividing the team physically as well as psychologically. Out in front at Camp IV, Wiessner and Dudley Wolfe felt that with its clearing they would be able to press on for the top. Below them the rest of the team were shaken and disillusioned by the battering they had received and, ominously, were already thinking of home. There does seem to be a sea change on every expedition when the dominant mood swings from 'thinking up' to 'thinking down'. Ideally this should only occur when the summit is reached. Unfortunately, it sometimes happens before and once it does it is hard, if not impossible, to reverse. Wiessner was possibly the only person who possessed the sheer force of character to stop the rot, but out in front he grew steadily more fixated with the summit and less aware of the house of cards slowly collapsing beneath him.

Progress was being made, albeit slowly. On 30 June Wiessner climbed House's Chimney with Pasang Kikuli and the next day Dudley Wolfe was almost winched up to join them. Camp V was established as another three-day storm started. Supplies up the mountain were poor to non-existent. Tony Cromwell was proving to be an inadequate deputy and vacillated at every decision, endlessly delaying carries for the feeblest of reasons that could not hide his own lack of commitment. Higher up the mountain Jack Durrance seemed to be forever caught between the Devil and the deep blue sea. Wiessner, above, was always criticising him while driving ahead with Dudley Wolfe, the one man who Jack Durrance, with his guide's experience, was most concerned for. Below, the expedition was running rapidly out of steam. Durrance himself had found it hard to acclimatise and had been plagued early on by useless boots and cold feet. He was now suffering sleepless nights worrying about the way Wolfe was almost being conned ever higher up the mountain.

And yet Wolfe *was* still going up, slowly and clumsily, however long he spent trying to recuperate at each camp. It is important to remember that in 1939 there was still only a very vague understanding of acclimatisation and the then current theory (which was to persist well into the second half of the century) was that each stage of acclimatisation could only be achieved by spending prolonged time at any given altitude. Today the policy of 'climb high, sleep low' is well established, even if it is still often disregarded, sometimes with dire consequences. Now it is recognised that one deteriorates faster than one acclimatises during time spent above 6000 metres. Dudley Wolfe, once he left Base Camp, never returned, and he was to spend an extraordinary amount of time above 7000 metres. These days it is a known fact that permanent life is impossible above approximately 5500 metres and physical deterioration leading to death is dramatically accelerated above 7000 metres; so much so that the summit of Everest, at 8848 metres, is right on the limit for human survival and then only for a matter of hours rather than days. But in 1939, and doubtless thinking he was doing the right thing, Dudley Wolfe determinedly pressed ever upward in the footsteps of the seemingly indefatigable Fritz Wiessner.

Only once did Wiessner descend to Camp II to find out what, if anything, was going on. Exhorting his weary men for an all-out effort, he urged everyone capable to do a carry to the highest camp.

By the time they reached Camp IV below House's Chimney Wiessner, Durrance and Wolfe were the only ones capable of further progress to Camp VI, on the Black Pyramid. Jack Durrance was now acutely worried about Dudley Wolfe's ability and fitness. He was already showing slight signs of frostbite on his feet which should, to a more experienced man than Wolfe, have spelt out the need for an immediate retreat. But when Durrance 'strongly' advised this, Wolfe sought Wiessner's opinion which was predictably hostile to Durrance, assuming he was jealous of Wolfe and wanted to go higher himself.

In fact Jack Durrance would have been only too happy to see the expedition abandoned altogether. He was all too aware that Wolfe would find the descent difficult, if not impossible, without help. But his concern was to no avail, and the next day on the way to Camp VII he himself was in trouble, beginning to show symptoms of oedema: a violent headache, faintness and an inability to get his breath. Wiessner, as usual, thought he would recover almost immediately but, after an appalling night at Camp VI, Durrance wisely descended to Camp IV, then all the way down to Camp II and in doing so probably saved his own life.

This left Wiessner and Wolfe out on a limb. Between Camp II and Camp VII stretched a line of well-equipped camps but with only minimal Sherpa support. Since the early Everest expeditions of the 1920s the Sherpas had shown their worth as brave, sometimes heroic porters. But they were not the experienced mountaineers they are today. They were very dependent on obeying orders, often frightened on difficult ground, easily discouraged and, on top of this, their command of English was poor. It was asking too much of them to take all the day-to-day decisions high on the Abruzzi Spur without supervision.

By 17 July after yet another short storm, Fritz Wiessner, Dudley Wolfe and Pasang Lama, the strongest of the Sherpas, had established Camp VIII just below the Shoulder, and they set out on what they hoped would be the beginning of their summit bid. As soon as they crossed a bergschrund they immediately met bottomless snow. Poor lumbering Dudley Wolfe just couldn't make any progress, floundering in the others' tracks, and returned to Camp VIII. He would either try again with 'another party', in Wiessner's optimistic words, or stay and maintain contact with the rest of the team. Neither actually happened and for five days Dudley Wolfe was to be entirely on his own.

In the deep snow Wiessner and Pasang Lama only managed to gain the crest of the Shoulder before camping well short of their intended site and the next day it still took them several hours to reach a campsite on the flat top of a rock pillar, at around 8000 metres. This was presumably the site spotted by Petzoldt the year before and marked the end of known ground. Above reared the rock buttress and above that was the great frozen wave of the sérac band. Wiessner's camp was to the left (west) of the crest of the Shoulder and well out of the line of sérac fall.

His campsite and, more important, the route the following morning, were chosen because Wiessner was first and foremost a brilliant rock climber and would remain so until well into his seventies. Instinctively, rock was his first choice; he was inexperienced and uncomfortable on steep ice and the sérac band seemed to be a very obvious danger. On Nanga Parbat a sérac had collapsed under him, causing him a twenty-metre fall into a crevasse from which he was extremely lucky to escape alive. Wiessner therefore resolved to climb the broken rocks above his camp, traversing left under the steepest section of the rock buttress and turning in at its western extremity. From there he hoped to gain the much easier summit snow slopes.

The alternative would have been to bear right from the top camp and follow a snow gully, now known as the Bottleneck, cutting through the rocks directly underneath the sérac. From there a dangerous-looking left-hand traverse would lead to the same summit slopes. Understandably, Wiessner rejected it. Had he chanced his arm on 19 July it is possible that he would have changed the course of Himalayan climbing.

Wiessner and Pasang overslept and left Camp IX late, at nine a.m. This was regrettable, for the rock climbing on verglassed rock proved to be more difficult than it looked and the hours slipped by. Wiessner led all day on mixed ground far harder than anything previously climbed at that altitude. He graded it Six which was the highest grade given in the Western Alps at the time. As nobody has ever tried to repeat Wiessner's route it is impossible to verify this, but at that altitude it must have been an incredible performance.

At last, late in the day, only a short traverse separated him from the summit snows. He was at around 8365 metres, less than 250 vertical metres from the summit. In his words:

It was six p.m. by then. I had made up my mind to go for the summit despite the late hour and climb through the night. We had found a safe route and overcame the difficulties, and with the exception of the traverse had easy going from now on.

The weather was safe and we were not exhausted. Night climbing had to be done anyway, as it would take us a long time to descend the difficult route up which we had struggled. Much better to go up to the summit slowly and with many stops and return over the difficult part of the route the next morning. Pasang however did not have the heart for it; he wanted to go back to camp once he realised night was not far. He refused to go on, even did not pass my rope when I started the traverse. His reasoning and my lack of energy made me give in.

Did Pasang Lama, who had performed extremely well all day, rob Fritz Wiessner of the summit, or was his the voice of reason? It could well have been both, for had Wiessner pressed on, he would possibly have made the top, but to climb up and down through the night with no bivouac gear would have been a very hazardous gamble. Wearing leather nailed boots would have almost certainly led to severe frostbite and, however good the rest of their equipment may have been, the cruel cold air of a clear night on the summit of K2 would have tested them to the absolute limit. No wonder that it was later said that Pasang Lama dreaded the wrath of the mountain gods that inhabited the summit snows of K2!

Although forced to retreat, Wiessner told Pasang that they would try again. On their way up the broken buttress earlier in the day he had studied the gully on their right below the sérac barrier and realised that it was probably much safer than he had first thought. It would also take far less time, and he resolved to try it. But on their descent, by now in darkness, they had to make a difficult abseil. Pasang got tangled in the ropes and in trying to free himself he managed to dislodge the two pairs of crampons he was carrying on his rucksack which dropped away into the black depths below. This misfortune set the seal on their summit ambitions, though they didn't realise it immediately.

July 20 dawned fine and clear. But the pair at Camp IX were in no state to try again for the summit and they spent the day resting. It was so calm that at 8000 metres with the tent door open, Wiessner lay naked on his sleeping-bag. He was determined to set out on the 21st, this time via the Bottleneck Couloir. How realistic an attempt this might have been if they had been wearing crampons is hard to guess. Wiessner himself was always convinced they could have done it, but after so much time spent at altitude it is quite likely that he was deluding himself. Nevertheless, leaving at six a.m., he and Pasang traversed right and up towards the Bottleneck. Wiessner describes reaching 'a short steep slope just beneath the ice cliff' which would require step-cutting, '. . . a full day's work at this altitude so again we return . . .' Just how far up the Bottleneck he went is difficult to say.

After yet another night (the fifth) at 8000 metres, Wiessner decided to go down to Camp VIII and pick up spare crampons, more food and fuel and also a fresh Sherpa, for Pasang was now very tired. As they regained the camp Dudley Wolfe emerged from his tent. No one else had made it to Camp VIII, he had run out of matches, and was resorting to melting snow for water in the folds of the tent.

Wiessner was puzzled. Why had no one come up? But he did not seem as worried as he should have been that nine days had passed since they had last seen anyone else. They all decided to go down to Camp VII which was well equipped. On the way down Dudley Wolfe trod on the rope, which pulled Wiessner off. Suddenly all three were falling towards the huge 2000-metre drop to the Godwin-Austen Glacier, and only a desperate ice-axe arrest from Wiessner managed to stop them twenty metres short of disaster. Wolfe lost his sleeping-bag in the fall, and only Pasang had carried his down from Camp IX. Wiessner had left his, thinking he would be returning the same day. In twilight they reached Camp VII to find it abandoned. The tents were full of snow, the poles of one tent had broken and there were no sleeping-bags or mattresses.

The three had a miserable night and the following morning Wiessner made the fateful decision to leave Dudley Wolfe and descend with Pasang Lama to Camp VI to see what was happening. By doing this Wiessner split his team and left the weakest member on his own with everyone else below him. Whether or not Wolfe wanted to stay there for another attempt, as Wiessner later claimed he did, it was, at best, a lapse of responsibility by the leader quite likely caused by his prolonged stay at altitude. Wiessner must have known that Wolfe would be unable to descend unsupervised from so high on the mountain, and it seems almost unbelievable that, given the state of Camp VII, he still did not appear to realise that something was seriously amiss below. The only explanation must be that Wiessner was still fixated by the summit and just not prepared to accept the need to plan a safe retreat. Judgement, reflexes and perception were dulled by being too high for too long. A situation that would occur again on the Shoulder of K2.

All through 23 July Wiessner and Pasang descended, passing through four more abandoned camps. No sleeping-bags, no mattresses, and no American members or Sherpas. After another grim night at Camp II they managed, by this time on their last legs, to make it back to Base Camp. Barely able to speak but apoplectic with rage, Wiessner laid into the hapless Tony Cromwell. Why had they been abandoned? Why had the tents been stripped? What had happened to the Sherpa support?

The answers to these questions and the accusations that followed were to haunt the American climbing establishment for years to come. But at the time Wiessner, despite his exhaustion, seemed to be mainly concerned that he had been temporarily robbed of the summit. For several days after his return to Base Camp Wiessner planned another attempt, even hoping it would be possible to pick Dudley Wolfe up on the way. Gradually, though, it began to dawn on him that not only would he not be able to regain his high point but that saving the forlorn Dudley Wolfe was the only thing that mattered.

By now only the Sherpas were in any sort of condition to go high. Jack Durrance tried, but soon developed signs of the pulmonary problems that had beset him before. Wiessner was still unable to set out and in the end only Pasang Kikuli, by far and away the most experienced Himalayan climber on the expedition, Tsering Norbu, Pasang Kitar and Phinsoo were still willing and, what's more, fit enough to return. Pasang Kikuli and Tsering Norbu in fact climbed from Base Camp to Camp VI in one day – over 2000 metres of ascent! It was an astonishing performance, more in keeping with the 'speed ascents' of the 1980s. On 29 July, almost a week after Wiessner had left him, three of the Sherpas regained Camp VII and found Dudley Wolfe still alive but in a bad way. Bodily waste soiled the tent and he had again run out of matches. The Sherpas made him tea and managed to get him outside the tent but he refused to go down and told them to come back again the following day when he would be ready. The Sherpas, for whom blind obedience to the Sahibs was still ingrained, didn't argue, and went back to Camp VI, where it stormed for a day. On 31 July the same three, Pasang Kikuli, Pasang Kitar and Phinsoo set out one last time, either to rescue Dudley Wolfe or at least make him write a note that absolved them of any further responsibility. They were never seen again.

Whether they reached him and all four fell or were avalanched on the descent or whether the three Sherpas failed to make it to Camp VII is academic. What is virtually certain is that the attempt was doomed to failure from the start. Dudley Wolfe would be incapable of helping himself and three men would never have managed to lower the sick man all the way down to the Godwin-Austen Glacier. Anyone who has been involved in mountain rescue, and its complex techniques evolved since the Second World War, is aware that unless the victim can move himself it takes more men and equipment to evacuate a casualty than Wiessner's team could possibly muster. During the first week of August the weather had broken down completely and on 8 August any faint hope that there would be survivors was finally abandoned. K2 had claimed its first four victims.

The recriminations were not long coming. As is almost inevitable in disasters of this nature the arguments were compounded by guilt, sorrow, revenge and ignorance. Time and time again, the same potent brew would surface over accidents on K2, producing long-running sagas in which the original, often complex, circumstances were buried under huge volumes of half-truths and prejudice.

The 1939 controversy was particularly vitriolic and soon to be compounded by Wiessner's German origins and the outbreak of war. At its heart were two simple issues. Why had the camps on the Abruzzi been abandoned and stripped of their sleeping-bags and, given that set of circumstances, why was Dudley Wolfe left on his own?

To attempt to answer the first question let us return to 18 July, the day Fritz Wiessner and Pasang Lama are establishing their final camp. At the bottom of the mountain Jack Durrance is still recovering from illness. At Base Camp Tony Cromwell is preparing for the imminent return journey and porters from Askole are due to arrive on the 23rd. Jack Durrance receives a note from Cromwell asking him to bring down 'all the tents and sleeping-bags you can'. This is actually easier said than done, given the limited manpower, but Durrance, safe in the knowledge that there are still Sherpas high on the mountain above Camp IV, and all the camps are well stocked, does what he can – the more gear removed from lower down the mountain now, the less to be carried down by the (hopefully) successful climbers in a few days.

But unknown to Durrance, the Sherpas above, unsupervised, unclear as to their role, with little understanding of English and with
rapidly sinking morale, have failed to keep supplies moving upwards.
On 20 July Tendrup is the only porter to venture above Camp VII.
Alone and nervous he shouts up to the site of Camp VIII and
(not surprisingly) gets no reply.

Convincing himself that everyone above is dead, there is now
no point in staying up. Tendrup persuades the other Sherpas at
Camp VII that the best thing to do is descend with as many of
the most valuable bits of gear as they can carry. Sleeping-bags
have always been the most precious commodity on expeditions for
Sherpas, to be traded or used later at home. Once persuaded, the
deed is done rapidly. And so, almost by accident, the mountain is
stripped simultaneously by two teams, both hoping they are doing
the right thing, but all obeying their natural instincts which are to
go down and go home.

A mystery which has never been resolved concerns a note that
Fritz Wiessner alleges Jack Durrance wrote to him, congratulating
him on reaching the summit and saying he had had all the sleeping-
bags brought down from Camp IV by Kikuli and Dawa and that
they would descend with these and the ones from Camp II to Base
Camp. There would be no sleeping-bags at all from Camp IV down
as Wiessner, Wolfe and Pasang would have their own with them.
This note was allegedly left at Camp II for Wiessner on his way
down.

The problem was that no trace of the note has ever been found, and
Jack Durrance has no recollection of writing it. Andy Kauffman
and Bill Putnam surmise in *K2, the 1939 Tragedy* that there are
three possible explanations. First that Wiessner made the story up;
second that Durrance *did* write it and it was later lost or thrown away
and third that Wiessner mistook the note that Tony Cromwell wrote
to Jack Durrance. Wiessner didn't mention the note at all until 1955.
It seems unlikely that he deliberately lied, though it is just possible.
Durrance on the other hand is certain that he didn't write it. Perhaps
the most likely explanation is that Wiessner wrongly assumed that a
note addressed to Jack Durrance was *from* him not *to* him. In the
aftermath of such a fraught expedition it is easy to give the note
more meaning and importance than it deserves.

After the expedition Cromwell became the focus of all Wiessner's
anger. He in turn held Wiessner totally responsible for the deaths

– adding fuel to the flames by stating publicly on his return to America that Wiessner had murdered Dudley Wolfe. On his own return Wiessner tactlessly told reporters that 'on big mountains, as in war, one must expect casualties'. Given that war had just broken out in Europe, this remark gave his detractors, many of whom were anti-German, another stick to beat him with. Perhaps the most outspoken critic of Wiessner was Kenneth Mason who wrote the classic Himalayan history, *Abode of Snow*. 'It is difficult to record in temperate language the folly of this enterprise,' was his summing-up of a very one-sided account of what happened.

Jack Durrance was appalled at the feud between Wiessner and Cromwell and decided from an early stage to keep a dignified silence. This he maintained for fifty years, during which time both Wiessner and public opinion turned against him instead of Cromwell. The American Alpine Club was torn by the controversy and in 1941 Wiessner resigned. He was readmitted in 1966 after a lot of persuasion from his friends, becoming an honorary member for his services to American climbing generally. But he never returned to the Himalaya. He died in 1988.

Durrance, in the end, emerges with credit. His diaries show that his concern with the performance of Dudley Wolfe was motivated by responsibility not jealousy and that the sleeping-bag removal was instigated by Cromwell and compounded by the Sherpas' lack of direction.

In the end Wiessner must be judged as neither saint nor sinner, but as a brilliant, single-minded climber, who was temperamentally unsuited to the demands of leadership. Chris Bonington, who has had more experience of leading major Himalayan expeditions than most, is firmly of the opinion that the leader must be prepared to carry out his role by spending most of his time behind and below the lead climbers, whose drive and commitment will invariably prevent their having a totally objective view of the whole venture. By leading from the front Wiessner cut himself off from his team both physically and psychologically.

And yet it could so easily have turned out differently. If Wiessner had decided that the Bottleneck Couloir was worth risking on 19 July, K2 might have been climbed. The descent would have been carried out with Sherpas still placed in high camps and most of the tensions existing within the team would have been forgotten in the euphoria of success. The ascent, without oxygen, would have made K2 the first of the fourteen 8000-metre peaks to be climbed and could well have changed the course of Himalayan climbing after the war. Ironically, the choice of route was a decision that Fritz Wiessner made for the best possible reason – safety. How sad that it should, albeit indirectly, have provoked such a terrible outcome.

8

Strangers and Brothers

The Second World War put paid to any further expeditions and after the war came the Partition of India in 1947 and the creation of the Muslim nation of Pakistan. In the turmoil of its birth, expeditions to K2 near the controversial new border with Kashmir were out of the question. This did not deter Charles Houston who had wanted to return since 1939. Despite his constant efforts it was not until 1952 that he made any progress. Even then it took the influence of the American Ambassador to Pakistan before permission was at last granted for an attempt in 1953. By this time Charlie Houston was one of America's most experienced Himalayan climbers. He had taken part in the first reconnaissance of the south (Nepalese) side of Everest in 1950 when with Bill Tilman they reached the foot of the Khumbu Icefall that bars access into the Western Cwm of Everest. This was to be the key to the eventual success.

On K2, Houston was again accompanied by his oldest and best friend Bob Bates. William House had to pull out but Houston and Bates were still able to select a strong and experienced party of eight men, two more than 1938, and for a very good reason. After Partition, Sherpas were unwelcome in Pakistan and local Hunza porters would have to take their place. Hunzas had already proved themselves on pre-war Nanga Parbat expeditions and were a hardy mountain race, though not quite as experienced as the Sherpas were rapidly becoming. Houston guessed that they would find the Abruzzi Spur beyond their ability and only planned to use them for carries from Base Camp to Camp II. So the team was increased, but not doubled or trebled, for Houston and Bates knew that campsites on the Abruzzi were difficult to find and more numbers would not necessarily make the climb easier. It was a lesson that other teams would have done well to heed in the future when some truly colossal expeditions

would arrive at Base Camp. But Houston and Bates remained true
to their pre-war alpine-style ethic.

They interviewed a lot of good people, trying to choose a com-
patible, rather than a brilliant, team that would work together.
Choosing the right people was one of the reasons that they were later
able to survive an appalling and protracted ordeal. Their team was
made up of Bob Craig, mountaineer and ski instructor, from Aspen,
Colorado; Art K. Gilkey, a geologist from Iowa; Dee Molenaar,
also a geologist and artist; Pete Schoening from Seattle; George
F. Bell, a physics professor at Cornell University; and an English
army officer, Captain H. R. A. Streather, who would be transport
officer. Since Partition Streather had served with the Chitral Scouts
and had already climbed Tirich Mir with a Norwegian expedition,
though on his own admission he was then a complete novice. Tony
Streather was considered for the 1953 Everest expedition, but turned
down because of his lack of Alpine and technical climbing expertise.
Charlie Houston's invitation to K2 arrived almost the same day
as his rejection letter for Everest. Ironically, he had been turned
down for an expedition to a technically simple route, and invited
instead to attempt a far harder one.

Like Houston's 1938 expedition it was a harmonious and happy
party that gathered in Rawalpindi towards the end of May. After
picking up their liaison officer, Colonel Atta Ullah, and Tony
Streather and completing a hectic week of engagements, they flew
to Skardu and in an hour and a half did what in 1938 and 1939
had taken two weeks of hard walking. Since Partition the old
approach from Srinagar was out of the question. Now Skardu
had trebled its population, both civilian and military, acquired a
hospital and an airport, and become the jumping-off point for all
future Central Karakoram expeditions.

The day they left for Skardu the expedition heard that the British
had succeeded on Everest. They must have had mixed feelings about
this and certainly the motivation for Houston's comparatively small
expedition to succeed must have been turned up a few notches.

The walk-in seems to be unique in that there is no record of a
porter strike! Twenty-six days after leaving America they arrived at
Base Camp in good spirits and soon work on the lower part of the
Abruzzi Spur was smoothly under way. To see if he was technically
up to it, Charlie Houston diffidently asked if anyone would mind
if he led House's Chimney and, with its ascent, felt that he could

K2 from Windy Gap. The Duke of the Abruzzi's classic 1909 photograph, often mistakenly credited to Vittorio Sella. (*Museo Nazionale della Montagna, Turin*)

Lieutenant T. G. Montgomerie, R.E., who designated the mountain K2 in 1856.

Godfrey Thomas Vigne made at least four journeys into the Karakoram.

Captain Henry Haversham Godwin-Austen, the first European to penetrate the Baltoro Glacier.

Roberto Lerco, the first to get a close look at the South-East Spur as early as 1890.

Captain B. Grombczewski,
agent to the Tsar,
Younghusband's 'opponent' in
the Great Game.

Sir Francis Younghusband saw
the north side of K2 on his epic
crossing of the Old Mustagh
Pass.

William Martin Conway
epitomised the romantic
explorer-mountaineer.

A.D. McCormick's painting of
Conway surveying from the
summit of Pioneer Peak.

McCormick's painting of K2 from the Throne Glacier. McCormick was one of the last expeditioning artists in the field at a time when photography was beginning to take over the duty of record.

The first expedition to attempt to climb K2 in 1902. *Above left*, Oscar Eckenstein, maverick equipment designer and leader. *Above right*, Aleister Crowley, diabolist and unconventional mountaineer. *Below*, the team: left to right, Wesseley, Eckenstein, Dr Jacot-Guillarmod, Crowley, Pfannl and Knowles.

Above, Vittorio Sella's classic 1909 photograph of the Mustagh Tower from the Upper Baltoro Glacier, a picture that was to inspire a future generation of climbers. (*Museo Nazionale della Montagna, Turin*). *Below left*, the Duke of the Abruzzi, the impressive leader of a talented team. *Below right*, Vittorio Sella, the grandfather of mountain photography.

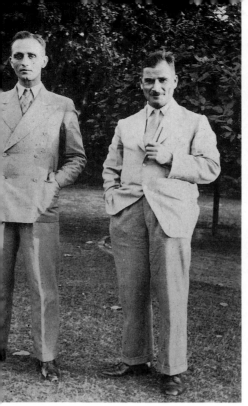

Above left, Eric Shipton and Bill Tilman, the most impressive partnership of the 'thirties, before setting out on their extensive explorations north of K2 in 1937. *Above right*, Houston's team reconnoitre the Savoia Glacier below the West Face of K2 in 1938. *Below*, the 1938 American expedition: back row, left to right, Petzoldt, Bates, Burdsall; front row, Houston, Streatfeild, House.

Above, Charles Houston. He and Petzoldt were the first climbers to reach the Shoulder. Houston was to return to the challenge of K2 after the Second World War. *Left*, the Americans' Camp V at the top of House's Chimney, 1938.

cope with anything else K2 had to offer. A pulley system was rigged at the top of the Chimney to haul loads up the outside walls. The weather was much worse than in 1938, with frequent short storms. Nevertheless progress was slow but sure, as the old campsites from 1938 and 1939 were reached and made habitable.

The higher they climbed the more apprehensive they became, for the mystery of Dudley Wolfe and the three Sherpas had never been resolved. Tony Streather remembers his unspoken fear that they would find their remains. At the site of Camp VI, which the Sherpas had left on their last attempt to rescue Wolfe, they found some sad remnants. Inside the wrecked tents were the Sherpa sleeping-bags neatly rolled up and ready to be carried down with the stricken Wolfe. A stove, fuel and a small bundle of tea wrapped in a handkerchief were the only other poignant reminders of the three brave men. Nothing else was found higher up to shed light on what might have happened.

As on the previous expedition the Black Pyramid provided sustained and precarious climbing. The expedition had taken longer to reach Camp VI than in 1938, and supplies, while not becoming critical, were certainly starting to cause some anxiety. Even matches, which had been such a problem in 1938, were beginning to get low and Houston had nightmares about running out again. The climb was becoming a struggle. 'Gone were most of the jokes; the banter had become more serious. We were more determined than ever, but the picnic was over.'

By the end of July Schoening and Gilkey had pushed the route out in poor weather to establish Camp VIII just under the Shoulder of K2. On 2 August the whole team arrived there, all safe and well with enough food for a serious summit bid. But the weather was breaking down and soon a full-scale storm was raging.

Much has been written about the monsoon not reaching the Karakoram. But it seems clear that in heavy monsoon years, of which 1953 was certainly one, the weather on K2 is affected by it and there have been some prolonged and ferocious storms on K2 in the last days of July and the first ten days of August. 1986 is another case in point.

At first Houston's little team were in good spirits: 'Bob Bates read aloud to us for hours. Dee Molenaar painted. We all wrote diaries.' They were still thinking upwards, so much so that Houston, true to his democratic roots, took a secret ballot to decide on the summit teams. '. . . When I crawled back from the other tents through the blizzard I was prouder than ever before of my party. When the ballots were counted Bell and Craig were to be the first team, Gilkey and Shoening the second.' As on Nanda Devi all those years before, Charlie Houston hoped that the names of the would-be summiteers would be kept secret. 'We hoped to report, "Two men reached the top" – no more, no less.'

During the fourth night of storm George Bell and Charlie Houston watched their tent start to disintegrate. At dawn it collapsed completely and Bell crawled in with Molenaar and Craig, while Houston remarked, 'Streather and Bates pretended to be glad to have me crowd into their tent, a French model with lining which made it very cramped even for two.'

By the afternoon of 6 August they were dispirited and discussed a partial retreat for the first time. They had radio contact with Colonel Atta Ullah at Base Camp with whom they had all become very close. He was tuned into Radio Pakistan weather forecasts which were grim. Could they descend to Camp IV, regroup, rest, rehydrate, then have another attempt? It seemed a forlorn hope and was to be cruelly dashed the next day.

August 7 was less windy and brighter. Everyone crawled from their tents and 'stumbled around like castaways first reaching shore'. But Art Gilkey suddenly collapsed and passed out. He came round quickly: 'I'm all right, fellows; it's just my leg, that's all . . . I've had this Charley horse [cramp] for a couple of days . . . I thought it would be gone by now. It's sure to clear up in another day – isn't it?'

Houston examined him and knew that disaster had struck. Art had developed thrombophlebitis – blood clots in the veins of his left leg. At sea level his condition could be serious with a possibility of clots breaking off and being carried into the lungs. But at that height, around 7800 metres, Gilkey's chances of survival were virtually non-existent. Houston tried to reassure Gilkey while 'trying to hide my awful certainty that he would never reach Base Camp alive'.

Now thinking downwards was all they could do. Tony Streather, interviewed forty years after the event, summed up his own feelings then, feelings that were almost certainly shared by everyone else.

I think we had deteriorated to the extent that we didn't think anything very logically, we just did what was obviously necessary at the time. We thought Art was going to die. We didn't think he would ever live. I don't think we kidded ourselves or didn't admit it to ourselves. As far as we were concerned, while he was still alive, we were trying to carry him down . . . in retrospect I don't think there was ever any chance.

Despite everyone's deep foreboding there was never any question of leaving Art Gilkey. Somehow every effort must be made to save him. They discussed their options: 1. try to get Gilkey down; 2. Gilkey and Houston to stay in camp while the others went down for more supplies; 3. all sit it out until the weather cleared, by which time Art Gilkey might be dead.

Hastily they packed up. Charlie Houston with ingrained good habits attempted to clear the campsite, throwing supplies of food away and dismantling the tents. He was stopped – no time for that now – and they started down. After a very short time it became obvious that they were pulling Gilkey on to textbook avalanche-prone slopes: feet of powder snow lying on hard ice with no chance to consolidate. There was no choice but to return to the camp – mercifully still intact. But it took a major effort to get Gilkey back up.

By now they had spent seven nights at Camp VIII and faced an even longer stay at an altitude which would eventually kill them all if they remained there. In despair Bob Craig and Pete Schoening explored the descent of a steep rock rib that seemed to lead eventually to Camp VII and give some security from avalanches. The next day was slightly better and Houston thought that the weather was now on the change. They decided to wait one more day in the hope that it would really improve. As a last gesture of defiance Craig and Schoening set out on a forlorn gesture – climbing *up* the Shoulder for some 150 metres before returning to the tents.

On 9 August the storm returned at full force. No one could move and for the first time Houston thought that they might all die. During the night Art Gilkey had begun to cough and his pulse rose to 140 per minute. Clots seemed to have carried to his lungs. Art apologised for being a burden and talked about the others making a further summit bid: 'Art said nothing of himself. He had never talked about his death, though he was too wise not to see its imminence.'

August 10 dawned cold, grim and windy. Conversations had to be yelled to be understood. Art *had* to descend, a clot was forming in his other leg and he couldn't survive much longer at that height.

Quickly the others packed up, taking the lightest of the tents, 'in case of emergency', as Bob Bates wrote. (One has to wonder just what *would* constitute an emergency, if not their present predicament.) Then they set off. 'Each of us realised that he was beginning the most dangerous day's work of his life.'

The nightmare descent began. In freezing, numbing spindrift Gilkey was first pulled through deep snow then, when the angle increased, lowered. Every manoeuvre demanded the utmost concentration and the seven battered men began to realise the enormity of their task. Art Gilkey, strapped into a makeshift stretcher of a wrapped tent, a rucksack and a rope cradle, was uncomplaining but silent, his face a bluish grey. But whenever anyone asked how he was he would force a smile. 'Just fine . . . just fine.'

Painfully slowly they lost height. At one stage they set off a powder-snow avalanche which nearly swept Craig and Gilkey away, but the rope from above held. At last they got to a point on the rock rib where they could start to traverse across to the abandoned site of Camp VII. Pete Schoening was belaying Art Gilkey and Dee Molenaar. Above them were Houston and Bates and Bell and Streather. Craig had unroped from Gilkey and crossed to the shelf on which the camp had been placed.

Suddenly George Bell slipped on hard ice and fell out of control. Streather was pulled off and the two of them cannoned into Houston and Bates who were traversing below them. All four hurtled down the slope with nothing to stop them going all the way to the Godwin-Austen Glacier – nothing, that is, except the rope from Art Gilkey to Dee Molenaar, which somehow caught and snagged Tony Streather. Molenaar was plucked off and all five carried on falling until the strain came on to Art Gilkey and that in turn came on Pete Schoening belaying him above with an ice-axe jammed into snow behind a rock. Miraculously, Schoening held them all. Miraculously, no rope broke.

The whole jumble of tangled rope and bodies slid to a halt in total confusion. Far below George Bell minus rucksack, glasses and mittens staggered in confusion. Bob Bates and Dee Molenaar were tangled together and were almost cutting Tony Streather in half. And Charlie Houston lay crumpled and unconscious on a ledge poised over a huge drop. Bob Bates soloed down to him and Houston came round, concussed and confused. 'Where are we?' he kept repeating. 'What are we doing here?'

Bob Bates, knowing that if Charlie Houston couldn't help himself no one else could, looked his old friend in the eye. 'Charlie, if you ever want to see Dorcas and Penny [his wife and daughter] again, climb up there *right now!*'

Mechanically Houston obeyed and climbed brilliantly. Bates followed slowly to reach Dee Molenaar, trying to answer Charlie's insistent question, 'What are we doing here?'

Stunned, shocked, facing frostbite and, above all, exhausted, it was essential to get a tent up quickly. Gilkey, who had not fallen and was probably the warmest of them all, was anchored securely by two ice-axes in the gully he was being lowered into when the accident had occurred. The others moved across and tried to get Bell and Houston warmed up in the tent. Now Pete Schoening, the strongman of the party, seemed on the verge of collapse and was coughing uncontrollably. Art Gilkey had been shouting to them but in the wind they couldn't understand what he was saying. At last Bob Bates and Tony Streather returned to the gully to try and bring him down. Bob Bates wrote, 'What we saw there I shall never forget. The whole slope was bare of life. Art Gilkey was gone.'

It has often been surmised that Art Gilkey had somehow cut himself free in an attempt to save the others, but Charlie Houston firmly believes this to be impossible.

Memories aren't clear about Gilkey's shouting. If he did it was only once or twice and muffled by the gust of wind. He was almost unconscious the last time I spoke with him (and, I believe, I gave him another shot to ease his pain) . . . there was no way he had the strength, freedom or intention to struggle himself free: he was almost dead by then – at least that's what I believe and the others feel similarly.

There seemed to be a faint groove in the gully that had not been there before. Gilkey had been avalanched. The two men, disbelieving and crushed by this last and biggest blow, returned to the tents.

The survivors had a horrendous night. Charlie Houston was severely concussed, hyperventilating and trying to cut a hole in the tent saying they would die from lack of oxygen. He kept asking the same questions: 'How's Pete? How's Tony?' Somehow the long night passed and the seven exhausted men emerged to fight another day.

Art Gilkey's death, however harrowing, undoubtedly saved them. Now they only had to fight for their own survival and it would take them the whole of the next day just to get down to Camp VI, which was still over 7000 metres. On the descent Tony Streather recovered a small bag, believing it belonged to Art Gilkey. But it didn't, it belonged to George Bell and miraculously contained a spare pair of unbroken glasses which cheered him up immensely. There was no sign of Gilkey except for some blood-streaked rocks, a tangle of ropes and an ice-axe shaft jammed in some rocks. No one mentioned this on the way down and it was not until the team was reunited that they all admitted they had seen those remnants.

George Bell's feet were badly frostbitten and, as Houston's concussion faded, Bell became the one to worry about. All the next day they descended carefully, aware that they were still not safe. At the top of House's Chimney Houston, insisting as leader on 'first up, last down', belayed everyone down in the dusk and supervised the lowering of all the rucksacks. By the time everyone else was safe in Camp IV just below it was dark.

Houston then had to abseil into the void but couldn't tell which, amongst the remnants of old ropes that littered the chimney, was the new one. He knelt in the snow and recited the Lord's Prayer, then climbed down without using them. Thankfully, he rejoined his companions in the camp below.

The descent to Camp III was more tedious than dangerous and there the exhausted men found plenty of food. After a decent meal they decided to go on to Camp II. Here the Hunza porters were waiting and, in an emotional reunion, many tears were shed and the Hunzas spontaneously said a prayer for Art Gilkey. It was, said Bob Craig, 'the deepest experience I've ever had with a human being'.

Back at Base Camp at last they received another heartfelt welcome from Colonel Atta Ullah, who, through regular radio contact, had become a vital part of the team. They made an hour-long tape-recording that evening of all that had happened. As Charlie Houston concluded, 'We entered the mountain as strangers, but we left as brothers.'

The day after their return, the Hunza porters built a memorial cairn that still stands on a tiny saddle of an outlying spur of rock at the confluence of the Savoia and Godwin-Austen Glaciers. It commands a superb view down to Concordia and across the South Face of K2. The team limped the four hundred metres to the cairn. They laid mountain flowers, the flags they had hoped to take to the summit, a favourite poem and Art's own ice-axe which he had given to Bob Craig just after the multiple fall. Bob Bates read a passage from the Bible and said a prayer. Then they turned away and began the preparations for the long journey home. George Bell had to be carried in a makeshift stretcher, but in the end lost only one small toe and half a big toe.

Unlike the bitterness surrounding the Wiessner expedition, the 1953 American K2 expedition became a symbol of all that is best in mountaineering. Today the team are still united in friendship and their shared ordeal brought them a depth of understanding and insight that is very apparent in their reunions. For Houston himself the expedition was a turning point. For many years he found it hard to come to terms with Art's death and suffered depressions, even, on one occasion, amnesia on the anniversary of the accident. Initially, he wanted to return in 1954 and was mortified to find that 'his' mountain had been booked by a large Italian expedition. Although he had permission for 1955 he didn't take it up and 1953 marked the end of his serious mountaineering. Instead he turned to the study of high-altitude medicine and in the last forty years he has become one of the world's greatest authorities on every aspect of the subject. It is surely no accident that his desperate attempt to save Art Gilkey has in a sense continued, for his research has surely saved many, many more lives since then.

Exactly forty years later, in 1993, Art Gilkey's remains were found just above the site of the presentday Base Camp. Several pieces of clothing, including a down jacket, and fragments of skull and other bones were positively identified as his. Eight years earlier an old ice-axe had been found at the base of the mountain, its shaft snapped below the head. It was in all probability the other end of the shaft that the 1953 team noted on the descent. Gilkey's bones were returned to the United States for burial in the family plot. As well as Gilkey's remains, the bones of a very small Asian were found further up the glacier. They were almost certainly the remains of Pasang Kitar who was apparently well below the average size of Sherpas.

When Charlie Houston's team left for home it was the middle of August. But K2 was to be visited again that year, and again the next. With Everest and Nanga Parbat climbed in 1953, how much longer could the Mountain of Mountains hold out?

9

A Sahib Is About to Climb K2

When Houston's team returned to Rawalpindi they met a man who also had continuing designs on K2. Professor Ardito Desio, the geographer on the Italian 1929 expedition, had been as persistent as Houston in applying for permission and in 1953 he was allowed to make a reconnaissance. Quite what its purpose was is not clear, for after three serious attempts on the Abruzzi Spur by the Americans, who had in their turn based their efforts on the Duke of the Abruzzi's explorations, there seemed little point in travelling all the way to the foot of K2 and back, apart from the strategic value of staking a claim for future attempts.

Professor Desio was, and still is, one of the great authorities on the Karakoram but makes no claims to be a mountaineer. Deeply involved in both the scientific programme and in fund-raising and all the political manoeuvring in Italy and Pakistan that mounting a major national expedition entailed, it was natural that he should look to an experienced climber to accompany him on the reconnaissance, and possibly appoint him as climbing leader if and when a fullscale expedition came about. Riccardo Cassin was an obvious choice, yet indirectly it would lead to a series of controversies that highlighted the differences between scientific exploration and mountaineering and, perhaps more important, the differences between a largely obsolete, authoritarian style of leadership and the democratic intimate rapport that the Americans had shown so effectively in 1953.

The reconnaissance was funded by two bodies: the Italian Research Council, who paid for Desio, and the Italian Alpine Club who met most of Cassin's expenses. This division led to travel arrangements in which Cassin invariably came off worst. At forty-four Riccardo Cassin was already the doyen of Italian climbing with a track record in the Alps and Dolomites second to none. Yet Desio appeared to treat him as a second-class citizen. Throughout the trip Cassin had to take the train while Desio flew. In Pakistan this meant a gruelling thirty-six hours across the Sind Desert from Karachi to Rawalpindi where, on his arrival, Cassin was excluded from a reception given by Colonel Atta Ullah for the returning American expedition. Desio went alone to pick their brains, while Cassin had to make do with seeing the team off at the airport two days later.

This couple made an uneventful journey up the Baltoro late in the season and merely confirmed, as if it was necessary, that the Americans had indeed attempted the Abruzzi Spur. Then they travelled home, Cassin once again suffering the train to Karachi before the flight to Rome.

Back in Italy permission quickly came through for an attempt in 1954. Initially Desio was to be the leader with Cassin as head of the mountaineering team. But Desio soon persuaded Cassin to resign from the organising committee, which then declared that as a result of medical examinations Cassin was unfit to take part in the expedition! It seemed to be a not very subtle ploy by Desio to exclude Cassin, possibly because as a star performer he would take media attention away from the respectable, scientific research and leadership that Desio himself would provide.

Here in a nutshell was Desio's dilemma. He wanted, above all, for K2 to be climbed. Yet in his final expedition plan, dated 5 December, 1953, his first aim was scientific, his second the 'conquest'. He realised that the two aims should be independent but might in reality overlap. Rather ominously he wrote, 'The expedition will of necessity be organised along military lines, in a sense that will be familiar to all who have spent some part of their lives – especially under wartime conditions – in our Alpine regiments.' Within such rigid parameters it is hard to imagine how the volatile flower of Italian mountaineering could blossom. Cassin's exclusion left him understandably bitter. It also made Desio's task harder. Cassin's presence and the respect he would undoubtedly have generated from the younger climbers might well have prevented or minimised the controversy that was to scar the expedition for years to come.

Desio eventually left Italy with a well-prepared and tested climbing team. It consisted of Enrico Abram, Ugo Angelino, Walter Bonatti, Achille Compagnoni, Cirillo Floreanini, Pino Gallotti, Lino Lacedelli, Mario Puchoz, Ubaldo Rey, Sergio Viotto and Gino Solda. Four scientists, a doctor and Mario Fantin, a climber and film-maker, made up the team. Even allowing for Cassin's absence it was probably just about as good a selection of Italian climbers as was possible, though none of them had any previous Himalayan experience.

Perhaps the most interesting choice was that of Walter Bonatti, at twenty-four the youngest member of the team. He had already amassed a formidable list of Alpine climbs including the Walker Spur on the Grandes Jorasses, the North Face of the Badile, the East Face of the Grand Capucin (a first ascent), and a winter ascent of the North Face of the Cima Grande di Lavaredo. There was no doubt that Bonatti was the most talented climber selected by Desio, but would he perform as well at extreme altitude? Would his youth and inexperience of working with a large team count against him?

Desio openly modelled his organisation on John Hunt's successful Everest expedition of the year before, though comparisons are revealing. Hunt's team probably had far less technical climbing expertise but of the eleven climbers (the same number as Desio's) all bar two had been to the Himalaya before and, of course, they had a very experienced group of Sherpas led by Tensing, a veteran of seven previous Everest expeditions.

Desio, determined to learn from the British experience, had no hesitation in taking and using oxygen, the first K2 expedition to do so for other than medical emergencies. Nowadays it may be seen as a retrograde step, but at the time the prevailing mood was that on the really high mountains no holds were barred. The problem with oxygen however is that once the decision to use it has been taken, the whole logistical build-up is increased exponentially. The deadweight of cylinders (in 1953 each complete set weighed around forty pounds) has to be carried to the highest camp before it can be used and the growing pyramid of carries needed to do this is reflected all the way back to Base Camp and even to the number of porters used on the long walk-in. This partially explains why the big oxygen-based expeditions to K2 like Desio's have used up to seven hundred porters, and in one case a mind-boggling fifteen hundred. (Alan Rouse, the leader of the 1986 British K2 expedition and an ex-Cambridge University mathematics student, once tried to persuade me that if the walk-in to K2 was four or five days longer it would take the entire population of the world to carry enough food and fuel to get an expedition to Base Camp!)

When Desio's team arrived in Skardu he managed to wangle a flight around K2. This was undertaken in an unpressurised DC3, using the expedition's own oxygen sets and masks and must have been an exciting couple of hours. They flew up the Baltoro Glacier, to Concordia, then north past the Abruzzi Spur and over Windy Gap at around 7000 metres, before turning sharp left to fly back past the North Ridge of K2 down the Sarpo Laggo and the Trango Glaciers towards Askole and over the Skoro La to Shigar and Skardu. It was the first time K2 had been circumnavigated by air, and may well be the last, as it infringes Chinese airspace. As a reconnaissance flight it must have been of even more dubious value than Desio's brief visit the year before, for the Abruzzi was passed so quickly that nothing important was noted. In any case Desio had not thought to take any of the climbing team with him. He did, however, take a unique aerial photograph of the North Face which revealed that the North Ridge is not as steep as earlier pictures (including his own) had shown. It was to be another thirty years before this would have any significance.

Desio's huge expedition left Skardu in two parties and by 31 May they were all reunited at Base Camp, after bad weather had caused the main party several delays. One incident that Desio knew nothing about at the time was a spectacular mishap to his brightest star. Walter Bonatti was asleep in his sleeping-bag at Urdokas when Lacedelli jokingly picked him up and wrestled with him but Bonatti, stark naked, slid out of the bag and rolled down the steep boulder-strewn hill below, knocking himself out and severely bruising himself in the process. Both men were appalled at the thought of Desio's reaction if he found out, and Bonatti spent several days confined to his tent with 'stomach trouble' until he could walk again.

The advance party of Compagnoni, Gallotti, Puchoz and Rey established the first two camps on the Abruzzi and by 14 June Camp IV had been reached, as usual at the foot of House's Chimney. Then on 18 June Mario Puchoz, a thirty-six-year-old guide from Courmayeur who had emerged from the medical tests as one of the strongest and fittest expedition members, developed what seemed to be a throat infection at Camp II. It was not thought sufficiently serious to return to Base Camp but after two days Puchoz, by now on antibiotics and oxygen, did not appear to be any better, though his condition still didn't seem particularly grave. Then, early in the morning of 21 June, 'after a very brief agony', Puchoz died. It does seem likely that he had developed pulmonary oedema, not the pneumonia for which he was being treated. Oedema does not respond to antibiotics and it was still not realised that immediate descent is the first and most important action to take. The Italians were devastated and, to make matters worse, the weather broke and Puchoz's body had to be left at Camp II until 26 June, when it was brought down and buried at the Gilkey memorial the next day. Morale, which had been at rock bottom, recovered somewhat with the vow to continue the expedition in his memory.

Learning from Houston's expedition the Italians used a winch to ferry loads up House's Chimney. Unlike the Americans, they relied much more heavily on their Hunza high-altitude porters whose performance ranged from enthusiastic loyalty to 'capriciousness' as Desio delicately describes it. Language problems undoubtedly played their part and here Colonel Attah Ullah, who had once again taken up the difficult position of liaison officer, proved invaluable in keeping both sides happy.

As seemed to be the norm on K2, the weather remained poor and the expedition gradually turned into a war of attrition. A further disaster was only averted by luck when Floreanini, descending on old American fixed ropes below Camp III, pulled out the anchors and took a horrific, bounding 250-metre fall before stopping on a ledge just above Camp II. Bruised and bleeding, but amazingly with no broken bones, he was carried down to the camp by a Hunza porter where he spent several days recovering from his injuries and severe shock.

Desio at Base Camp could do little directly to affect events on the mountain except send a series of notes exhorting the climbers to do their best: 'The honour of Italian mountaineering is at stake,' concluded message number ten which, true as it may have been, wouldn't have helped much to overcome the Black Pyramid.

By 12 July morale was again sagging and the weather was once again poor. Desio took it upon himself to deliver 'message number eleven' in person at Camp II. This he did though its contents are not revealed in the expedition book. Desio returned the same day to Base Camp where message number twelve quickly followed. This put the forty-year-old Achille Compagnoni in charge of the summit attempt and gave Ugo Angelino the responsibility of co-ordinating the supplies to all the camps. It ended on a quasi-heroic note: 'Remember if you succeed in scaling the peak – as I am confident you will – the entire world will hail you as champions of your race and long after you are dead. Thus, even if you never achieve anything else of note, you will be able to say that you have not lived in vain . . .' Mussolini himself couldn't have put it any better!

It is not hard to guess the reactions of any presentday expedition, whatever its nationality, on receipt of such a message, which shows just how much times have changed. But in 1953 it appeared not to cause any paroxysms of laughter from on high and, suitably inspired, the lead climbers pressed on. It would be fascinating to know whether they took such imperious exhortations for granted or whether they felt the voice was coming from a long-gone generation. It is inconceivable that John Hunt would have sent such a message, and even the somewhat Colonel Blimpish Everest expeditions of the 1920s would probably have drawn the line at such blatantly chauvinistic sentiments.

Whatever the cause, things began to improve and the air of failure lifted. On 14 July Camp V was established and two days later Abram and Gallotti got to Camp VI. On the 18th Compagnoni, Rey, Gallotti and Bonatti ran out seven hundred metres of fixed rope to a point between the top of the Black Pyramid and the foot of the Shoulder. It was the Italians' Camp VII and had been a magnificent day's work. Here they found the remnants of Houston's Camp VIII – a tent, full of snow, but still standing a year later, a silent testimony to the heroic attempt to evacuate the stricken Art Gilkey.

Then once again the expedition seemed to run out of steam. Compagnoni, Lacedelli and Rey needed a rest, the weather was still very changeable and the ferrying of loads up the mountain was still sporadic. It was not until 26 July that Compagnoni, Abram, Bonatti, Lacedelli, Gallotti and Rey spent the night in Camp VII and under fine, clear skies the stage seemed set for the last act of the drama. Inevitably, though, the weather had other ideas and the six men spent the next day sitting out a storm during which Bonatti developed a stomach upset (real this time). So when on the 28th the others set out for Camp VIII at the foot of the Shoulder proper, he was left, weak and wretched, cursing his bad luck.

As the day wore on Bonatti forced himself to eat at all costs. Rey descended early, also stricken with the same trouble. Late in the day Gallotti and Abram returned shattered, having helped Compagnoni and Lacedelli to dig out the site of Camp VIII at 7740 metres. The plan was for the leading pair to pitch a last camp at over 8000 metres and return to Camp VIII where further supplies, plus two oxygen sets, would be taken up. It was, perhaps, an unnecessarily protracted arrangement and, like all complex plans, stood a good chance of going wrong. More seriously, though, it left the leading pair to spend at least four nights at around or above 8000 metres. As in 1939 and 1953, the effects of prolonged stays at very high altitudes were still not really appreciated.

The first setback was the condition of Rey who was too exhausted to contribute anything more and set off down to Base Camp for the last time. Gallotti, too, was almost at the end of his tether, but on the 29th he managed somehow to follow a revitalised Bonatti up to Camp VIII, where they found Compagnoni and Lacedelli tired and depressed. They had managed only a hundred metres or so that day and had left their rucksacks on the Shoulder. Another tent was pitched and the four discussed what to do next. In the end it was agreed that Bonatti and Gallotti would descend to Camp VII, pick up the two oxygen sets, and then climb up to the proposed site of Camp IX. Bonatti insists that Lacedelli and Compagnoni agreed to lowering this from immediately below the rock band to a point some hundred metres down the Shoulder. Compagnoni seemed exhausted and hinted that Bonatti might have to take his place in the summit bid.

It seems clear that the expedition by now was barely in control of events. To descend, return and climb up to Camp IX in a day seems to be the result of very muddled thinking. The oxygen sets surely should have been a clear priority from much earlier on. They were more important than the extra tent at Camp VIII. Indeed Bonatti thought that all four might be able to cram into the top camp the following night.

Early next morning the pair descended unladen, and trying to make a track to reascend later, they took short steps and stamped them down firmly. They picked up the sets at Camp VII and met two of the best Hunza porters ascending, Mahdi and Isakhan. Mahdi was the strongest and most determined of the high-altitude porters and on their return to Camp VIII, only he, Abram and Bonatti were capable of going any further. Bonatti freely admits that he deceived Mahdi, promising him the chance to go to the summit if he completed the carry of oxygen sets to Camp IX. 'We put the proposal to Mahdi, giving him the impression that he might be able to go to the summit with me, Lacedelli and Compagnoni. It was a necessary deception which had, however, a grain of truth in it.' Mahdi agreed and was kitted out with clothes from Gallotti and Abram, except for high-altitude boots, the lack of which was to be critical. One wonders what scheme was at the back of Bonatti's mind, for presumably with only two oxygen sets, they would have had to try for the summit without their help. Neither of them took sleeping-bags so it is hard to believe that Mahdi was really taken in or that Walter Bonatti was any more than vaguely contemplating a summit bid himself. But in the light of allegations made long after the expedition it is important to try to understand what Bonatti might have been thinking.

It was half past three before they left Camp VIII and only four hours of daylight remained for them to climb to the top tent. The next twelve hours have been the subject of so much controversy (including a libel action) that forty years later it is virtually impossible to find out exactly what happened and it seems invidious to try to judge which of two stories is true. Bonatti, as already stated, claims that there was prior agreement to drop the height of the final camp to make their last carry easier, but Compagnoni and Lacedelli make no mention of this in their account. As soon as they reached the lower end of the Shoulder Bonatti started shouting, 'Lino! Achille! Where are you? Where have you pitched the tent?'

'Follow the tracks,' came the not terribly helpful reply. At half past six Abram, totally exhausted, gave up and descended in the dark. Bonatti and Mahdi pressed on up the Shoulder.

They still could not see the tent but Bonatti assumed that it was hidden behind a rock. The tracks veered leftwards towards the spot where Wiessner had camped. At last, in almost total darkness, Bonatti reached the rock and was horrified to find no tent and the tracks leading on upwards over steep ground and out of sight. He could get no reply to his shouts by now littered with curses. Mahdi, faced with impending nightfall and no tent, seemed to be losing his senses and broke into incomprehensible shouting and terrible howls. Whatever Bonatti suggested Mahdi seemed to ignore and there was a very real danger of him falling off.

Then suddenly a light appeared above them and Lacedelli's voice, seemingly quite near, asked them if they had the oxygen, hardly the most perceptive question, one would have thought.

'Yes,' replied Bonatti.

'Good! Then leave it there and come up at once!'

'I can't! Mahdi can't make it.'

'What?'

'I said, Mahdi can't make it. I can look after myself but Mahdi is out of his senses and is crossing the face right now.'

Mahdi, transfixed by the light, had risen and set off across the steep ice slope. Then the light went out. Mahdi yelled in despair, 'No good, Lacedelli Sahib! No good, Compagnoni Sahib!' But the light never came on again and there was no further communication from above.

Bonatti managed to quieten Mahdi and they resigned themselves to a bivouac at 8000 metres. It was bitterly, grimly cold and time, as always, even on a good bivouac, stood still. But even in his frozen misery Bonatti was able to admire the star-studded night with a huge sea of cloud rising gently up from below so that all but the highest summits were slowly blotted out. Then the first gust of wind and snow hit them and suddenly they were right up against it.

Each of us was now fighting for himself, drawing on his last resources. Then suddenly I heard a howl alongside me, a human howl and not the howling of the wind and I instinctively stretched out my hand towards a flying shadow. I was only just in time to stop Mahdi making for the precipice.

At long last came the dawn. The wind dropped and it stopped snowing. As soon as it was light enough to see, Mahdi lurched off downhill. Bonatti couldn't stop him and watched with his heart in his mouth as he negotiated the long steep slope. Eventually Mahdi reached the flatter part of the Shoulder and Bonatti could relax a bit, waiting for the sun to hit him. When it did a little warmth seeped into his frozen limbs. It was, says Bonatti, a few minutes to six. There was no sound from above and Bonatti was still unable to spot the tent. As he descended he heard a cry but couldn't see where it came from.

Remarkably unscathed, Bonatti regained Camp VIII where to his relief he found that Mahdi had returned safely, though he had signs of severe frostbite. As they were ministered to by Abram and Gallotti their thoughts turned to Compagnoni and Lacedelli. What was happening on this, the hoped-for summit day?

In *The Ascent of K2*, Compagnoni and Lacedelli made a point of stating that they wanted to pitch their camp as high as possible, right up against the foot of the rock band that Wiessner had almost climbed in 1939. They reached it at about three in the afternoon and settled in. As the shadows lengthened they spotted Bonatti, Mahdi and Abram now on the Shoulder, well below the point where they would have to start traversing left over steep ground to reach the tent. As it got dark they heard shouts. 'Unfortunately the high wind made conversation extremely difficult.' At last, however, Lacedelli thought he understood what they were saying. It seemed to him that the shouts came from Bonatti and that he was telling them that he could manage by himself. Mahdi, on the other hand, apparently wanted to return to Camp VIII. '"Go back," we shouted, "Go back! Leave the masks! Don't come any further!" It did not even occur to us that our colleagues could be thinking of spending the night at such an altitude without a tent or even a sleeping-bag.'

They spent a cold, uncomfortable night in their tiny tent, occasionally brewing camomile tea and talking about the day ahead of them. At dawn they were flabbergasted to see a figure receding in the distance. They yelled and he stopped and turned round, then resumed his stumbling downward progress. 'Try as we might we could find no solution to the mystery. We thought of all possible explanations except the right one.'

At five a.m. they were ready to start but first they had to descend to pick up the abandoned oxygen sets. At six fifteen they retrieved them and started climbing. (If these times are right Bonatti must have started down considerably earlier, otherwise they would have surely come within easy hailing distance if not actually met.)

On oxygen now, but still moving slowly through deep snow, they first tried the Bottleneck Couloir that Wiessner had found so time-consuming without crampons. But now the snow was dangerous and unstable. They thought it madness to try and climb it and turned to the rocks on the left (still nowhere near the first line tried by Wiessner much further to the left). They spent two hours trying to force a way up, Compagnoni at one point falling off, luckily into soft snow and without hurting himself. In the end it was Lacedelli who led a thirty-metre pitch of broken rock that he found harder than anything else on the whole climb. It brought them out on to the steep ground immediately below the sérac band. Cautiously they started a long traverse leftwards, half-expecting the whole ice wall to collapse on top of them. Their first oxygen bottles were already empty but at the end of the traverse they expected the worst to be over. In fact a very steep fifteen-metre slope of treacherous snow took Compagnoni fully an hour to climb and it was with huge relief that they at last laid hands on solid rock.

They were now higher than anyone had ever been on K2, climbing
the easier-angled slopes that Wiessner had just failed to reach on his
first attempt. There was only about another two hundred metres
to go. Surely it was in the bag? But progress was still painfully
slow and the hours sped past. Through a break in the clouds they
caught a glimpse of the tents of Camp VIII and two tiny figures
beside them, which encouraged them. Then suddenly, within a few
seconds, they were each struck with impending suffocation. Their
oxygen had run out. Tearing off their masks and trying to control
their breathing they checked each other's condition by identifying
mountains around them. 'That's Broad Peak over there. Its summit
is now some distance below us. Therefore we can't be far from the
summit of K2.'

They carried on with the burden of empty oxygen sets weighing
them down. It seems almost inconceivable that they didn't simply
abandon them but they listed four reasons why they kept them on.
First, getting them off was not so easy, and involved lying flat in
the unstable snow. Second, they thought they had almost reached the
summit. Third, the sun was sinking and every minute was precious.
Finally, they were not averse to leaving something solid on the
summit as evidence of their achievement. But the top refused to
arrive. Climbing what they hoped was the final hump, another long
slope awaited them. They were taking three or four steps at a time,
then halting, bent over their ice-axes. The only unusual thing was a
buzzing in their ears, but their minds still seemed to be functioning
properly. Suddenly a patch of blue sky appeared above them and the
mountain was lit by evening sun. Ice crystals danced in the air and
the cold was piercing. It was almost six p.m.

The last steps were up a wide, easy-angled snow slope.

All of a sudden we perceived that the slope was becoming less
pronounced: the snow was getting firmer and, thank God, we
were no longer sinking into it. The angle of the slope continued
to diminish, by this time the ground was almost flat – now it
was flat!

A few minutes before, below at Camp VIII, the porter Isakhan
entered the tent where Bonatti, Abram and Gallotti were waiting
and announced in perfect English, 'A Sahib is about to climb K2!'
They rushed outside, Bonatti with a great lump in his throat. Two

tiny dots were slowly and steadily advancing just below the summit, blue in the twilight.

On the summit Compagnoni and Lacedelli removed their gloves to shoot a short piece of movie film and stills and plant the Indian, Pakistani and Italian Alpine Club flags in the snow. Compagnoni almost immediately showed signs of frostbite and a glove blew away but Lacedelli gave him one of his own. After half an hour and 'one more look at the summit, that windswept solitude where it would probably be true to say that we had both just experienced the greatest moment of our lives,' they turned to go. Soon it would be completely dark.

They descended by the dim light of the stars, weariness increasing every minute until they reached the traverse beneath the sérac wall where Compagnoni took a short fall. Again he landed in snow unharmed. Then, gambling everything, they plunged straight down the Bottleneck Couloir which mercifully did not avalanche. They stopped at the point where they had picked up the oxygen and Compagnoni discovered he had a small flask of cognac in which they drank each other's health. Although it was only a few drops each, it went straight to their heads. Descending the Shoulder they both fell over a crevasse and cleared the lower side, Lacedelli losing his ice-axe in the process, and at last they reached a sérac overlooking Camp VIII. Compagnoni, descending in the dark, fell off again and Lacedelli could not hold him. His luck held for the third time and, half buried in the soft snow in which he had landed, he expected Lacedelli to come hurtling down out of the darkness on top of him – skewering him with his crampons. But Lacedelli managed to check himself and Compagnoni guided him towards an easier-angled slope which Lacedelli could slide down. At eleven p.m. they reached Camp VIII and fell into the arms of Bonatti, Gallotti and Abram. Their frostbitten hands were thawed out and began to throb. Sleep was impossible. 'It was another night of suffering, anxiety and bitter cold: the most stupendous night of our lives.'

On the morning of 1 August the weary team left Camp VIII. Desio had instructed them to leave anything that was not essential in order to get down quickly and safely – no thoughts then of conservation! Compagnoni, unroped, fell two hundred metres out of control before hitting a patch of soft snow. This was his *fourth* fall in twenty-four hours and shows the sort of state he must have been in. At forty years of age the time and effort he had expended at that altitude was taking a severe toll. His hands were badly frostbitten but Mahdi's condition was a lot worse, eventually resulting in the loss of most of his feet and fingers.

Compagnoni and Lacedelli reached Base Camp on 2 August and by the 3rd everyone was safely off the mountain. Then Desio issued an emotional message (number thirteen):

> Lift up your hearts, dear comrades! By your efforts you have won great glory for your native land, whose name, following the announcement of your triumph over our camp radio, is on the lips of men throughout the world . . . You have deserved well of your country and today all Italians are rising to acclaim you as worthy champions of your race . . . Remember to keep secret for the time being the names of our two indomitable colleagues who actually scaled the peak . . . now I must leave you without delay in order to turn my attention to the scientific programme . . . Good-bye then, until we meet again in Italy in a few months' time.

And so the first ascent of K2 was over. At home Compagnoni and Lacedelli were awarded gold medals for gallantry, as was Mario Puchoz posthumously. Desio was made a Knight of the Grand Cross and Bonatti received a silver medal for gallantry. The whole team had an audience with Pope Pius XII and it would be nice to think that they all lived happily ever after, but they didn't. Slowly resentment and quarrels rose to the surface.

The most serious was the differing accounts of the events on the Shoulder given by Bonatti, Lacedelli and Compagnoni. Bonatti was appalled that the official report played down the bivouac, and that the height of Camp IX, the place and height of his bivouac, and the time the summit team claimed they set out were all wrong by his recollection. Bonatti increasingly felt he had been abandoned by the summiteers who had deliberately ignored his cries for help. Initially he hoped for 'a gesture of some kind, a word to put the record straight, maybe in a face to face discussion'. Then the film was finished which made no reference to the bivouac at all. Bonatti protested and the film was altered.

Bonatti eventually wrote his autobiography (*Le Mie Montagne*, 1962) which gives his side of the story in great detail. But three years later, during the celebration of the tenth anniversary of the first ascent, an article in the *Nuova Gazzetta del Popolo della Domenica* was subtitled 'How Bonatti tried to reach the top before Compagnoni and Lino Lacedelli'. The text accused him of abandoning Mahdi and of using some of the oxygen. Furious, Bonatti brought a libel action against the writer, which he won. Bonatti repeatedly tried to get the Italian Alpine Club to admit its mistakes in its official report and in 1992 on the fortieth anniversary of the first ascent he did get an apology from Roberto de Martin, the club's president.

This acknowledgement of Bonatti's case has incensed Compagnoni, now in his eighties, who commented, 'You can't change history after forty years.' He thought that Bonatti had been foolhardy in trying to reach Camp IX. 'The tent was a flimsy thing with barely room for two – Lacedelli and I slept with our feet sticking out of the flap.' He adds that on their return to Camp VIII everyone congratulated them – Bonatti included. 'Everyone knew it had been a team effort . . . the fact that it happened to be me and Lacedelli is academic.'

To the outsider it does seem to be something of a storm in a teacup. The high siting of the top camp could easily have been a misunderstanding but was surely not a deliberate move to outwit any summit ambitions Bonatti may have harboured. Above all, Compagnoni and Lacedelli needed the oxygen, and playing high-altitude hide and seek was not the way to ensure its safe arrival. It is quite possible that they were not overkeen to leave the warmth of their tent when Bonatti was shouting to them, but once again it seems more like an example of the cock-up syndrome than a deliberate abandoning of Bonatti and Mahdi to their fate. As for the discrepancy in the times that they left for the summit on 31 July, it is clear that either Bonatti, or Compagnoni and Lacedelli, were mistaken; it doesn't matter much which, as neither party was close enough to communicate successfully when the small, stumbling figure was spotted on the Shoulder.

Overriding the whole controversy are the twin factors of reasoning and memory at high altitude which are invariably impaired, sometimes seriously. Add to that the effects of the passage of time and, after forty years, who can tell how accurate recollections are? In a recent letter from Charlie Houston, who is himself over eighty, he writes of the reissue of his *K2, the Savage Mountain*: 'It's amazing how much my recollection has changed since writing the story forty years ago!'

This was not the only post-expedition trauma. As ever, money, or lack of it, caused problems. The expedition and Desio were involved in lengthy disputes with the Italian Alpine Club over funding for the scientific part of the expedition. The Club's role as organiser, the accounts, the expedition leader and the money itself, were all subjects for controversy.

Perhaps the most incongruous affair was instigated by Compagnoni who, as a result of the summit filming, had lost fingers from frostbite. He therefore sued the Italian Alpine Club and the film company for a share of the film rights! It was a case that carried on for three years, during which time the other expedition members publicly dissociated themselves from him. In the end, hardly surprisingly, Compagnoni lost. It was also rumoured that both Lacedelli and Compagnoni needed extensive treatment for mental damage caused by oxygen deprivation on the summit day.

All in all it ended very differently from the British Everest expedition the year before, which certainly had its tensions and arguments but ones that were successfully resolved or at least suppressed in the years that followed. Perhaps, in the end, the 1954 Italian K2 expedition itself was something of a dinosaur, a symbol of an age and attitude almost extinct in post-war Europe.

Interestingly only one member ever *did* do 'anything else of note', in Desio's words, and that was, of course, Bonatti himself. After a period of intense depression following the K2 expedition, Bonatti soloed the South-West Pillar of the Petit Dru above Chamonix, an astonishing feat at the time. The Bonatti Pillar quickly became one of the all-time classic Alpine routes. And in 1957 he returned to the Karakoram with, amongst others, Riccardo Cassin to attempt the unclimbed Gasherbrum IV. Bonatti and Carlo Mauri reached the summit of that beautiful mountain which is arguably even harder than K2. Bonatti was probably the greatest mountaineer of the late 'fifties and early 'sixties when, after soloing a new route on the North Face of the Matterhorn, he retired from climbing to become a traveller, photographer and explorer.

With K2 climbed at last and Kangchenjunga also falling a year later, the big three had all been climbed within three years. The rest of the unclimbed 8000-metre peaks quickly followed, except for Shishapangma, situated entirely in Chinese-occupied Tibet, which held out until 1964. What would be the future of these giants? Would anyone bother to return once they had been ascended or would man turn his attention to lower but possibly harder prizes? Many people felt that the time and effort and cost of their conquest was out of all proportion to their importance. K2, remote and aloof, was left alone. Apart from a low-key German–American attempt in 1960 led by W. D. Hackett, which got no further than the Black Pyramid, it was to be twenty-two years before a major expedition visited the mountain. By then a lot would have changed.

10

A Teams and B Teams

During the mid to late 1950s attention in the Karakoram focused on the superb collection of spectacular but lower peaks scattered right across the range. The Mustagh Tower, Gasherbrum IV, Gasherbrum II, Broad Peak, Hidden Peak (Gasherbrum I) and Rakaposhi were major scalps, and all climbed within the space of three years. Then, in 1961 Pakistan closed the whole of the Central Karakoram to expeditions. The reasons were complex. The Kashmir question had never been properly resolved since Partition in 1947. Tension between Pakistan and India increased and the whole area was felt to be too sensitive to allow expeditions to enter. Pakistan also managed to tighten her grip on the contested northern border by signing a shrewd agreement with the Chinese Government, giving her large neighbour a strip of land thirty miles wide. K2's North-West and North-East Ridges actually defined a small part of this border. By accepting the deal, China in effect acknowledged Pakistan's claim to the land to the south.

So during the 'sixties and into the 'seventies Nepal became the focus for expeditions, even though she too closed her doors from 1966–70. Then, with the improvement in equipment and technical standards, innovative expeditions like that to the South Face of Annapurna (1970) and the South-West Face of Everest (1975), showed what could become possible on 8000-metre peaks, and suddenly every face and ridge in the Himalaya seemed up for grabs. Inevitably, the forbidden Karakoram became the most sought after range in which to put these developments into practice. All the major mountains had only one route and below them were some of the most desirable unclimbed smaller peaks in the world. Names like Uli Biaho, Paiju, Trango Tower, the Ogre and the Latoks epitomised the huge untapped potential of the area and climbers the world over fantasised over the day when access would be permitted. Naturally, K2 with its huge unclimbed ridges and buttresses and only one successful ascent came high on the long list of 'Last Great Problems'.

Over the years the tension eased and very gradually a few expeditions trickled back to outlying peaks. In 1974 Bob Bates and H. Adams Carter, both over sixty, trekked with their wives up to K2 Base Camp. It must have been an emotional journey for Bob Bates, thirty-six years since his first visit and twenty-one since Art Gilkey's death, as he and Ad Carter went up the Savoia Glacier for another look at the North-West Ridge. They both felt that, even with the big advances in technical gear, the route from the Savoia Saddle would be extremely difficult and they suggested an alternative approach to the ridge via a hanging glacier and a mixed snow and rock wall that gave access to a prominent snowfield at around 7000 metres. This would bypass the jagged rock towers immediately above the Savoia Saddle. Bob Bates and Ad Carter had indeed spotted the route that would be taken by three of the four subsequent expeditions to the North-West Ridge, but somehow their advice was either not communicated or understood or perhaps simply ignored by the first of these.

In 1975 the Baltoro area was opened up and an avalanche of applications landed in Pakistani embassies around the world. Nineteen were successful and suddenly, too suddenly, the invasion began. Expeditions from France, Holland, Italy, Poland, Switzerland, Britain, America, Austria and Japan were hastily assembled and throughout the summer there was a more or less continuous procession of porters ferrying supplies and equipment up the Baltoro Glacier. The result was chaos. After so long an absence of expeditions, porter stages, load sizes, fees, rest days, etc., all became open to negotiation and almost every expedition was dogged with strikes, go-slows and thefts. Some expeditions even failed to reach Base Camp and a vast amount of ill-will was generated. In retrospect it would have made more sense for the Pakistan Ministry of Tourism to have rationed the numbers, and made its sometimes labyrinthine regulations simpler to understand by both expeditions and porters. As it was, the expeditions felt continuously ripped off, and the porters, sensing that they had the upper hand, held them to ransom with a neverending series of demands that could not be met. A favourite ploy was to carry as far as the Baltoro, get paid off when the going got hard and return quickly to Askole to pick up the next expedition.

Set against this background came the biggest and most ambitious expedition of the year. Led by 'Big Jim' Whittaker, the first American to climb Everest, and organised under the auspices of the American Alpine Club, permission was granted for the North-West Ridge, an imaginative project, given that K2 had not yet had a second ascent and, for Americans in particular, success on K2 was a long-overdue event.

The team was chosen, ironically in the light of what was to be a particularly acrimonious expedition, for its compatibility. Early on Alex Bertulis, one of the founder members, was dropped on the basis that he was unable to relate well to the others and was suffering a recurring back problem. Though most of the members had outstanding climbing records, there was not a lot of Himalayan experience between them. The final team was made up of Lou Whittaker, a mountain guide and Jim's twin brother, Jim Wickwire, a Seattle-based lawyer who was the instigator of the expedition, Leif Patterson, a mathematics professor, Robert Schaller, a Seattle surgeon, Fred Dunham from Ellensburg, Washington, Fred Stanley, Galen Rowell, a leading mountain photographer and writer, Steve Marts, who was climbing cameraman, and Dianne Roberts, Jim Whittaker's wife, who was also a professional stills photographer.

It is sometimes hard for the British to appreciate the cultural differences between ourselves and our American cousins and doubtless as hard for them to understand us. Small wonder then that when the expedition book, Galen Rowell's *In the Throne Room of the Mountain Gods*, was published it was received in Britain with amazement verging on horror. How could climbers behave in such a way? Where were team spirit, stiff upper lip and gallantry? Why was everyone so devastatingly and cruelly honest about each other?

Rarely has an expedition book described in such detail the day-to-day trials and tribulations of an unhappy expedition. The vitriolic resentment of almost every member towards almost every other is exposed for all the world to see. It relies very much on all the expedition diaries made freely available to the author and so, despite any inbuilt bias that Rowell himself might add, it has to be a reasonably accurate reflection of the whole sorry experience.

The sacking of Alex Bertulis was the first of a long succession of incidents that plagued the expedition. Almost unbelievably it took nearly two months from its departure from the USA to establish Base Camp on the Savoia Glacier. The first delay was in

Rawalpindi where it took eleven days before the weather was fine enough to fly into Skardu. When they arrived Whittaker managed to get a flight in a huge Hercules C-130 up to K2, staying on the Pakistan side of the border. Due to a misunderstanding as they approached K2, Galen Rowell was ordered back from the cockpit window where Dianne Roberts took, in Rowell's words, 'exquisite aerials; I felt as if someone had robbed me of a priceless possession.' Galen and Dianne didn't get on, not really surprising given the presence of two competing stills photographers on the same expedition. Most of the team were worried about what they perceived as her overambitious ideas about her role on the mountain. She was inexperienced as a climber but had put in a lot of planning work before the expedition started. In her words: 'I feel I've earned my place on the team. I've paid my due.'

The flight to K2 seemed to achieve one important piece of information. Lou Whittaker and Jim Wickwire thought they had spotted a snow ramp on the north (Chinese) side of the Savoia Saddle that bypassed the gendarmes on the ridge crest. It was to be an observation that would significantly contribute to the eventual failure of the expedition.

A problem that seemed to haunt the members throughout its tedious crawl to Base Camp was the pecking order on the mountain, in particular the possible summit team or teams. Unlike most British expeditions, where walk-ins are traditionally opportunities for laid-back relaxation after the stress of expedition organisation and departure, the American team competed in heavy-load carrying and raced from stage to stage. The unfortunate Rowell, sprinting ahead with a lightish sack of photographic gear, was ridiculed. 'At lunch stops my pack was frequently hefted by Jim, or Wick, or Lou. One would say, "Wow, that's light. Not over thirty-five pounds." Another would lift it and say knowingly, "More like thirty."' This, hardly surprisingly, was a tactic that seriously undermined confidence.

The 'Big Four', as Jim and Lou Whittaker, Jim Wickwire and Dianne Roberts were nicknamed, became increasingly isolated from the rest of the team, who resented their exclusivity and high-handed decision making. The potential for going high on the mountain seemed to have been assessed on the flimsiest of evidence. More time was being spent visualising the climax of the expedition than appeared to be given to the reality of climbing the not inconsiderable chunk of mountain between Base Camp and the highest camp.

The porter strikes delayed the team for so long that many members succumbed to illness and defeatism before they reached the mountain. Jim Wickwire's diary describes a famous incident: 'Jim [Whittaker] finally told them we would burn the money and pay no one unless we got to Base Camp. Lou suggested burning a ten rupee note in front of them. Jim concurred. Digging the note out of the money sack, he held it up and I lit it with my lighter. With that dramatic gesture we walked out of their encampment back to our tents. Here we wait while the noisy debate goes on across the way.' The action horrified the liaison officer who took it as an insult to his country, but it did seem to work and the expedition lurched on another stage. At Concordia many of the porters were paid off and loads were ferried by the remainder, first to the usual Base Camp on the Godwin-Austen Glacier, then up to the site on the Savoia Glacier under the West Face of K2, where the Americans set up their own Base Camp.

It had been mooted by Lou Whittaker that the expedition cut its losses and simply go for the Abruzzi Spur. But lawyer Jim Wickwire countered this with the thought that if the expedition didn't actually attempt the North-West Ridge, as they had intended and publicly stated, they could possibly face lawsuits on their return to the States from expedition donors and sponsors! That the thought of legal action should influence the route taken on a Himalayan mountain seems almost unbelievable. In the end it was resolved to go for the North-West Ridge as planned, but only about 70 of the original 650 porters ferried loads to Base Camp. The team was already half beaten.

Meanwhile the dissent over the attitude of the 'Big Four' was growing. While Lou Whittaker was taking a tent down he had incurred the wrath of Fred Dunham, the occupant at the time, who wrote in his diary, 'There is only one way to handle a guy like Lou who shoves his weight and size around. That is to say what you think to anyone and if he resorts to physical strength he should end up with an ice-axe in the back of his head or a bullet between the eyes. There is no other way for a smaller person to get justice.'

On 5 June Base Camp was set up on the glacier, almost seven weeks after leaving the USA, and still not all the loads had arrived. Work began immediately on finding a route up to the Savoia Saddle. Leif Patterson and Galen Rowell skied up the glacier towards the col. Suddenly it all looked feasible. The ridge looked long but climbable and Rowell found himself thinking, 'For the first time in weeks the mountaineer in me lusted for the summit.'

Unlike on the last attempt in 1938, the saddle was quickly climbed using twelve-point crampons and fixing rope. It was Lou Whittaker and Jim Wickwire who first reached the col, the same two who had enthused in the aircraft reconnaissance about the possible snow ramp on the Chinese side. Like the Duke of the Abruzzi sixty-four years previously, all they could see was a cornice and a huge drop down to the K2 Glacier. Above the saddle there was a steep open face for a couple of hundred metres with the corniced drop to the left. For the next two weeks they probed the cornice which hid their view and the possible ramp line, but it was to be early July, when the first pinnacle on the ridge was at last overcome, that they realised there was to be no easy way. To rub salt in the wound they found that the col was 450 metres lower than it was marked on the map, at 6220 metres, instead of 6670. This, combined with a recent survey which calculated (erroneously) that K2 was around 8750 metres high, suddenly added almost six hundred metres to the climb and would probably mean an extra high camp, throwing a logistical spanner into the complex works of moving food, fuel and tents up the ridge.

It is easy to criticise after the event but one cannot help wondering why the Americans stubbornly persisted over the next month to climb across the convoluted towers and gaps above the saddle. It was clearly going to be a nightmare route for load-carrying and time was running out. They did have at least two alternatives open to them, had they made a quick decision: to try the hanging valley and ice face, a climb that would bring them out well above the pinnacles at around 7000 metres, or at least to investigate the West Ridge of the mountain instead, conveniently situated above their Base Camp. But in Jim Wickwire's words: 'We did talk about the West Ridge, but there wasn't much enthusiasm for that alternative on the part of any of us. We had rolled the dice with the complete North-West Ridge, lost and that was that.'

Tensions within the team continued to increase with the two Freds, Dunham and Stanley, assuming the role of the underdogs. They had both been ill and Rowell describes their condition: 'Their behaviour resembled that of unskilled labourers who believe they have no chance of advancement in their jobs. When they were healthy they were willing to work, but not too hard and not too long. If they felt sick . . . they simply took sick leave.' Rowell himself had been suffering from bronchitis which had turned into pneumonia. Progress on the mountain was minimal and the weather was as poor as it seems to be most years on K2: short spells of good weather followed by three- or four-day storms. In the odd good spell, Jim Wickwire led up the ridge, searching for the non-existent snow ramp but gradually admitting that it didn't exist and the ridge would have to be taken direct. If nothing else, the Americans showed that the value of aerial reconnaissance for climbers seems minimal. Angles and spacial relationships are difficult to judge from the air, and to base a whole expedition strategy on a briefly glimpsed view from a cockpit window was clearly a mistake.

As if there wasn't enough bad news, one of the high-altitude porters fell ill. Akbar Ali was infested with roundworm which had caused an obstruction then a perforation of the small intestine. Peritonitis developed into septic shock and in the chaotic Base Camp conditions, complete with a howling blizzard, Dr Rob Schaller was faced with a situation as grim, if not grimmer, than the one faced in 1939 by the young Jack Durrance when Chappel Cranmer had his pulmonary oedema. All night Schaller fought to keep an intravenous drip from freezing up. Akbar was clinging on by a thread, and his blood pressure barely registered. He survived the night but then had another crisis and Schaller plied him with intravenous antibiotics. For the next three days he hovered between life and death, then slowly turned the corner. But on 9 July he had a relapse. A helicopter rescue seemed the only thing that would save him, but none was forthcoming. In the end Akbar was carried to Concordia and eventually walked out from Urdokas under his own steam. The power of antibiotics and the remarkable strength and stamina of the Baltis were combined with a simple will to survive. Ironically, at Paiju a helicopter *did* arrive for Akbar and only just in time. However, it wasn't Akbar who climbed in but another porter, Jaffar, who had collapsed with a perforated ulcer. He was evacuated to Skardu and also made a complete recovery.

During the dramas at Base Camp, the inevitable occurred on 3 July, and the attempt on the North-West Ridge was formally abandoned at a high point of around 6700 metres. As a consolation prize Rowell and Leif Patterson wanted to climb the Angelus or Angel Peak, the elegant small satellite of K2 easily accessible from Base Camp. But the ascent was vetoed by Jim Whittaker, to Rowell's disgust: 'What a pity it is to have to beg to climb!'

The Americans returned to Skardu where they were stuck for three days as flights to and from Islamabad were cancelled due to bad weather in the Indus Gorge. Returning expeditions began to pile up, completing everyone's frustrations with mountaineering in general and the Karakoram in particular. Eventually a C-130 arrived and four expeditions were taken out to a great cheer from inside the aircraft.

The American dream remained unfulfilled on K2. The expedition had achieved little and had suffered great internal strife. But they were not alone, for successes in the Karakoram in 1975 were few and far between. However, the expedition book and, to a lesser extent, the film, were instrumental in bringing a heightened awareness of the area to the climbing world in general. A magnificent double-page spread of dawn sunlight on the Trango Towers taken by Galen Rowell, published in an issue of *Mountain* magazine devoted to the Karakoram, said more than any words could ever do, and despite the negative experiences of so many expeditions, the Karakoram was *the* place to go in the late 'seventies. Trekking quickly took root and the Concordia to K2 Base Camp adventure became the most demanding and popular walk in the Karakoram. As a climbing objective K2, still awaiting a second ascent, remained a highly desirable prize. But with the sudden awareness of the incredible potential for high-standard climbing the area had to offer, it was the superb granite architecture of the lower Baltoro and Biafo Glaciers, epitomised in Rowell's picture, that would rival the challenge of the big black mountain at the head of the Godwin-Austen Glacier.

There was one more event in the Baltoro region in 1975 that changed the course of mountaineering history. While climbers flooded to the area to put the lessons of the big technical face climbs, learnt in the Alps, Yosemite and Nepal, to ever harder tests in a new region, two young climbers were prepared to push a new philosophy on to the centre stage. Using no oxygen, no fixed ropes and no porters Italian Reinhold Messner and Austrian Peter Habeler climbed a new route, the North Face of Gasherbrum I (Hidden Peak) using what quickly became known as alpine-style tactics. This major climb sent shockwaves around the climbing world. It instantly gave the couple superstar status, and set a new benchmark for expedition ethics. Slowly, the old expedition-style began to look out of date, cumbersome and unnecessarily expensive. But it was to be several years before Messner and Habeler's methods were to gain any general acceptance and, at the time, many people, while admiring the superb physical achievements of the pair, felt that the margin of risk in such an ascent was far too high. So with this major success an unsatisfactory Karakoram season came to a close. But already even more teams were jockeying for position for 1976.

During the 1970s the climbing world witnessed the rapid emergence of the Eastern Bloc countries, particularly Czechoslovakia and Poland, as forces to be reckoned with. The Polish climbers in particular seemed to take to the Himalaya and from the mid-'seventies to late 'eighties were a major driving force both in terms of successful expeditions and in producing world-class climbers like Jerzy Kukuczka, Voytek Kurtyka and Wanda Rutkiewicz. Mountaineering was one form of combined escapism and rebellion that was just about tolerated within the rigid Communist society of the day. The Polish climbers became pastmasters at using and outwitting 'the system'. The local clubs had large membership and provided a tremendously supportive group identity. Many Polish climbers earned a living by doing high-access maintenance work – painting factory chimneys, high-rise flats, etc. – from abseil ropes. Their large, well-ordered expeditions were always undertaken on a shoestring budget with antiquated and patched-up equipment which was however very functional. Jerzy Kukuczka once compared Polish and Western expeditions to cars in the East and West. The shiny high-performance cars run well on good roads, but when the roads get rough and rutted the old Polish bangers just carry on regardless.

In 1976 the Poles attempted the long North-East Ridge of K2, like the Americans the year before shunning the opportunity to make a second attempt via the Abruzzi. Their leader was Janusz Kurczab and his team was made up of nineteen climbers – the largest number by a long way to try K2, but they employed no high-altitude porters at all.

The Polish expedition coincided with my own first direct interest in K2. In 1976 I was a member of the British Trango Tower expedition. We flew to Skardu with the Poles and spent a couple of days in their company before we started our own walk-in. I vividly remember their friendliness and good humour as well as their desperate efforts to keep their porter wages to a minimum. At one point, to save weight, they were seriously considering doing without the inners of their double boots! One member of the team was well known to British climbers. Janusz Onyszkiewicz had married an English climber, Alison Chadwick. In 1975 they, with Wanda Rutkiewicz and Krzysztof Zdzitowiecki, had climbed Gasherbrum III, at that time the world's highest unclimbed mountain. Tragically, Alison was killed in 1978 on Annapurna I. Janusz Onyszkiewicz became heavily involved in Solidarity, the banned trade union movement led by Lech Walesa, and he was imprisoned for a time. Later he was a member of the Polish government after the ousting of Communism, becoming Minister of Defence.

When the Poles arrived at Base Camp in 1976 they were greeted with a month of fine weather! They systematically fixed ropes and camps on a lateral rib leading to the crest of the North-East Ridge proper, just below the critical knife-edge section – almost half a mile of corniced gendarmed ridge. This took ten days to climb from Camp III and a young Voytek Kurtyka took a fifteen-metre fall through a cornice, injuring a leg. From Camp IV, at the far end of the knife-edge, easier featureless climbing led over a snow dome towards the right-hand slopes below the summit headwall. As Camp V was about to be occupied the weather broke and for a week there was no progress on the mountain. It wasn't until 12 August that the camp was occupied and then in a quite extraordinary couple of days all nineteen climbers reached it with loads, an amazing achievement that speaks highly both of the teamwork necessary to carry out such a logistically complex effort, and of the acclimatisation programme that enabled all the climbers to get to 7700 metres. (The Americans in 1978 felt that some of the heights given by the Poles were optimistic.)

On 13 August Cichy and Holnicki, the first summit team, pressed up to establish Camp VI with four other climbers and on the 14th set out for the summit. They climbed a sérac barrier, but were turned back at 8250 metres below the main obstacle, a sixty-metre rock and ice step.

The following morning Chrobak and Wojciech Wröz cracked this barrier, but it took them most of the day. Using oxygen they pressed on over steep snow slopes leading to little rocks and easy snowfields below the summit. But at six p.m., tantalisingly close to the top at 8400 metres, they were nearly out of oxygen and the weather was threatening. Less than a couple of hours at most from the top, they retreated, but even so they didn't regain their top camp until one a.m., completing the last abseil in a violent storm that completely justified their decision to turn back. No further action took place until about the end of August by which time five members had fallen ill. But the top camp was never reached again and on 8 September the expedition was abandoned. Nevertheless it was a determined and well-managed effort that, with a spot more luck, would have succeeded. For Wojciech Wróz this was to be the first of three expeditions to K2, in which he reached over 8000 metres each time. The last one was to end in success and tragedy.

If the Polish team was, by contemporary standards, rather large, it was nothing compared with what was to follow in 1977. A truly colossal fifty-two-man Japanese expedition laid siege to the Abruzzi. Fifteen *hundred* porters carried to Base Camp. The leader, Ichiro Yoshizawa, was seventy-three years old. Six Japanese climbers reached the summit including Takayoshi Takatsuka, who had led a seven-man reconnaissance to the Abruzzi Spur the year before. For the first time a Pakistani, Ashraf Aman, reached the summit of the highest mountain in his country.

This, then, was the long-awaited second ascent of K2: a total anticlimax. If it proved anything it was that with enough money and manpower success was almost guaranteed. This, however, had already been demonstrated on Everest several times over. Even in 1977, the expedition was seen as a dinosaur, totally out of step with current thinking epitomised by Messner and Habeler two years earlier. The ecological impact of such huge numbers traipsing up the Baltoro was perhaps not such an issue as it would be today, though the idea of sending a small army to repeat a climb that in 1954 was achieved with far less manpower (but even then seen as a large expedition) seemed quite pointless. Compared with many other climbs in the Karakoram in the mid to late 'seventies K2 was proving something of a damp squib. It seemed too big and too hard to be climbed in anything other than expedition-style, yet what was the point of repeating what was already known to work?

This was the essence of the problem that Chris Bonington tackled in 1978. Bonington was then at the height of his considerable organisational powers, having masterminded a series of successful high-profile expeditions. Annapurna South Face and Everest South-West Face had undoubtedly pushed forward the limits of what could be done on the highest mountains. But by 1978 it was possible to sense that Bonington himself was growing disenchanted with the big expeditions. In 1977 he had climbed the Ogre with Doug Scott, an epic which had nearly killed both of them. Despite that, it was easy to see that Bonington often hankered after small close-knit groups of friends going for big, but not outrageous, projects. His climbs on Changabang, Brammah and Shivling have received far less publicity, yet were probably more enjoyable than the endless computer-based logistical extravaganzas for which he has become so well known. Both on Everest in 1975 and K2 in 1978, he had originally planned a lightweight approach, Everest by the South Col and K2 by the Polish route on the North-East Ridge. On each occasion he had been persuaded to change his mind and go for broke on a more ambitious project. Dougal Haston and Doug Scott had been instrumental in his decision to go for the South-West Ridge of Everest and in 1978 Peter Boardman and Doug urged him to try the unknown West Ridge of K2. Both meant a radical rethink and ended up as fixed-rope expeditions. Given that Doug, in particular, was soon to become a devout apostle of the alpine-style ethic, it is interesting that on these two expeditions he was partly responsible for changing to the tactics he was soon to decry.

Faced with the problems of the West Ridge, which looked to be at least as hard and probably harder than the South-West Face of Everest, Bonington was determined to try it with a smaller team. He toyed with the idea of putting fixed ropes on just the lower half of the climb and then mounting an alpine-style push for the top. But none of his projected logistical plans seemed to work out. 'In the end I abandoned trying to climb the mountain by computer with the thought that we would have to rise above the logistic barriers – one usually did!'

In the end he settled for a team of just eight climbers (the same as Charlie Houston in 1953). They were mainly the old guard who had been with him on Everest: Doug Scott, Nick Estcourt, 'Tut' Braithwaite, Peter Boardman and Dr Jim Duff, with the addition of Joe Tasker who, with Pete Boardman, had made an outstanding first ascent of Changabang West Face in 1976, and film-maker Tony Riley. As I had hoped to be included on this expedition I watched them go with envy tinged, however, with a very real apprehension. It is, of course, too easy to be wise after the event, but I can remember feeling that after Everest and the Ogre, K2 seemed to have become a part of the expedition treadmill, the next on a long list of challenges, and something was not quite right in the attitude of some of the team members. For Nick Estcourt, the expedition appeared to hang over him. He was in the process of changing jobs from the security of a computer programmer at Ferranti to the unknown challenge of running a climbing shop in south Manchester. His personal life was mildly chaotic and he seemed more resigned than enthused about the prospect of another long and arduous trip. Somehow I couldn't look him in the eye when we said goodbye.

Whatever doubts were secretly harboured, the expedition soon met its first potentially serious situation. Tony Riley, driving overland in charge of the expedition gear, became caught up in what proved to be the opening salvoes of the war in Afghanistan when the two vans were buzzed by low-flying MiG fighter planes and met tanks on the streets of Kabul. They were briefly impounded before being escorted to Jalalabad and the Pakistan border. On the walk-in there had been a porter strike at Paiju campsite and, like the Americans before him, Bonington had some trouble in getting the loads as far as the Savoia Glacier. Compared with 1975, however, porter problems were trivial. The whole team plus equipment were established on 1 June, only three weeks or so after leaving the UK.

Nick Estcourt and Pete Boardman made a quick reconnaissance up the Savoia Glacier past the foot of the West Ridge to see if there was an easy route bypassing the first steep buttresses on the northern slopes. There wasn't, but the pair went as far as the Savoia Saddle where Nick celebrated by urinating into China! Doug Scott and Joe Tasker had more luck, exploring the small glacier below the West Face, the Negrotto Glacier, and finding a likely-looking line that led to the crest of the West Ridge well beyond the initial outlying buttresses.

Over the next few days Camp I was established and ropes were fixed and Chris Bonington and Joe Tasker reached a point just below the ridge proper. Here an easy-angled snow basin seemed to provide a quick and simple route to the pyramid of K2, bypassing the rocky crest of the ridge itself. Bonington, who had previously thought the route should follow the ridge, urged the short cut and Tasker agreed. Unroped they crossed to the far side and at 6400 metres they found a site for Camp II.

The following day the climbers drew lots for the lead above Camp II. Pete Boardman and Joe Tasker won and so were thrown together for the first time since their epic Changabang climb. Supported by Bonington, Estcourt and Quamajan, a high-altitude porter, they all climbed to Camp II where Boardman and Tasker were left to establish the route ahead. The weather had been excellent but that night clouds arrived from the west and it snowed for two days, pinning the occupants of each camp down. On the third day it cleared somewhat though it was still windy and Boardman and Tasker, in the lead where they wanted to be, made good progress running out around 250 metres of rope over difficult mixed ground. From Camp I Scott, Estcourt and Bonington failed to make it to Camp II in the new snow and abandoned their loads below the traverse across the basin. They radioed the lead pair and said they would set off early the next morning, for supplies at Camp II were running low.

On 12 June Bonington woke with a streaming head cold and Scott, Estcourt and Quamajan set off without him. Above, Boardman and Tasker regained their high point and started out on new ground. During the morning Jim Duff arrived at Camp I to break the news that Tut Braithwaite, who had been having trouble with a recurrence of a chest complaint, had decided to go home. It was an unwelcome but not totally surprising piece of news. Meanwhile Pete Boardman, in the lead, had stopped to warm a numbed foot, and later wrote vividly in his diary what happened next:

Dark figures moved across the slope, very slowly, very late it seemed. I took my boot off and warmed up my big toe and then put my boot back on. Ate a Milky Way and Sesame Snap. Then a great rumbling roar. 'Joe, Joe, look!' The whole bowl of snow started moving slowly. Because of the concave slope it accumulated around the lower part of the slope. The two figures were about a hundred feet above the sérac wall. One figure completely enveloped. I nearly took a photograph, checked by revulsion, horror, couldn't believe it. A great cloud of snow right across to Angel Peak, a slab avalanche five hundred feet wide, three hundred feet high. Thousands of tons of snow. The figure in the middle struggled and was overwhelmed and disappeared from view. Three thousand feet to the glacier, the end figure fifty feet from the tent of Camp II, slid and struggled and fell thirty feet spinning and then stopped. The memories are chemically vivid. Cold calm thoughts – and I must hate myself for this, I suppose – came. Someone's been killed – Chris, Nick – QJ – can't be Doug. I'm sure the surviving figure, by movement, is Doug. Joe didn't seem to have noticed it properly. I had seen it all. Descend. The figure shouted 'Nick'. It must be Nick. Nick is dead. But we don't know. 'Don't let that bloke go back across the slope, Joe.' [He'd be there first.] So easy for someone involved in an accident like that to do something quickly, irrationally, particularly if it's Doug. Don't do anything stupid, unclip, clip descendeur. Joe arrives first at CII which the figure has regained. 'Nick's copped it, youth.'

Doug Scott had come within a whisker of death. On reaching the basin he and Estcourt had decided to fix a rope across for extra security. Nick Estcourt had simply been using the thin fixed rope as a handrail but Scott, who was running it out, was tied to it. When the avalanche started the rope pulled him inexorably backwards into its path. Scott turned somersaults backwards and resigned himself to death.

> There was no fear. I registered only curiosity at being in my first big avalanche and contemplated the prospect of dying. Time was in suspension during those few seconds until I suddenly stopped – my heavy sack anchoring me firmly in the snow sufficient to snap the rope. I stood up and watched, horrified, as the avalanche with Nick in the middle of it poured down the cliffs to the glacier below.

At Camp I Chris Bonington had seen the huge cloud of billowing snow pass by and, unaware of the possibility of anyone caught up in it, had started taking photos until Jim Duff suddenly realised what might have happened. Gripped with doubt and horror they kept the radio open. It crackled into life and Scott's voice, distorted with static and heavy with emotion, broke the news. Distraught, Boardman, Tasker and Scott retraced their steps across the basin, quite safe now on the firm underlying snow. At the far side Quamajan was waiting in deep shock. He showed them his hands streaked with burn marks where he had tried to hold the rope. He had been about to set off across the slope when Nick, with whom he had been sharing a cigarette, said he would go next.

The next day everyone descended to Base Camp. Doug set off early in a dull cloudy dawn to search the avalanche debris in a futile attempt to find Nick's body. Later that day everyone got together to try and decide what to do next. It would have been an easier decision to reach had the accident occurred later in the expedition. But after only twelve days on the mountain retreat seemed a horribly abrupt end to everyone's hopes and dreams. Pete Boardman was quite clear in his own mind – he wanted to carry on. But Doug Scott, Jim Duff and Tut Braithwaite had no doubts that the expedition should be abandoned. Pete was aghast.

I can't believe my ears that Doug and Jim want to stop the climb. It was a mistake that could have been avoided. The route should be a safe one. Joe, amazingly, is non-committal, I'm astonished he's not more determined. Only Chris and I seem to want to go on. Nick would certainly have gone on . . . I really want to give the mountain everything I have, to struggle amongst overwhelming beauty above 25,000 feet.

Initially, Bonington also wanted to go on, despite the grief of losing his best friend. Tony Riley wished to continue and make his film, though he realised that he could not influence the decision as he was only a support climber. But Doug Scott, who had come so close to death, felt he could not possibly carry on and pointed out the agony their wives would have to go through if they continued.

With only three people in favour of going on, the expedition was abandoned. Bonington and Scott left for home immediately to see Carolyn Estcourt, and the others were left to pack up and return in dribs and drabs.

I was in the Karakoram on another expedition as the subdued team members arrived in Skardu, and can vividly remember the determination that Pete showed as he told me that he was going to go back as soon as possible. Pete was clearly as upset as the others about Nick's death, but he could dissociate himself from it and concentrate on his own future ambitions. Joe was far more circumspect, but I had no doubt that the two of them would soon return.

11

An Old Score Settled

When Chris Bonington and Doug Scott got back to Skardu, they met Jim Whittaker and a strong team preparing to leave for their own attempt on K2. Almost as soon as the Americans got home after the 1975 débâcle, plans were being made for another expedition. Once again Jim Wickwire was a driving force in its conception, and Jim Whittaker, now approaching fifty, was leader. But his twin brother Lou would not be going with them. In 1975 the Big Four had suffered their own internal tensions, mainly centred on the difficulty Lou had experienced with Jim's new wife, Dianne. From now on Jim and Lou would go their separate ways.

Determined to avoid the mistakes of 1975, particularly in his sometimes high-handed and inflexible decision-making, Jim Whittaker had set about recruiting a stronger team for 1978. But it seemed that his criteria for selection were primarily to do with past successes rather than compatibility, and the final choice was a group who almost all had summit aspirations. It is hard not to compare Whittaker's policy with Chris Bonington's team choices on Annapurna and Everest, where several members were included mainly for their ability to work well together in a supporting role. The Poles were an even better example of teamwork and it was their route on the North-East Ridge that Whittaker was attempting. The party was made up of Whittaker himself, his wife Dianne Roberts, Jim Wickwire and Rob Schaller, all from the 1975 expedition. Newcomers were Craig Anderson, Cherie and Terry Bech, Chris Chandler, Skip Edmonds, Dianna Jagersky (Base Camp Manager), Lou Reichardt, Rick Ridgeway, John Roskelley and Bill Sumner. All had excellent track records and nearly all had been to the Himalaya. Whittaker 'wanted the best, toughest, meanest climbers in the United States'.

Initially, the Americans had been refused permission for K2 in 1978 because the mountain had already been booked by Chris Bonington, and only some high-level lobbying by Senator Edward Kennedy, a family friend of the Whittakers, who went straight to President Bhutto, had the Ministry of Tourism's initial decision overruled. This was to be the thin end of the wedge: the first time two expeditions were to be allowed on K2 in the same year. By 1986 it had grown to nine. The Americans were given a permit for late in the season, to avoid porter congestion on the walk-in, and so long as they went for a different route to the British. Whittaker had hoped to try the West Ridge, but when the British opted for this themselves the North-East Ridge was an obvious second choice. It would be a worthy objective for the Americans who, if the 1960 American–German expedition is counted, had now made five unsuccessful attempts on the mountain.

Whittaker's team was subdued by the news of Nick Estcourt's death which brought home to many of them, even before they had started the walk-in, the reality of climbing on big Himalayan peaks. Right at the beginning there was a misunderstanding when half the team drove off from Skardu in a cloud of dust leaving an embarrassed Whittaker at a farewell ceremony with the District Commissioner. Their liaison officer threatened to quit on the spot and Whittaker had to plead with him to stay on. Not a good start. But Whittaker was bending over backwards to be democratic, sometimes to the point of allowing too much discussion and dissent. By the time the Americans arrived at K2 Base Camp on 5 July there had been far less internal strife than in 1975, and porter problems, thankfully, were far less serious.

But once work began on the North-East Ridge, and Whittaker started to sort out who was to lead what, almost immediately some of the climbers read hidden agendas into his plans. Rick Ridgeway, author of the expedition book *The Last Step*, was as frank in describing the problems as Galen Rowell had been in 1975. Ridgeway chided himself for succumbing to the temptation of questioning every decision:

I realised how ridiculous it was, mapping all those scenarios of who would climb with whom. Time and again, all of us had told each other we would avoid the jockeying-for-position, the game-playing that happens on big expeditions, and here I was indulging in it already, at that early stage. It was ludicrous. I had to laugh at my own gullibility. Anything could happen

– sickness, injury, storms – to change any sequence of events planned in advance.

And yet for others the feeling grew that there was already, as in 1975, an 'A' and a 'B' team. Cherie Bech, writing about the expedition philosophy later, said it would have been more honest to say, '"A certain number of you are chosen for the summit, the remaining members are here to carry loads" . . . Instead everyone was encouraged actively to believe that we all started out with a chance of reaching the summit.' But on a large expedition people simply *do* perform with differing degrees of efficiency at different times and, despite her contentious assertion that during a seven-day spell of good weather the whole team could have got to the top, any expedition leader has to organise his resources in the best possible way to optimise his chances. On a climb as long as the North-East Ridge of K2 it is hard to see how the logistics could be arranged for more than four to six climbers to make a summit bid. In the event it was only four who had the opportunity, but this was to be a long way off.

As work started shifting gear to Advance Base it quickly became apparent that Cherie Bech was being viewed critically both as a climber and for her judgement. She had set off from Base Camp with a sack weighing over ninety pounds, a colossal load that was quite unrealistic. John Roskelley, a self-confessed redneck from Spokane, Washington and one of the strongest climbers in the world, was scathing: 'Every single time I go on one of these big climbs with women it's the same story . . . I've seen them kill themselves trying to prove they are as strong as men . . . People criticise me for being down on women on expeditions, but I've never yet been on a big mountain with one that's worth a damn.' Harsh words indeed. Sexism was not yet a high-profile issue in 1978, but one does not get the feeling it would ever have inhibited Roskelley. Cherie Bech was an incredibly determined climber who had, with her husband Terry, made a highly creditable (if illicit) effort to climb Dhaulagiri in 1972. They had reached nearly 7500 metres before giving up in the face of bad weather. Cherie had carried huge loads all the time, as well as being five months pregnant. Whether it was wise to try and repeat her carrying feats on a large expedition was open to question. What was certainly a lot more controversial was her increasing friendship with Chris Chandler. They climbed together and were constantly in each other's company. It was a relationship that, as the expedition carried on, threatened to cause real problems.

Initially the expedition made reasonable progress, soon establishing three camps below the knife-edged section of the ridge before sitting out a storm. Knowing that it had taken the strong Polish team ten days to climb it, Rick Ridgeway and John Roskelley were under no illusions as to the difficulty. On 30 July they made a spectacularly good start and ran out almost four hundred metres of fixed rope, only stopping at five p.m. and regaining the tents of Camp III in twilight. Ecstatic, they radioed their progress to Jim Whittaker who responded, 'Unbelievable – you guys are real tigers!'

The next day they regained their high point at seven thirty a.m., and continued their rapid progress, occasionally using old Polish fixed ropes. But they had been too optimistic and the end of the traverse was further than it looked. On 1 August Jim Wickwire and Bill Sumner pressed ahead through light snow but again didn't reach the site for Camp IV, still two hundred metres away. On the 2nd Roskelley, Wickwire and Ridgeway reached the end of the knife-edge but had difficulty in finding the spot where the Poles had pitched their camp. They pressed on in thick cloud, worried that they might have to turn back yet again. At last the clouds parted briefly and Roskelley in the lead shouted down the good news to the others that he had found a site good enough for three tents. It had taken only four days to climb and fix this, the most technical section of the ridge. It was a brilliant demonstration of the levels of difficulty now undertaken in the Himalaya almost as a matter of course, and provides an interesting yardstick to measure progress over the years. Eckenstein's expedition didn't get to the start of the knife-edge ridge. Houston's expedition in 1938 considered the whole of the North-East Ridge too long and difficult to attempt. Though Vittorio Sella recommended Wiessner's expedition to give it a try in 1939, they were unconvinced. By 1976 the Poles felt confident enough to climb it, though it had taken ten days. Now, only two years later, it had taken just four. Doubtless it will eventually be soloed by someone climbing up the North-East and down the North-West Ridges.

Instead of the accolade they felt they deserved after the break-through, the tired occupants of Camp III were berated for indulging in a rest day by Lou Reichardt and Jim Whittaker when they arrived with heavy loads at Camp III. One cannot help feeling that all too often the Americans felt giving vent to their feelings would help solve their problems but invariably it made them worse. On

Himalayan expeditions it is quite often worth exercising a bit of restraint at close quarters. Whittaker's leadership on both expeditions was flawed on the psychology front and his basic man-management was at times naive. It could not have been made any easier by the presence of his wife. Dianne Roberts was a fiercely independent woman who wanted to be taken seriously as a climber. Once again it was John Roskelley who was prepared to voice any misgivings at the thought that Whittaker was trying to get her further up the mountain (to Camp IV) than her ability deserved. 'I was under the impression Dianne was supposed to be the photographer on this trip, not a climber. Everybody here knows the only reason she's along is because she's your wife.'

But it really wasn't as simple as that. As in 1975, Dianne Roberts had thrown herself into the organisation of the expedition and performed well on the lower slopes of the mountain, in her view earning her the right to go as high as she possibly could. A problem was developing that would increasingly crop up on further expeditions, indeed had already occurred with tragic results on Everest. This has nothing to do with women or sexism but ability. Using fixed ropes and jumars it is quite possible that fit, strong but comparatively inexperienced climbers can get very high on big technical climbs quite easily. When putting one foot in front of the other and sliding a jumar up a rope is all that's needed, it is beguilingly tempting to see just how high you can go, which is fine so long as nothing goes wrong, or you don't misjudge your endurance, and that the fixed ropes do not have awkward horizontal sections. But on a long traverse all three circumstances can simultaneously occur and then it takes skill and experience to avoid trouble. In 1972 on the West Ridge of Everest Harsh Bahaguna froze to death on a horizontal set of fixed ropes simply because he couldn't manage to change a karabiner over a belay point due to cold hands. A trivial situation rapidly became desperate, then tragic. Roskelley in his forthright way was voicing a real concern.

With the question of Dianne Roberts unresolved, the weather, which had been slowly deteriorating, broke down completely. On returning to Camp I Ridgeway was accosted by a furious Terry Bech who accused him of trying to malign Chris Chandler by spreading rumours about a relationship with Cherie. Ridgeway apologised for meddling in other people's business but the problem was far from going away.

When the storm eased, Camp IV was established. With the fixed ropes in place and a well-trodden trail it was possible to do the carry from Camp II to IV in just two hours of exhilarating climbing poised high over the Chinese side of the ridge. On 10 August Jim Whittaker made the fateful decision of who to pick for the summit attempt. Unsurprisingly, the four names were Jim Wickwire, Lou Reichardt, Rick Ridgeway and John Roskelley. All had in Whittaker's opinion 'worked the hardest, shown the most strength' and possessed 'the most drive to make it all the way'. All four expressed the wish to climb without oxygen, though Ridgeway was more doubtful about his chances than the others.

It fell to Chris Chandler and Skip Edmonds to push the route out to Camp V situated on the broader section of the ridge. At Camp IV Cherie Bech and Craig Anderson were in support. But they failed to reach the site of Camp V as another bad storm moved in. The four were marooned on the far side of the knife-edge ridge, a potentially serious situation, for they were eating the provisions that had cost so much energy to carry, and at that height and position it was not a good place to get stuck for any length of time. Urgent radio calls from Camp III to descend were easier to make than obey. On the morning of 12 August, after a violent radio argument, Craig Anderson and Skip Edmonds set out while Chris Chandler and Cherie Bech took down the tents to stop them blowing away. But Craig and Skip, exposed to the full force of the storm, had to retreat. The tents were repitched and the four sat it out for another day. On the 13th they made an epic crossing. It took over eight hours to return to Camp III and on the way Chris Chandler was avalanched midway between two anchors. Unlike Nick Estcourt, Chandler was saved by the fixed ropes, which held.

The storm lasted another three days. On the 16th it cleared but to the frustration of those below, Terry Bech and Bill Sumner decided it was too dangerous to return from Camp II to Camp III where Chris and Cherie felt the same about the traverse to Camp IV. This time any criticism seemed without justification. Even on fixed ropes it is unwise to move for at least twenty-four hours after heavy snowfall and the death of Nick Estcourt was still on everyone's minds. But the leadership felt that if quick progress to Camp V wasn't made soon the big guns like Wickwire and Roskelley would soon have to be unleashed.

The following morning saw a tense meeting at Camp III. Chris Chandler and Cherie Bech had started across the traverse but soon turned back, fearing windslab avalanche conditions. Roskelley, Reichardt and Wickwire powered up from Camp I and Whittaker and Dianne Roberts soon followed. Whittaker suggested that the next day Roskelley and Ridgeway should break trail across to Camp IV, followed by Chris and Cherie who would open the route to Camp V. Lou Reichardt openly doubted whether Cherie was strong enough to reach Camp V without oxygen and angry words were exchanged before an uneasy truce. Once again there was a tendency on both sides to rise to the bait, a temptation, no doubt, succumbed to under the strain of so long at altitude and the increasing urgency of making real progress as time was running out. It was noticeably colder and the autumn storms might not be far away.

The route to IV was reopened and next day, still tense and bickering, Roskelley, Reichardt, Ridgeway and Chandler pressed on up and over a featureless snow dome looking for a site for Camp V. Towards the end of a long and exhausting day Chris Chandler and John Roskelley had a vitriolic stand-up row about Chandler's relationship with Cherie. It reached quite surreal proportions when Lou Reichardt, belayed by Chandler, broke through a snowbridge into a crevasse. Neither Chandler nor Roskelley paid any attention to his plight but carried on arguing face to face. Ridgeway went to help Reichardt, laughing at the absurdity of this high-altitude farce. An hour later they arrived at the site of Camp V at around 7700 metres. It was a crucial achievement, for failure to make it that day could have so dispirited everyone that the expedition might have foundered there and then.

That evening at Camp IV the weather broke yet again but this time it was distinctly warmer – wet snow turning to rain low down. Roskelley and Ridgeway stayed up at Camp IV to hold the fort. Once more the rest baled out. Morale hit a new low. The A and B teams were barely communicating. Earlier Ridgeway had asked Terry Bech what A and B stood for: 'Best and Asshole' was his blunt reply.

It proved to be the worst storm of the summer, four days of whipping winds and snowfall threatening to wreck Camp IV. Cooped up in lower camps there was plenty of time to argue about summit plans when (or if) the fine spell arrived. At Camp IV Roskelley and Ridgeway proposed that they should simply go for it alpine-style. The plan was predictably a red rag to a bull and bitterly resented by the lower camps but it indirectly had the effect of provoking a crisis meeting back at Camp I of all the team (minus, of course, Ridgeway and Roskelley who by now had been forced back to Camp III).

Jim Whittaker opened the discussion with a heartfelt apology for his heavy-handedness in the past and the unfairness of some of his decisions. He appealed to all of them to pull together one last time to get someone, anyone, to the top of the mountain to fulfil the forty-year dream of an American ascent. Terry Bech felt that the B team had been treated like porters and had been excluded from any chance of the summit, while Chris Chandler pointed out that measuring summit potential simply by how fast people carried loads between camps, or how much leading they had done, was no indicator of their performance above 8000 metres, where willpower and sheer desire for the top were probably the decisive factors. Then it was proposed by Jim Wickwire that the summit team should be rechosen after Camp V was fully stocked on the basis of everyone's performance at the time. This was approved and Terry Bech then brought up another problem. Everyone was aware that the direct finish, as it had come to be called, so nearly climbed by the Poles in 1976, would be technically difficult, probably needing some fixed ropes and almost certainly only allowing two people to the summit. Bech suggested that the B team traverse left to the Shoulder of K2 and finish via the Abruzzi. It gave a better chance of success for the B team, and could provide a safer and easier descent route for anyone completing the direct finish. Logistically it was a complicated plan but it did provide a fallback position. If the direct finish was too hard, it could go a long way to unite the team and, if all else failed, would be the only option left. Terry's plan was given approval, and after Whittaker once again called for a united last effort the meeting broke up.

Peace lasted two whole days, then with the storm still blowing, another meeting ended in dissent with Lou Reichardt calling for a decision to be made on one route or the other, stating that, given the weather and their limited resources, even one route would stretch everyone to the limit. Chris Chandler left the tent in protest and it was left to Terry Bech to keep pushing for the dual ascent. The arguing was abruptly cut off on the evening of 25 August when, quite suddenly, the storm cleared, the temperature dropped and stars pierced the night sky. The following day was pivotal. Lou Reichardt had proposed to go from Camp I to Camp IV in a single day. This was ostensibly to save a day, but also to catch up with Ridgeway and Roskelley who would be starting out from Camp III. Jim Wickwire, Craig Anderson, Jim Whittaker and Dianne Roberts were in on the plan but the rest of the team was kept in the dark. Lou then requested the wrench to tighten oxygen cylinders from Chris Chandler. A suspicion began to grow that the B team were being duped. The A team were regrouping. It was quite true, they were. What seems so obvious to an outsider reading the differing accounts of the expedition sixteen years later is how unnecessary and destructive these subterfuges and others like them were. How could it possibly help to climb the mountain when half the team were locked in combat with the other half? And why, after nearly two months on the mountain, were so many people still deluding themselves they could reach the top?

The day nearly produced a disaster. From Camp I at 6000 metres to Camp IV at 7500 metres was an enormous distance and height to cover. To help those below at Camp III Ridgeway and Roskelley broke trail downhill until about halfway to Camp II then returned and set off for IV. Though fine, it was still blowing hard from the Chinese side and it took four cold and exhausting hours to break trail across the knife-edge. Luckily neither of them seemed frostbitten, but feet, hands and noses were numb. Behind them Lou didn't leave Camp III until after two p.m. Jim Wickwire, Jim Whittaker, Dianne Roberts and Craig Anderson stopped for a brew and it was three p.m. before they set out on the exposed windswept traverse. As they met the full force of the wind it dawned on Anderson that they were out on a limb. He also began to worry that the B team would arrive in Camp III and, finding it deserted, would realise that they had been deceived. But he had to put these worries behind him as the afternoon sped by, the wind and spindrift blew over the ridge and darkness beckoned.

It was a shattered and exhausted procession that finally staggered into Camp IV suffering the first signs of exposure and barely able to speak. Roskelley was, predictably, fuming at the bad judgement of Jim Whittaker in allowing Dianne to cross, but even he was impressed that she had got the drive and strength to make it. Despite the wind and nearly being benighted, they were all safe but far too shattered to progress further the next morning. It was still blowing hard and, radioing back to Camp III, Roskelley told the lower party not to come on across the knife-edge. There was no room for them at Camp IV.

This, unsurprisingly, caused a furious response and a two-way-radio slanging-match ensued. Terry Bech threatened to cut away all the fixed ropes and burn the tents but was calmed down by Cherie and Chris Chandler who pointed out that he might face murder charges! An uneasy calm descended on the camp as they dully accepted their rest day. It was broken by a loud explosion as Chris Chandler, making tea, blew up a half-full gas cartridge while changing cylinders. It removed his eyebrows and half his beard and moustache. It was the last straw. Chandler quit the expedition and returned to Base Camp to sit it out until the others returned.

The wind dropped and the next day, 28 August, everyone was on the move. Those at Camp IV moved up to V and the occupants of III traversed to IV. For Dianne Roberts the carry to V was the personal highlight of two expeditions. Disparaged and resented for so long, she had proved herself by getting to over 7500 metres, a height record for American women.[1] Buoyed by optimism that now at the last moment everything was going well Rick Ridgeway slept soundly. He awoke early, pleased to find that he was rehydrated enough to want to relieve himself. Half asleep and pushing his way out of the tent into the night, it took him a few moments to realise something was wrong. Silently, big snowflakes drifted down out of a starless sky.

Next morning everyone sheltered in the tents as snow and wind continued. What to do? Go up and establish Camp VI? Sit it out here? Or go down? Each course had something to be said for it; each could lead to the climb being abandoned. Eventually the seven occupants of Camp V chose all three options. Jim Whittaker, Dianne Roberts and Craig Anderson went down, Roskelley and Ridgeway stayed put and the indefatigable pair of Reichardt and Wickwire did a carry up to the site of Camp VI under the rock buttresses at the foot of the summit pyramid. They climbed above the bad weather and returned in good spirits. The camp was at the same site as the Poles' and wasn't as high as they had hoped, but there was nothing to be seen higher up and the ground soon became technical. It would have to do.

Amazingly, the A team managed to fit in a small row about the use of oxygen before the weather broke for the umpteenth time and the Big Four descended to Camp IV. Here Lou Reichardt found the energy to cross the knife-edge to talk to Jim Whittaker and return again the same day. The discussion was to reassure Whittaker that the A team were still one hundred per cent committed. On his return to Camp IV it was agreed that the four would go for the direct finish. The next day, which was still stormy, they also made it painfully clear to Cherie Bech that she wouldn't be going with them.

---

[1] It wasn't to last long, for only a few weeks later two American women climbed Annapurna I (8091m).

It stretches the bounds of credulity that grown men (and women) could have so many public changes of mind and baring of souls, but during the afternoon Wickwire broke the news that he had opted for the Abruzzi finish. This put Cherie and Terry back in the picture again. But on 2 September, when they all reascended to Camp V, Cherie and Terry arrived very late, hypothermic and exhausted. Cherie, in particular, was in a bad way and was given oxygen. Astonishingly, she made a good recovery and had 3 September to try and recover as it was snowing again. That evening the whole team prepared to accept the sixth American defeat on K2.

September 4 dawned bright and cold and sunny, and faced with this, the last chance, the six in Camp V prepared for one last big effort. Setting off it quickly became obvious that at last Cherie Bech had shot her bolt. Lou Reichardt wrote with sensitivity of that moment:

She realised she had reached the limit of her endurance and turned back. She had never hesitated during the expedition to carry the same loads as men nearly twice her weight . . . we were struck by the tragic dichotomy between willpower, which would have carried her anywhere, and her body which was made of the same weak flesh as the rest of us.

And Rick Ridgeway was also moved:

I still held that image of her standing above watching us slowly walk away. She stood there stripped of pretensions, her final dreams dissolving before her eyes, and like the rest of us at that final hour of the expedition, naked before the mountain.

And what of Cherie herself? She wrote from a rather different perspective:

. . . We started out for Camp VI. My hands were starting to freeze up again and I wanted to adjust my glasses but as Lou was jerking impatiently on the rope, all I could do was stumble along as best I could. I faced the biting cold of the best snow plateau at 7700 metres and imagined I could see Chris's figure standing there bathed in the soft golden light of early morning . . . my heart ached to be with him. The time had come for me to turn round. The vision of Chris standing there and the feeling we had shared together on the mountain stood in stark contrast to my present companions with whom I shared nothing. I unroped and walked back to camp alone.

Not for the first time, and certainly not the last, perceptions of the same event at high altitude could be very different, yet still true for each individual.

At a prominent rock below the final pyramid the five remaining climbers assembled. Ridgeway and Roskelley would be going straight up, while Reichardt, Wickwire and Terry Bech started their long traverse left to the Shoulder of the Abruzzi. The two parties split, wishing each other well. Ridgeway and Roskelley ploughed a furrow through waist- and even shoulder-deep snow to the site of Camp VI which Reichardt and Wickwire had reached a week before. Progress was desperately slow and soon they heard the others shouting to them. The snow was too deep to cross to the Abruzzi and they were caching their loads before retreating to Camp V. They would join them in the morning on the direct route.

But Ridgeway and Roskelley were not having it any easier. At last they reached the site of Camp VI and had to dig for hours to find the loads left by Reichardt and Wickwire. Then they spent the evening melting snow, brewing, melting snow, brewing. At last Ridgeway prepared to sleep before their summit attempt.

'We have got to start early – we should get the stove going at one thirty.'

'I'll let you know when it gets to that time.'

'What time is it now?'

'Twelve thirty.'

Somehow they managed to get the stove lit on time, but in those grim, predawn hours Ridgeway could feel that the urgency needed for their supreme effort just wasn't there. It was past six a.m. before they got started, much too late already and, after less than a rope-length, Roskelley retreated. Avalanche danger was extreme with huge banked-up slopes of unstable powder snow. Ridgeway had a brief look and confirmed Roskelley's decision. A radio call to Jim Whittaker at Camp III gave the bad news. The expedition seemed to be finished, unless the three at Camp V could come up with something.

Below, Wickwire, Reichardt and Bech left Camp V uncertain what to do, but soon, looking up to the direct finish, they saw that

Roskelley and Ridgeway were struggling. Then they saw an avalanche sweep part of the route ahead, and knew that they would be wasting their time if they climbed up to join them. There was no alternative but to try again to cross the deep snow to the Shoulder and hope that conditions improved when they got there. Lou Reichardt regained the abandoned loads from the day before but decided to break trail unladen. By doing this he made better progress and the three decided that if the leaders took turns in trail-breaking without a pack, they could return to pick it up when the tracks were stamped out. In this way, first Lou then Jim led across, and later in the afternoon Jim at last reached a point where only a forty-five-degree slope led to the Abruzzi. To his delight the conditions suddenly improved. Jim returned for his sack, and Lou with Terry, who was selflessly carrying a very heavy load in support, climbed up on to the Shoulder. Jim returned and following in their tracks soon caught them up.

It was far too late to climb as high on the Shoulder as the Italians had done in 1954 and the Japanese the previous year, and they pitched a tent at about 7900 metres. It was seven before the three crammed into it for a short, nearly sleepless night before their big day. Wickwire twice fell asleep and knocked the pan over, spilling precious fluid over his sleeping-bag and, worse still, his fibre-pile mittens. Now he only had woollen gloves with a nylon shell. At four a.m. in the bitter cold night he and Reichardt prepared to leave the tiny tent. As they left Jim dropped his water bottle which skidded down the icy surface and out of sight. Terry Bech silently watched them go, knowing that he had done everything possible to help them on their way and now his own chance was finally gone. When the sun came up he would go down to Camp V and wait with Cherie for the returning climbers.

Lou and Jim crunched up the hard snow of the Shoulder. Both men carried oxygen and at seven thirty a.m. Wickwire decided it was time to start using his. But to his horror he found that the cylinder was only two-thirds full. In order to make it last to the top he would have to regulate the flow to one litre a minute. (This would in fact only just offset the effort it took to carry the set in the first place.) At the top of the Bottleneck, before the left-hand traverse under the sérac band, Lou Reichardt decided it was now time to use his oxygen. But even with the flow at a maximum rate of eight litres a minute he was getting no value at all. He discovered that a rubber tube had been punctured in several places, and he had nothing to repair it with. In disgust he abandoned both the set and his pack and set off after Wickwire, now climbing slowly and deliberately up beyond the sérac barrier and, they hoped, above all difficulties. Jim saw that Lou had left his pack and stopped to wait for him.

'I'm going without oxygen . . . watch me and tell me if I exhibit any bizarre behaviour.'

Wickwire agreed, then added, 'You realise, though, that I'm going to the top regardless?'

They continued, finding snow conditions on the upper slopes worsening, deep and unconsolidated as it had been on the north-east slopes. At one stage both men forged separate tracks in their desire to find firmer snow. Despite his lack of oxygen, Lou led for a while and Jim found it hard to keep up with him, even with oxygen. But the gap slowly closed and Jim overtook him. Late in the afternoon the sun disappeared behind the summit ridge and the temperature dropped sharply. Lou, without oxygen, and without his jacket left in his rucksack, started to get cold. Surely the top couldn't be far away? Jim, almost in a trance, plugged on, thinking of all his family who had supported him in his quest for the summit. He thought of the five unsuccessful expeditions before him and suddenly stepped into the late evening sunshine. The summit was only yards away.

Lou joined him. 'We've come this far. Let's make the last step together.' It was five fifteen p.m. on 6 September, 1978. The American dream was at last realised.

Far, far below at Camp I watchers through a big telescope had viewed their progress throughout the day. Feuding forgotten, excitement mounted and when the two tiny figures disappeared over the summit ridge wild cheering broke out. Then, drama. One figure quickly reappeared and descended rapidly – almost running it seemed. But where was the other? Time slipped past. No sign – had there been an accident? Could one of them have fallen or was there a crevasse on the summit? Forty long minutes passed and the sun had set. A red alpen glow lit the summit pyramid. The descending figure was well down the summit slopes. Then to everyone's joy a second dot appeared below the summit and started descending. But was he too late? Red faded to grey and snow started to blow off the summit as the wind got up and night fell. The dot below the summit was faced with a bivouac in the autumn cold at 8500 metres.

When Reichardt and Wickwire had reached the top, Lou had barely posed for a photo and taken one of Jim, before quickly setting off down to retrieve his jacket and rucksack. Jim had lingered. He had tried to change a film, get out the flags and perform all the various summit rituals. Suddenly, it was past six p.m. Night was almost upon him. As he left the summit he realised he wasn't going to get down without a bivouac. With no sleeping-bag, it was going to be a long, cruel night.

Early on 6 September Ridgeway and Roskelley had woken at Camp VI on the direct finish determined to give it one last try. Again they had started the stove early but this time they were even later setting off. Like the day before, the snow was potentially lethal. It was quite unjustifiable to continue. Then in the early-morning radio call they heard that Lou and Jim were well on their way to the top. They had only one option: to pack up, follow Lou, Jim and Terry's tracks to the Abruzzi and try it themselves the next day. It would be their third night above 8000 metres. They contemplated the huge loads they would have to ferry round to the Shoulder and decided to abandon all the climbing gear, except for one rope which they would leave at the junction with the Abruzzi Spur. Even so it was a gruelling carry and they had resorted to towing their sacks through the snow, arriving on the Shoulder at around three in the afternoon. They had passed Terry Bech on his way down to Camp V but the Abruzzi Camp VI was empty.

As night fell the wind blew across the Shoulder of K2. The hours passed, seven, eight, and no sign of Jim or Lou. At nine they were worried and blew a whistle and flashed a torch. At last they heard a faint reply. Lou Reichardt had passed the camp in the darkness and was a hundred metres below them, preparing to spend the night in a crevasse if he could find one. Now he had to climb back up and arrived desperately tired, on the verge of collapse, encrusted with ice and unable to speak.

When he managed to speak coherently he told them he had last seen Wickwire on the summit. Gradually, the gravity of the situation dawned on Roskelley and Ridgeway. Preparing to leave early, as Jim and Lou had done, they didn't know if they were setting out on a summit bid, a rescue or to retrieve a body. They started the interminable preparations to leave. It was bitterly cold, but what would it be like just below the summit of K2? Could Jim possibly survive?

High above, Jim Wickwire was still very much alive. He had a nylon bivouac sack that at least kept him out of the worst of the wind but he was still racked with bitter cold. He had found himself slipping slowly down the slope below the summit and was pleased that he could still think clearly enough to anchor the sack by pinning his ice-axe through the fabric in one corner into the snow and using his ice-hammer in the other. 'Good thinking, Wickwire – not bad under these conditions. Now you won't slide any more.' Feeling more secure he tried to keep the circulation going in his feet and fingers. 'But you will survive. You have made the summit. You have gone this far. It is all downhill from here. It is that simple. Keep moving your toes and your fingers. Shift your arms, your legs. Keep the circulation going. The night will end. You will survive.'

Like Bonatti and Mahdi almost a quarter of a century before him, Jim found himself on the extreme limits of survival. It was undoubtedly much colder than Bonatti's bivouac but Wickwire's equipment was probably better. He believes the key factor in his survival was the fact that he had made it to the top. 'There was an incredible lift in my spirits knowing that a lifelong dream had been realised. Accordingly, I would make it through the night somehow. If I had turned back short of the summit, then been forced to go through the kind of night I experienced, I doubt I would have made it out of the bivouac the next morning. In this regard, Bonatti's bivouac – while not alone – may have been more difficult psychologically. He knew he would not be going up in the morning with Compagnoni and Lacedelli.' Even so, sheer bloody-minded willpower was essential. Sleep was the great enemy. Relax, and there would be no awakening. Racked with paroxysms of shivering, Jim Wickwire stuck it out until the first grey light of dawn seeped through the thin nylon fabric enshrouding him. He *was* alive, he *would* survive.

Below, Rick Ridgeway and John Roskelley had left Camp VI at three thirty and made steady progress up the Shoulder and through the Bottleneck. They both decided not to use oxygen until they had to. As they climbed they wondered what they would find, and the higher they climbed the more they feared it would be a body. Roskelley was out of sight ahead and behind him Ridgeway describes climbing into his line of vision.

How far is John? Look up. I should see him now . . . There he is, but wait. I stare at the scene mesmerised: I am not prepared for what I see . . . Frozen in the scene two figures. One below the other, blue suited and moving slowly – John. The second standing above, no apparent movement, legs slightly spread,

arms down, a scarecrow figure yet also godlike, still not moving
– frozen solid? Jim Wickwire.

Jim had made it through the night but, come the dawn, he had been in
terrible danger. As the first rays of sun hit the bivouac, still bringing
no warmth, he began to relax:

> . . . OK. One crampon on. Sun feels good, but it is still so cold.
> My fingers are awfully hard. I wonder how the toes are inside
> that boot. Wait a minute, Wickwire. Look at your boot. The
> crampon is loose. Two steps with that rig and it would pop off
> and so would you. A long fall. All the way to Base Camp.
> Ha, ha. That's funny.
> Who needs crampons anyway? Just lie back and relax. You
> can go down later. Put the crampons on later. You prob-
> ably don't need them anyway.
> Feel the sun. Things seem so strange.
> Relax . . . Go down later . . . Sit up, Wickwire. Focus.
> You're in bad shape. Snap out of it. Concentrate, Wickwire,
> concentrate . . .

Stiff with cold, his clothes cracking with frost, Wickwire got it
together to start descending and at last met the second summit
team just above the Bottleneck. He seemed to be OK and prepared
to descend. His movements were mechanical, 'like the Tin Man of
Oz with no oil', as Ridgeway described him.

As he started down the steepest section Roskelley shouted to him,
'Wick, when we get back remind me to enrol you in my climbing
school. You could use a few lessons.' Jim looked up and grinned.
Reassured, the two pressed on upwards.

Above the Bottleneck Ridgeway decided it was time for oxygen.
But to his surprise Roskelley unloaded his and dumped it in the
snow. 'There's no way I'm hauling that thing to the top. I know I
can get up without it.' Ridgeway had his doubts, but like Reichardt
the day before, he simply couldn't get his own set to work. The mask
wouldn't fit and, however he adjusted it, kept falling off his face.
Furious, bemused and frustrated Ridgeway saw Roskelley pulling
away from him. He too dumped the oxygen and decided to go
without. Trying to control his breathing, but now free of the weight
of the set, he followed Roskelley up on to the final slopes of K2.

At three thirty they too stood on the summit of the second highest point on earth. Like Lou and Jim they had walked arm in arm almost to the top. Then Roskelley baulked at the last few feet. 'It may be corniced.' Beyond rational thought, for Lou and Jim had been there only the day before, Ridgeway crawled the last feet on his belly with Roskelley holding his ankles. There was no cornice and they sat on top, euphoric, for an hour. Ridgeway tried to capture the moment in his mind, a memory to replay when he was an old man. But his oxygen-starved brain refused to take it in properly.

The descent was uneventful and they regained the camp on the Shoulder before nightfall. As they luxuriated in the warmth of sleeping-bags and the shelter of the tent Ridgeway dozed while Roskelley changed gas cylinders on the stove. Suddenly their world fell apart. A violent explosion, flames everywhere, the tent burning, hair singeing, sleeping-bag a mass of sparks and feathers. Then amongst the charred wreckage they were suddenly outside in the biting cold of night. No tent and a sleeping-bag gone. Somehow they crammed into the other tent and the four exhausted men spent a ghastly night together.

It took them until midday to get going, all of them overcome with torpor. Willpower ebbed and the temptation to do nothing was overwhelming. At last they staggered off, abandoning everything not essential to their survival. What should have been a leisurely two-day descent to Advance Base turned into yet another epic as a storm broke, trapping them at Camp III. By the time the exhausted summit pairs arrived at Advance Base Jim Wickwire was in a bad way. Pneumonia had set in and by the time he reached Base Camp his condition had worsened. There was no time to lose and Wickwire was evacuated the next morning and carried to Concordia and then down to Urdokas. At Liligo near the foot of the Baltoro Glacier a Pakistani army helicopter plucked him to safety.

So at last, despite the arguments, the storms, the endless setbacks, a major new American route was climbed on K2 and three of the four summiteers had made virtually oxygenless ascents against all the odds. Many of the team would go from strength to strength. John Roskelley and Jim Wickwire in particular have continued to perform at the highest level in the Himalaya, though both have turned their backs on large expeditions. So too did Chris Chandler and Cherie Bech, whose relationship had caused many of the problems on K2. They went as a pair to attempt a winter ascent of Kangchenjunga. Accompanied by only one porter, Chris Chandler died of pulmonary oedema and the other two suffered appalling frostbite and subsequent amputations.

Looking back at the five major American expeditions to K2, one cannot help but be struck by the extremes of behaviour produced under the democratic and open framework that Americans take such justifiable pride in. Were the differences between Charlie Houston's happy and united trips and Jim Whittaker's acrimonious ones simply what has to be expected in a democracy? Genuine friendships are not forged easily. Whatever the nationality, however an expedition is run, friendship, with the accompanying virtues of tolerance, loyalty and co-operation, makes all the difference. By luck and good judgement Houston's two expeditions had it in abundance but the others didn't. They were not alone: K2 had already soured expeditions other than American ones and would often do so again.

12

The Magic Line

By 1979 Reinhold Messner had climbed four of the world's 8000-metre peaks, including Everest, and all had been completed without oxygen. Inevitably, his attention turned to K2, though at that time Messner claims he had no thought of climbing all the 8000ers, a feat he completed in 1986. Messner himself needs no introduction. He was in his prime, without doubt the world's best, and best known, mountaineer. He was already courting and suffering massive media attention and had become as big a name in Europe as a world champion skier or star footballer. His lectures could fill stadiums and he was widely quoted (and misquoted). After his Everest climb with Peter Habeler the two had split acrimoniously and now Messner needed a challenge that would exceed Everest. He found the challenge on Nanga Parbat with a solo ascent that astounded the climbing world. What next? In his own words, 'I felt ready to take another of my "steps" forward: my new plan was to attempt the world's second highest mountain with a small team and by a difficult route. And for this I had selected the South Pillar . . . which we had christened the Magic Line.'

Messner's small team consisted of Alessandro Gogna with whom he later wrote the expedition book *K2, Mountain of Mountains*, and Renato Casarotto, who already had a reputation for difficult solo climbs. From the South Tyrol came Friedl Mutschlechner and from Germany Michl Dacher. The highly talented climber and film-maker Robert Schauer from Austria completed the team of six.

Perhaps it was the Messner publicity machine that raised such high expectations of the expedition. A poster of his Magic Line shows a rather baffling route that goes up the South Pillar to a prominent snowfield, the Mushroom, then, instead of continuing up the South-West Ridge, traverses diagonally up and right to finish up the final section of the Abruzzi. Whether the line was drawn for artistic reasons or whether Messner could have actually followed it is academic, for not long after his arrival at Base Camp he decided not to attempt it at all.

There were several reasons for this. The first was the death of a porter. Messner had wanted to start the climb from the Savoia Glacier, using the same Base Camp as the Americans and British. By going up the Negrotto Glacier to the Negrotto Col, he felt he could avoid the steep couloir that runs down the south-east side to the Filippi Glacier. (The couloir was to be the scene of a tragedy in 1986 when two Americans, John Smolich and Alan Pennington, were killed in an avalanche.) But on the way through the small chaotic icefall around the foot of Angel Peak, leading to the easy ground in the middle of the Savoia Glacier, a porter, Ali Kazim, fell in a crevasse and was killed. The others refused to carry on and Base Camp had to be sited at the traditional point on the Godwin-Austen Glacier. A quick reconnaissance by Messner seemed to indicate that the way via the Negrotto Glacier was not as safe as he had hoped after all. Another short investigation of an alternative South Face line well to the right of the Magic Line by Messner and Friedl Mutschlechner also came to nothing when a huge chunk of sérac broke off and swept their intended route. It was at this point Messner proposed that they settled for a quick ascent of the Abruzzi instead. Renato Casarotto was incensed. He was only interested in the new route. Gogna too was disillusioned. But they were overruled.

It may well be that Messner was having doubts about the Magic Line from a very early stage. In his defence, his judgement of its danger, particularly below the Negrotto Col, was to be proved quite correct. His doubts that a team of just six climbers could succeed on it was influenced by the knowledge that a massive French expedition would be arriving to try it in a few weeks, and that all his small group might achieve would be to prepare the lower section, then be forced to abandon it. It must also be said that over the years Messner's mountaineering judgement has been superb. It seems strange to describe the first person to climb all the 8000-metre peaks as a cautious climber, but Messner has weighed up all his climbs very carefully and retreated from quite a few when he considered the odds to be too high.

When Messner turned his attention to the Abruzzi the team made a fast and very competent job of fixing ropes to the top of the Black Pyramid and placing three camps on the way. On 11 July Messner and Dacher climbed on to the Shoulder and pressed up to just under

8000 metres where they found a flattish spot for a tiny two-man tent. During the night it stormed and delayed their start until seven. Michl Dacher had been convinced the night before that six hours would see them on top but once they reached the Bottleneck Couloir they met bottomless powder snow which stayed all the way to the top. Like Roskelley and Ridgeway the year before, they took no rope.

The day seemed neverending. Messner, uncharacteristically, appeared full of doubts: '. . . Endlessly, eternally, we climb through the snow. Why do I keep climbing if I know we shall never reach the summit? The sun is on the way down and it is already ice cold.'

Dacher likened his progress to '. . . some wretched little earwig scrabbling to get out of the bathtub'. But Dacher, aged forty-five, was on his third 8000-metre peak and as stubborn as Messner. On the final summit slopes Messner felt his strength ebbing but at last the snow conditions improved a bit. Quite unexpectedly he found himself standing in sunshine with only a short ridge separating him from the top. He made radio contact with Base Camp and told them the good news. 'I pass the apparatus over to Michl, he squats down, and as I plod up to the highest point on the ridgetop, I hear him ordering flowers for his wife.' It was four forty p.m. on a perfect sunny afternoon. In the east the shadow of K2 was thrown across miles and miles of the brown dusty hills of Chinese Sinkiang. Stars were appearing in the sky, even though the sun had not yet set.

To their surprise, the descent to the Shoulder only took two hours, and they regained their camp before nightfall. Too tired to cook or even brew they spent another cold and uncomfortable night, and set off down in the morning in deteriorating weather. At Camp III they met Robert Schauer, Friedl Mutschlechner and Alessandro Gogna on their way up, but after discussion the three decided the weather was too bad to sit it out so high on the mountain and all five descended to Base Camp. There were no further attempts.

Though the expedition was a success, Messner caused controversy with the presentation of his ascent of the Abruzzi. True, he had succeeded in climbing K2 with a small team. In reality it was the same size as Houston's 1938 expedition (minus Sherpas of course) and, like all the expeditions, used fixed ropes as far as the top of the Black Pyramid at 7400 metres. To claim, as Messner did in his book *All Fourteen Eight-thousanders*, that above the Black Pyramid the ascent was completed in pure alpine-style is also true, but not really so very different from the Americans on the North-West Ridge, nor indeed from what Houston's and Wiessner's expeditions were trying to do. What was irritating to many Messner-watchers was the increasing tendency for him to put the best possible gloss on his already formidable achievements when he had no need to. Thus it was reported in the normally staid Swiss newspaper *Neue Zuercher Zeitung* that Messner and Dacher 'stormed' K2 in only five days with three 'commando raid'-type camps (whatever they may be). The truth was that it took them twenty-one days from the first foray on to the Abruzzi on 22 June to the summit on 12 July, which was still very quick. In the end Messner and Dacher *did* climb the route in five days but, using that criterion, it could be argued that in 1953 Hillary and Tensing climbed Everest in only five days from Advance Base! As far as the 'three' camps are concerned, there were only three if you choose to describe the top camp on the Shoulder as a bivouac. But it *was* a tent, pitched and equipped in the normal way with stove, sleeping-bags and foam mats.

In the ever-increasing dependence on media attention and sponsor-gratification many expeditions have allowed themselves to fudge the exact details of their ascents. Numbering camps is one way of doing this. With ingenuity, Advance Base, Interim Camp, Dump Camp, etc., can be so named to make it possible to place Camp I almost at the top of a mountain! Using fixed rope left by other expeditions often doesn't count either (even when it is extensively used) in so-called alpine-style ascents. And to take the times of ascents from the moment you start the successful summit bid is simply misleading (a further extension to this is now seen in the reporting of some very fast climbs in the Alps where only the actual *climbing* time is recorded). If it was only the popular press that were misled it wouldn't really matter, but all too often the specialist climbing press as well will go along with the misreporting as a way of dramatising a story. It has always seemed sad that Reinhold Messner, who above all others has no need to oversell himself, should frequently appear to do so.

If Messner's ascent of K2 was something of an anticlimax for a public who had perhaps come to expect too much of one man, it was an acute disappointment for Renato Casarotto. He was fast becoming Italy's best-known solo climber with impressive ascents in Peru, Patagonia and elsewhere in the Karakoram. He was a purist – obsessed with climbing technically challenging and aesthetically appealing lines. He had played little part in the ascent of the Abruzzi and was clearly deeply annoyed that Messner had

'Simply splendid' was how Younghusband greeted the most impressive view of K2, from the north, here looking towards the arrow-like North Ridge. (*Adrian Burgess*)

Above, the terraced rampart of the West Face. (*Jim Curran*) *Below*, the classic view from Concordia which failed to impress Conway. The Abruzzi Spur is the last spur before the right-hand skyline. (*Doug Scott*)

Above left, Roger Payne climbing House's Chimney. *Above right*, typical steep mixed terrain on the Black Pyramid. *Below*, approaching the foot of House's Chimney. (*all Julie-Ann Clyma*)

Above, the difficult leftwards traverse above the Bottleneck and below the dangerous sérac wall. (*Jim Wickwire*) *Below*, looking up from the base of the Shoulder. The broken buttress climbed by Wiessner catches the sun. The Bottleneck is in shadow directly above the climber. (*Dick Renshaw*)

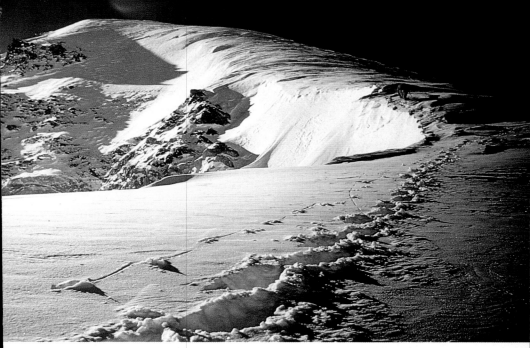

Above, on the edge of space. Lou Reichardt on the long summit snow slope still 150m below the top. (*Jim Wickwire*) *Below*, Doug Scott on his 1983 attempt on the South-South-East Spur, with the Godwin-Austen Glacier below, Concordia at the confluence and Chogolisa with its kilometre-long summit ridge beyond left. (*Roger Baxter-Jones*)

Above left, Yamashita high on the West Face during the successful 1981 Japanese West Ridge expedition. *Above right*, Nazir Sabir, the Hunza porter who was to become Pakistan's leading climber, fulfilled a personal ambition to reach the summit with the Japanese. *Below*, panorama from the West Face, with Chogolisa (7665m) left and Masherbrum (7821m) right. (*all Nazir Sabir*)

Above, on the North Ridge looking across to the line of the Polish route which was completed by Christophe Profit and Pierre Béghin. The diagonal ramp is clearly visible. *Below*, looking down the North Ridge from 6800m to the K2 Glacier. (*both Alan Hinkes*)

Crossing the long knife-edge section of the North-East Ridge. (*Jim Wickwire*)

given up on the Magic Line so quickly. In his turn Messner was disappointed by Casarotto's performance as a climber, feeling he was far too slow, which must have been a painful pill for Casarotto to swallow. Somehow the Magic Line began to assume almost grail proportions for him. One day he would return and solo it, proving himself to Messner once and for all.

While Messner's little expedition prepared to leave for home, another monster one had arrived from France. Led by Bernard Mellet, it had fourteen climbers, thirty tons of equipment and as many porters as the Japanese had taken in 1977. Amongst the stars were Yannick Seigneur, Ivan Ghirardini, Pierre Béghin and Jean-Marc Boivin. In their attempt on the Magic Line they climbed through August into September, fixing ropes and establishing seven camps. The last one was just over 8400 metres and was reached in mid-September, by which time the autumn storms had arrived. The expedition was marred by the death of Lhaskar Khan of a heart attack at 7150 metres. Seven of the fourteen climbers reached the top camp and five unsuccessful summit bids were mounted. A high point was reached less than two hundred metres from the summit.

Obviously the bad weather was the decisive factor but Messner, for one, felt that 'at the critical moment the French lacked the courage to press on into the unknown nothingness above them'. These are blunt words and may or may not be fair. By the end of September, when the climb was finally abandoned, it was clear that if the French pushed any further an accident would be almost inevitable. One man's 'lack of courage' is another man's 'wise mountaineering decision'.

The expedition was enlivened by a world paragliding record. Using a 'specially modified' glider (a euphemism, one cannot help feeling, for 'highly dangerous') that weighed only half the normal weight, Jean-Marc Boivin launched off from Camp IV at 7600 metres and landed at Base Camp thirteen minutes later. During the flight his tear ducts froze which must have been very unpleasant, but it did not deter Boivin from parapenting from near the South Summit of Everest a few years later and making a spectacularly stylish landing in front of a camera in the Western Cwm. Tragically, this charming and effervescent character was killed parapenting in Venezuela.

The French expedition, like the Japanese in 1971, seemed to fly in the face of current Himalayan thinking. This was epitomised earlier in the year when Georges Bettembourg, another leading French climber, joined Joe Tasker, Peter Boardman and Doug Scott in an attempt to climb the North Ridge of Kangchenjunga. Bettembourg had previously climbed Broad Peak with Yannick Seigneur in only nine days. Though Bettembourg did not reach the summit of Kangchenjunga, Boardman, Tasker and Scott did and, with the confidence that came of such an ascent, Peter Boardman was convinced that they could do the same on the West Ridge of K2 in 1980, even though it was steeper and technically harder than Kangchenjunga. Peter Boardman, Joe Tasker, Doug Scott and Dick Renshaw made up the team. Dick Renshaw had been with Joe Tasker on an epic two-man ascent of Dunagiri in 1975 and had suffered bad frostbite on his fingers. Now recovered, he was, and remains, an enigmatic figure. Incredibly self-possessed, with immense willpower, Dick Renshaw is, on first meeting, shy to the point of being withdrawn. He is a talented sculptor and woodcarver and brings a calm practicality to climbing. Compared to the other three, Dick Renshaw was almost a recluse and has never had any part in climbing aboard the media bandwagon that the rest of the team were all constantly involved in, whether they liked it or not. (For the record it was quite obvious that Joe Tasker *did* like it, Doug Scott didn't and still doesn't and Pete Boardman only tolerated it if it helped his next project.)

Though eventually the little team would fail on K2, it proved to be one of the most impressive small expeditions to go to the mountain. They had their problems before they got there when Gohar, a Hunza porter, fell in a snow-covered crevasse below Concordia. He was rescued, uninjured if badly shaken, but the porters, who had memories of the death of Ali Kazim on Messner's expedition the previous year, were demoralised and, on arrival at the Godwin-Austen Base Camp, flatly refused to carry round to the Savoia Glacier. So the team had to make their own ferries of gear up to the foot of the West Ridge.

As they had done on Changabang, K2 and Kangchenjunga, Boardman and Tasker were prepared to fix ropes on at least the lower half of the face. They avoided the critical snow basin that had avalanched Nick Estcourt, and all four carried to the ridge above. The line they then followed was always about 150–200 metres higher than the British attempt two years earlier. Initially, they were a reasonably united team, as Pete Boardman's diary illustrates: 'Drinking beef and tomato soup and listening to Clapton. Outside stars and cold. We are a bunch of old-timers, always comfortable, joking, enjoying ourselves as much as possible . . .'

It didn't last. Doug, Pete and Joe had probably been together now for too long. Pete Boardman and Joe Tasker were a formidable pair and exercised more power and authority than they themselves may have been aware of. Doug Scott remains a mighty force in British mountaineering and, though passionately committed to the idea of a democratically run expedition, in reality, he often finds it very difficult to accommodate others' points of view. Within a few days Boardman's diary has a very different tone, as bad weather forced them to sit it out. An argument broke out over sponsorship photographs:

> . . . Back in the tents we spent hours telling each other what we thought of each other! Doug has really cast me as a clever, scheming villain over the last months, whereas Joe is respected by him. All quite a shock but everything has to be so emotional with Doug. Joe is always restrained in such arguments but never open hearted . . . God knows what Dick thought of it all.

Unlike the American flare-ups in 1975 and '78 which were caused mainly by members discovering things about each other that were best left unsaid, the British problems were almost certainly the results of long-lingering resentments built up over too many expeditions together with too many shared experiences and too little discussion, too late. Like a long marriage that has lost its way, Doug, Pete and Joe had gone to K2 together for convenience rather than for a shared experience. Doug Scott certainly felt isolated from the other three and felt that Joe Tasker resented his presence as an older, more experienced climber.

When the route on the West Ridge had been pushed out to 7000 metres, Scott proposed an alpine-style push to the top. He found the capsule-style concept of fixing long sections, then pulling the ropes up and repeating the process, extremely boring and time-consuming. But the others disagreed and, faced with disunity over tactics, they decided to abandon the attempt on the West Ridge and, like Messner, go for a quick alpine-style ascent of the Abruzzi. On 18 June, after only three weeks on the ridge, they were back at Base Camp. Doug Scott later wished that they had made a more determined attempt to climb the route alpine-style, acclimatising more thoroughly first. His interest in the Abruzzi was quickly subdued.

After a first foray to the lower reaches of the route, and several days of soul-searching, he left 'without regret'.

By now it was the end of June and the remaining three were still at the foot of the mountain. This might not have mattered much were it not for the fact that Dick Renshaw was going to become a father for the first time at the end of August and, unbeknown to Tasker and Renshaw, Boardman was going to marry his girlfriend Hilary at much the same time. So when, on 2 July, they returned to the Abruzzi Spur, at least two thirds of the team must have been hoping for a quick ascent. It was not to be.

Peter Boardman later made the point, already stated in an earlier chapter, that he felt that the technical standard of climbing on the Abruzzi was far higher than anything done before the war. It was a view shared by Joe Tasker who wrote ruefully of their initial feelings.

> We were now expecting to be able to start from the bottom of K2 and reach its summit in a matter of days. We were not doing justice to the early pioneers. The route was extraordinarily difficult . . . the difficulties increased as we climbed higher . . . We could always climb sections but were overawed by the perseverance which must have been needed in the days when ropes were made from hemp and when boots were heavy with the nails in the sole for friction.

Ever pragmatic, the three climbed, if not in pure alpine-style, then certainly lightweight. They uncovered old but usable sections of fixed rope, and were prepared to put in the odd length of new rope over difficult sections of the route, but they were carrying everything themselves in a single push. It took until 11 July to get to the lower part of the Shoulder and here they were stopped for a day by poor weather. At five p.m. a detailed radio report picked up by their liaison officer, Major Nassar Sarwat, and intended for a Japanese expedition active elsewhere in the Karakoram, gave promise of a cloudy day on 12 July and fine weather the day after.

With this encouraging news the three, who had been considering a retreat to Base Camp, decided to go for it, getting as far as possible on the 12th and to the summit the next day. They set off up the Shoulder with gusts of wind blowing spindrift across the broad ridge. Visibility was poor but they still had faith that the weather forecast would prove correct. As they gained height up the Shoulder, Joe Tasker had a premonition of catastrophe: that an avalanche would billow out of the clouds and engulf them.

In the afternoon they reached the rocks at the foot of the Bottleneck Couloir and, as light faded and snow started falling in earnest, they began to look for a safe campsite. Boardman was leading, going strongly and ploughing through deep snow. The other two, following, couldn't match his pace. Every promise of a suitable ledge turned out to be useless. Renshaw had never been as high as this before and was finding the going very hard. Eventually, they found a small space on top of a rocky prow. It took two hours to clear a spot for the two-man tent into which all three squeezed. Renshaw hung over the edge and used rucksacks on the tent floor to support him. Boardman was in the middle, with Tasker pushed right up against the wall behind the tent. They tried to make brews but kept falling asleep. They were now at 8100 metres with only five hundred metres to go – if only the weather would clear.

Joe Tasker awoke 'to an instant awareness of a sordid death. All was black, the tent was collapsed on top of us. A heavy avalanche of snow was pouring over the tent . . . the snow crashed down on the back of my neck and my face was beaten inexorably closer to the ground.' He shouted to Pete and Dick – there was no reply. He lost consciousness for a few minutes and when he came round the avalanche had stopped. Convinced that Pete and Dick had been swept away, he was left alone and suffocating in a tiny pocket of air in the wrecked tent. Desperately, he fumbled for his Swiss Army knife in the breast pocket of his windsuit and eventually managed to cut a small slit in the tent fabric to breathe through. It says a lot for his presence of mind *in extremis* that he didn't enlarge the slit in case he damaged the tent unnecessarily. But what had happened to Pete and Dick?

When the avalanche of powder snow, accumulated from the summit slopes, had swept over the rock wall and hit the tent, it had been half knocked off the prow of rock it was anchored to. Renshaw was held in its folds, poised above a 3000-metre plunge to the Godwin-Austen Glacier with just the paper-thin ripstop-nylon tent fabric between him and oblivion. Boardman had been pushed to the edge of the ledge and was able to free himself and then pull Renshaw on to firm ground. In the cold, windy blackness they had shouted for Tasker, then started digging. Relieving the weight of snow off Tasker enabled him to gain consciousness and at last he could sit up and take notice. Desperately they tried to sort out the chaos of gear inside the tent and get some semblance of order, when with a dull hissing sound, a second avalanche came pouring out of the night. This time Tasker pressed himself against the wall behind the tent but Boardman and Renshaw, outside, were exposed to the full force. Pete Boardman was tied on to the belay pitons and he grabbed Renshaw and held on grimly, while the avalanche rushed past, leaving the three of them cold, shocked and terrified, sheltering in the half-demolished tent. Raw survival was now the name of the game. Hang on, don't give up, stick it out until dawn and see what that brings. Neither Boardman nor Tasker had any illusions. Pete Boardman: 'The mountain is completely impersonal, indifferent, we are irrelevant . . .' Joe Tasker: 'The second avalanche brought home to me how helpless we were, how tiny and insignificant our lives were on this mountain. There was no harmony with these forces of nature, we were specks in the colossal and uncaring universe.'

At first light they were still alive. There had been no further avalanches but it was still snowing. They packed up whatever they could retrieve from the tent which was just about usable. Joe Tasker led off down, wading through thigh-deep snow seemingly poised to avalanche. He was indifferent: there was no choice, though Pete Boardman behind him shouted for Joe to stick to the exposed rocks. But in doing this Joe had constantly slipped and stumbled, so he decided that ploughing straight down was the best bet. For once (perhaps the only time), Boardman seemed broken, descending in a daze and accepting his fate. Joe Tasker had rarely seen him in such a state, but when they reached the flatter part of the Shoulder, Tasker himself ground to a halt and the situation was reversed as Boardman dug up reserves of strength and ploughed a trail as the other two floundered in his wake. At last Pete found the spot where they had camped on the way up and they set about re-erecting their torn and battered tent. It had taken six hours to descend three hundred metres. Damp and chilled to the bone, they crawled into their sleeping-bags. Most of their food and spare gas cylinders had been lost in the avalanche and, using the pan lid, Joe melted enough snow to fill an aluminium water bottle to produce a woefully inadequate drink. Semi-conscious and barely able to register where they were, they nevertheless found themselves discussing the possibility of returning for another attempt. They were still in shock and unable to think straight, though occasionally it penetrated their befuddled minds that they were still in an appalling situation. One gas cartridge left and with almost no food, they simply *had* to descend, for to sit it out until the weather improved ran the very real risk of not getting down at all.

Pete Boardman wrote in his diary of his feelings at Camp V. 'Dick seems to be able to resign himself to such dangers but I very fiercely do not want to die. I think we have a fifty per cent chance of survival if we just launch ourselves downwards.'

At five p.m. Joe Tasker tried to contact Major Sarwat at Base Camp and made a poor connection. 'Our tent was destroyed in an avalanche and we are back at Camp V.'

Through the static Joe heard him reply, 'I get that you have reached Camp VI and are going for another try. Is that correct? Over.'

Joe fought back tears as he realised that there was to be no sympathy for their dire straits. But in the next days the Major at Base Camp was to fulfil an identical role as Major Atta Ullah had to Charlie Houston's team in 1953, a friendly voice in the world of the living, encouraging and willing his team down the mountain.

The similarity with 1953 did not end there for, as they were very aware, they were now camped in virtually the site of Art Gilkey's collapse and, in deep snow the following morning, Boardman was so worried about avalanche risk that he, like the Americans before him, took to the broken rock rib running down to the left of the ice slope above the site of Camp IV where they had left a spare tent and some food. When they reached the spot they thought their Camp IV had been they were faced with a white-out. Apathetically, they sat in the snow, prodding with their ice-axes in a futile attempt to find their cache of gear. At last Dick Renshaw uncovered a frozen turd, proof that they were near, and soon they dug up the precious spare tent, food and gas.

That night they radioed the Major again who said he had a surprise for them and would hand the set over to a friend of theirs. Georges Bettembourg, skiing in the area, came over loud and clear. ''Ow are you? You 'ave it difficult? When will you be down?'

The voice of their companion from Kangchenjunga the previous year put new heart into them and, in Joe Tasker's words, 'In spite of the feeling that we were in a condemned cell speaking on a telephone line to a free man . . . the warmth of his company was a bonus to look forward to on our return to life.'

After a night on sleeping pills the three had recovered somewhat and Tasker even had the willpower to film some of their retreat that morning. With still over 2000 metres to descend, their ordeal was by no means over, but below the Black Pyramid progress was steady and, with odd sections of fixed rope, it was rather safer. Tasker radioed the Major on the hour as Boardman and Renshaw drew ahead. At last the clouds broke and they caught the odd glimpse of the glacier still far below. The snow was melting on the rocks and in the grey murk the temperature rose. With fading willpower Joe forced himself down the last interminable slopes to two tiny dots. They were the two Hunza high-altitude porters, Gohar and Ali, whom the Major had sent round from Base Camp to greet them. At last, rocking on his feet, Joe reached them and, as at Houston's reception in 1953, tears of relief at their survival were shed.

The following morning, with Gohar and Ali carrying huge loads, they reached Base Camp and an emotional reunion with Major Sarwat and Georges Bettembourg. There, one would have expected the story to end. It was 15 July and they had given K2 their best efforts. 'Hammerfall', as the avalanche was referred to (after an incident in a sci-fi paperback that they were all reading during the expedition), had foiled the final summit day but they had come very close. So close that after three days to recover they had a discussion and found out that all three wanted to have another attempt. Even an attack of dysentery couldn't deter them and after only a week at Base Camp they returned for one last effort. This time they made uneventful progress up to their last campsite – repositioned out of range of avalanches – and prepared for the summit attempt the following day.

But yet again the fickle K2 weather broke down and after sitting it out for a day, with empty stomachs craving food that wasn't there, they finally gave up and made a long, but this time uneventful, retreat to Base Camp. The expedition had been a failure but no group of climbers had ever tried harder to get to the top. Some might say they tried too hard. The following year I accompanied Pete Boardman and Joe Tasker with Chris Bonington and Alan Rouse to Kongur in Chinese Sinkiang, only some two hundred miles north of K2. I was impressed, almost awestruck, at Pete and Joe's drive and commitment. The expedition succeeded when many others would have given up. Pete was the driving force and was entirely at home in the high-altitude environment he had made such a major part of his life.

He was still obsessed with K2 and, when China opened up its side of the mountain, the following year, he obtained permission to try the North Ridge in 1984. In 1982 Boardman, Tasker, Renshaw and Bonington went to the North-East Ridge of Everest. In a final effort to climb the Pinnacles, giant rock towers barring the way to the final summit ridge, Pete Boardman and Joe Tasker were killed. There was a sad irony in their deaths on Everest for both felt that their destiny was somehow inextricably bound up with K2. Pete had written on his way back from the mountain in 1980:

At last I can let myself go and look forward to many months without K2's shape standing in between. I understand the mountain better now. It's not like any other mountain, and grows, a symbol in my life. Strange how I'm not disappointed but happy – so different from '78.

13

The West Ridge

1981 got under way with a return visit by Yannick Seigneur to the South Face of K2 with a four-man team. They reached 7400 metres before retreating. Though the Face has now been climbed twice, in 1986 and 1993, there is no doubt that whatever line or variation is taken on this huge expanse it is all, as Messner had decided in 1979, threatened by avalanche and sérac fall. Any ascent would have to be quick and lucky.

But the major event of 1981 was the fifth ascent of K2. In 1979 a six-man expedition from Waseda University Alpine Club in Japan had made the first ascent of the North Ridge of Rakaposhi, and from its summit gazed at the distant black triangular fin of K2 and the idea of climbing the West Ridge was conceived. It is worth explaining that Japanese climbing is based around large firms and universities. They often have huge membership and many leading climbers continue their affiliation with university clubs long after graduation. Because of their numbers the clubs are strong enough and also wealthy enough to undertake their own major Himalayan expeditions, circumstances unimaginable in British universities with their long tradition of small, low-budget, low-key explorations.

Like the Americans in 1978 and the French in 1979 the Japanese had to wait their turn in the season as the small French South Face team had received first permission. The fourteen-man Japanese expedition was led by Teruo Matsuura who was the first Japanese to climb Everest, with Naomi Uemura, in 1970. He had been a major figure in Japanese Himalayan and Karakoram mountaineering for many years. They set up Base Camp on the Savoia Glacier on 19 June. Their liaison officer, Major Abdul Qayuun, had done sterling service in persuading three hundred porters to carry all the way up to this point given the recent problems experienced by Messner and the British.

The expedition was enhanced by the presence of Nazir Sabir, a Hunza who has made the transition from high-altitude porter to climber in his own right, rather in the same way as Pertemba Sherpa has done in Nepal. Nazir had been with the Japanese who made the second ascent in 1977. Then he had reached 8200 metres before being turned back by a storm. He still nursed a burning desire to climb K2, for himself and for the memory of his elder brother, killed in an army expedition to the region in 1980.

The expedition used fifteen porters to carry loads to Camp I at 5850 metres and the start of the West Ridge proper. The Japanese followed much the same line as the British had and by 30 June had established Camp III at 7100 metres, just below the high point of the previous expedition. Above this point are two large snowfields separated by a rocky band of slabs the Japanese called the Slide. Megumi climbed this and on 17 July Camp IV was reached at the top of the upper snowfield just below a Y-shaped gully. It seemed very avalanche-prone and it duly did on 19 July. Yabuta and Yamashita were just about to leave Camp IV but the avalanche missed them, sweeping the whole gully and leaving a firm bed of hard-packed snow. But getting up to the safe area was not easy as the bottom of the Y was a steep, wet hundred-metre stretch of rock shute. That was avoided by a traverse that gained the snow-filled right-hand branch of the Y and led to the prominent horizontal snowfield cutting right across the West Face at 8200 metres. The route involved five and a half kilometres (3.4 miles) of fixed rope. Out of fifty-two days spent above Base Camp twenty-one were bad enough to stop climbing. This may well be a realistic average for bad weather on K2 over the years on every route, though there does seem to be some reason to suppose the West Face gets slightly better weather than the exposed Abruzzi which catches the wind funnelling between K2 and Broad Peak.

As the route to Camp IV was being completed, an eleven-day storm moved in, which caused a logistical crisis as gas and food intended for higher up were being used before they reached their destination. The Japanese hoped to establish two more camps before the top but had to abandon the idea of Camp VI and put camps at the fork of the Y at just over 8000 metres. On 3 August Megumi and Iwata fixed ropes on the vertical rock above Camp V and on the 5th Otani, Yamashita and Nazir Sabir, using oxygen, traversed across the upper snow band of the West Face fixing sections of rope to the crest of the South Pillar at the top of the Magic Line. This they then joined at an altitude of around 8300 metres. They returned to Camp V and set out the next day, again with oxygen, for the top. By ten a.m. they had regained their high point, and were faced with what looked like difficult climbing ahead. Like the Americans on the Abruzzi, they dumped their oxygen as more trouble than it was worth. It took until six p.m. to climb a difficult face of mixed rock and snow. With no food, tent, sleeping-bag, stove or oxygen, they dug a miserable snow hole and spent a grim night which Nazir Sabir describes in an interview he gave to Greg Child in *Climbing* magazine in October 1987. 'We tried to warm ourselves with a candle. It seemed like the last source of heat and light on earth. In the middle of the night I felt my toes going cold and began to massage my feet. While doing that I hit the wall of the cave and then, no more cave! We were all on our own and not very sure of surviving the night.'

In the morning the weather was still fine and, moving desperately slowly through deep snow, it took over three hours to gain a hundred metres. Now, with the summit only about fifty metres of vertical height away on comparatively easy ground, there occurred a surreal incident which Nazir Sabir found bewildering.

'When I reached Otani he was on the walkie-talkie – Matsuura [the expedition leader] was asking us to go down because he thought we would be too tired to take the summit and return to Camp IV that day. For the next forty-five minutes there was a dramatic war of emotions, of confusions within confusions, between the higher heavens of K2 and basecamp.' One can sympathise with a worried expedition leader isolated far below, but his intervention so close to the summit seems quite extraordinary. Nazir Sabir clearly thought so. 'I couldn't believe it. I said, "Forget about what the leader said. I'm not going down because I missed K2 from so near last time." I said that in Pakistan we don't listen to a leader sitting far below. But the Japanese think of a leader as a god. I talked to the liaison officer three times on the radio – he abused me and wanted to throw all responsibility on to me if someone should die. I said I didn't care, I just wanted to go. Finally, the leader agreed to let us continue.'

Yamashita was exhausted and stayed behind. Nazir, breaking trail, reached the top after only another hour. Just below the summit he offered Otani the lead, but he declined. 'No, Nazir. K2 is your mountain, you make it first.' So, like Jim Wickwire and Lou Reichardt in 1978, they took the last step together. Otani by now was so tired he could not use the radio and Nazir relayed the good news down to Base Camp. They were the first to reach the summit by any other finish than the Abruzzi.

Returning to Yamashita, they made a desperate descent, exhausted, starving and, above all, dehydrated. Nazir's lips were so dry they bled, and at Camp V there was little to sustain them, just some hot water with a bit of sugar and some rice. By the light of the moon Nazir Sabir continued down to Camp III in the hope of finding more food and drink, but there was no stove and he had to wait until the others joined him. They had spent fifty-two hours above 8000 metres, sustained only by a cup of water and the rice. Nazir lost twenty-four pounds and suffered some memory loss for a few months afterwards.

It was a major success, even though, until the summit bid, it had been carried out by a traditional fixed-rope expedition. But in the end, as so many others had found on Everest, K2 and other Himalayan giants, commitment had been total. The summit push was as far out on a limb as any on K2. Nazir Sabir was not the first Pakistani climber to reach the summit, but he had undoubtedly been the key figure in the final push and it earned him a well deserved accolade afterwards. Since 1981 he has climbed Broad Peak and Gasherbrum II with Reinhold Messner. The three ascents put him into the ranks of world-class performers, but he has followed his own path, running a trekking agency and becoming an accomplished photographer and guide. He has travelled widely and, in Greg Child's words, 'Nazir Sabir is very much a modern Pakistani man.'

On 10 August, 1981, the same day as the successful summiteers returned to Base Camp, a long-awaited announcement was made in Peking. The Chinese Mountaineering Association gave permission for access to the north side of Mount Qogir, as they insisted on referring to K2. At last the mysterious North Face of the mountain, glimpsed by Younghusband and Grombczewski in 1887 and visited by Desio and Shipton, would be open to foreign climbers. It came as no surprise when, three weeks later, on 22 September, it was announced in Peking that a Japanese expedition would be attempting it in 1982. When the Chinese had first opened the Tibetan and Sinkiang mountains to foreigners they had done so to the accompaniment of horrendous peak fees. All expenses in China were anything up to four times higher than anywhere else in the Himalaya and when K2 was added to the list it was painfully obvious that such a major and remote objective would cost a small fortune to attempt. That the Japanese could book it and pay the peak fee within three weeks of the announcement was a reflection on the sheer professionalism and financial good footing of Japanese climbing, which was claiming a relentless rate of success right across the Karakoram and Himalaya.

Unlike the Waseda University expedition in 1981, the Japanese North Ridge expedition was a national one. The overall leader was Isaoh Shinkai but Masatsugu Konishi was in charge of climbers and tactics. Nine strong climbers were chosen for the mountain itself but there were thirty-three support climbers, whose role was to ferry gear to Base Camp. There are major logistical problems in getting to K2 from the northern approach via the Aghil Pass and the Shaksgam river. The first is that neither camels, yaks nor donkeys can get to the foot of the mountain and there is no local populace available, like the Baltis, to porter loads. On top of that the approach is effectively cut off for at least two months each summer by the volume of meltwater from the Shaksgam river. Consequently Base Camp is sited some ten miles below the foot of the North Ridge of the mountain, at a patch of willows called Suget Jangal which Younghusband, Desio and Shipton each describe in their various explorations, and all loads have to be ferried by the climbers up the K2 Glacier which, if anything, is even more convoluted and difficult than the Baltoro and Godwin-Austen Glaciers.

From the K2 Glacier the view is one of stunning simplicity. K2 is an almost perfect triangular wedge with the North Ridge bisecting the face straight from the glacier to the summit. The right-hand horizon is defined by the North-West Ridge which runs down to the Savoia Saddle, the American Towers being clearly visible. High on the North Face to the left of the North Ridge is a prominent hanging glacier in an amphitheatre formed by the North Ridge and another prominent ridge that descends in a knife-edge from the summit to around 7000 metres where it seems to have been cut off by some monstrous cheese slice. Below are what appear to be very avalanche-prone slopes and buttresses and the ridge, which could accurately be described as the North-North-East Ridge, seems a very unlikely project to be tackled direct, and equally difficult to traverse into from either side. The left-hand side of the mountain mass is defined by the upper slopes of the North-East Ridge, though most of the American Route is out of sight above the knife-edge ridge.

For the Japanese, the North Ridge was the obvious, if not the only, route to attempt. It took the whole of May for the team to transport the loads from the distant Base Camp to the foot of the ridge. Three of the support climbers stayed on and the remaining thirty returned to Japan lest they were cut off by the increasing volume of meltwater.

The climbing on the ridge was sustained but, perhaps surprisingly, fairly straightforward, and the angle, which seemed almost vertical when seen head on, was more like an average of forty-five degrees as Desio's aerial photograph in 1954 had hinted. Nevertheless it still took until 1 August to establish four camps and to fix ropes to 8000 metres. All the climbing members reached that point at least once – a fine achievement, similar to the teamwork of the Poles on the North-East Ridge in 1976.

Between 1 and 9 August the team rested, and it was during that time that a curious high-altitude collision took place with a Polish expedition which traversed across to the North Ridge from their intended objective, the North-West Ridge. Fixed ropes merged and a diplomatic incident occurred with a protest appearing to be made from the Chinese Mountaineering Association to the Pakistan Ministry of Tourism.

Poised for a summit bid, the climbing leader, Masatsugu Konishi, had very clear ideas about how this was to be achieved. He wanted all climbing members to reach the summit, without using oxygen. He placed great emphasis on individual responsibility, particularly in judging whether or not to press on or retreat during a summit attempt. Climbers were strongly advised to go to the top of the fixed ropes as often as they thought necessary to acclimatise before mounting the final push. Effectively, the attainment of the summit became a competition between all the eligible contestants, a far cry from Houston's drawing of lots or Whittaker's nominated teams.

Konishi issued a warning, brutal in its honesty and one that many Western climbers would find hard to swallow:

> Please calculate your strength against the difficulties to the top. If you miscalculate, naturally you could die. But the responsibility for the decision lies in yourselves. You are leading climbers. You are responsible for your judgement. If, for example, I should become exhausted at 8500 metres, you need not help me. It will have been my responsibility to have climbed to such an altitude. I should have descended sooner. Nobody can take care of others at high altitude anyway without an oxygen cylinder . . . The summit bid, I think, is just like the duelling

of the ancient Samurai. If you are inferior, even though only a slightest inferiority, you should put yourself to the sword.

In fact, setting aside the Samurai flourish, Konishi was really stating the obvious and his advice would be well heeded by any climber operating at his limits at over 8000 metres. On K2 in 1986 Adrian Burgess expressed much the same views before the British team was about to attempt the Abruzzi in one continuous push. At the time some members (myself included) found his comments ruthless and self-centred. In fact, as he explained later, it was a tactic designed to force everyone to face up to their own limitations and not put other lives in danger. If it had actually come to the crunch, Aid admitted ruefully, there was no way he could stand by and not do everything possible to save lives. And so it was with the Japanese on the North Ridge.

From their highest camp the Japanese traversed left into the huge snow basin below the final summit ridge. On 14 August Sakashita and Yoshino set off first, followed by Yanagisawa and Ozaki about an hour later. All climbed solo but Ozaki climbing up the centre of the hanging glacier was turned back by a sérac at 8200 metres and retreated. Sakashita, going strongly, exited on to the final slopes via a forty-metre step and reached the top just after eight p.m.[1] Yanagisawa was not far behind and Yoshino too summited at around nine p.m. They bivouacked some three hundred metres below the top but Yanagisawa had no down jacket with him. Sakashita, who was in the best condition of the three, tried to keep him warm and in the morning set off down while the other two waited until the second summit party arrived with hot tea and a rope. Descending slowly, Yoshino and Yanagisawa reached the top of the fixed ropes. Somehow Yanagisawa disappeared and, after a futile search, Yoshino descended to Camp IV. The successful four-man second summit team reached the top at four p.m. One of them, Tatsuji Shigeno, set a rather unusual high-altitude record by playing a mouth organ on the summit! All four were forced to bivouac but all made it down safely. On the way a small red object, thought to be Yanagisawa's jacket, was spotted in an avalanche-prone basin but his body was never recovered. One of the expedition doctors was also killed on a small peak near Base Camp while taking photographs.

[1] The *whole* of China runs on Beijing local time which means all north-side times are three hours later than the equivalent Pakistan times.

Once again the Japanese had employed siege tactics but this was probably their greatest success on K2. For the first time a major new route had been climbed at the first attempt, and without oxygen, by seven successful summiteers. Though the route proved to be somewhat easier than first appearances had suggested it was undoubtedly one of the great plums left in the Karakoram in 1982. It is curious to note however that Konishi evaluated the expedition as only thirty per cent successful. Six out of twelve climbers reached the top (fifty per cent) but the two deaths penalised them ten per cent – an inscrutable formula.

It may not have gone unnoticed that, with the exception of the Abruzzi Spur, all the routes achieved on K2 have made quite substantial variations to their originally intended line. The North-East Ridge avoided the direct finish, the West Ridge barely skirted the crest of the ridge before making a long traverse across the West Face to the top of the South-West Pillar, and the North Ridge traversed off at three-quarters height to cross the hanging glacier. But all three variants pale into insignificance compared with the line taken in 1982 on what is still inexplicably referred to as the North-West Ridge of K2.

Janusz Kurczab was once again leading an expedition, this time a rather unlikely combination of fifteen Poles and six Mexicans who made up a strong team. Learning from the experience of the Americans' defeat in 1975, the Poles explored the cwm to the right of the Savoia Saddle and climbed a seven-hundred-metre ice-face leading to the crest of the North-West Ridge at just below 6700 metres. The face was compared to the North Face of Les Courtes in the French Alps: but here it was just a minor feature on the side of the ridge. During the ascent a Mexican climber was avalanched, fell two hundred metres and suffered only a fractured forearm. The Poles placed their Camp II on the broad crest of the ridge and immediately started to follow the line of least resistance, leading inexorably across the North Face, and well on to the Chinese side of the mountain, for in reality, the Polish line scarcely follows the ridge for more than a few rope-lengths. The North-West Ridge, which from the K2 and Savoia Glaciers seems so clear cut, is on close acquaintance an ill-defined broad area of featureless rock and ice in which it is all too easy to opt for a leftwards diagonal line following the faults leaning towards the North Ridge. There is of course nothing inherently wrong with this – it is just that the appellation North-West Ridge is inaccurate and misleading. And on K2, due to the vagaries of border disputes, it is also trespassing!

And so the Poles pushed out their lines of fixed ropes deeper and deeper into China. On 5 August Jan Holnicki and Aleksander Lwow established Camp IV at 7550 metres near the crest of the North Buttress and the Japanese fixed ropes. Bad weather stopped them climbing until 11 August but, while the Japanese were making their successful summit bids, the Polish team failed to capitalise on the good weather, which by the 16th had broken again. It was not until 29 August (by which time the Japanese were off the mountain) that the Poles returned to find Camps III and IV destroyed. At last they pitched Camp V at 8050 metres on the North Ridge. On 6 September Leszek Cichy (the first person to climb Everest in winter with Krzysztof Wielicki) and Wojciech Wróz, who had got so high on K2 in 1976, made their summit bid. They reached round 8200 metres before a storm broke and they retreated with minor frostbite to toes and fingers. The autumn storms were building up and the expedition was abandoned. Once again Wojciech Wróz had been foiled close to his goal. The Poles fixed 3500 metres of rope on the route, some of which was still there in 1986 when the British team tried the same line.

There was another Polish expedition on K2 in 1982, a Polish women's expedition. The team of eleven climbers, including a French woman, Christine de Colombel, was led by the redoubtable Wanda Rutkiewicz, already Poland's, if not the world's, leading female Himalayan climber. Sadly, the expedition reached only just over 7000 metres on the Abruzzi Spur when Halina Kruger collapsed and died suddenly at Camp II at 6800 metres. The cause of her death has been reported variously as cerebral oedema or a heart attack. The expedition was abandoned and Kruger was buried at the Gilkey memorial. A small four-man Austrian team led by Georg Bachler helped in the evacuation of Halina Kruger's body and that expedition also gave up its attempt.

On K2, the years from 1983 to 1985 were low key. Expeditions came and went but no new routes were completed. There were, however, some highlights. In 1983 an Italian expedition led by Francesco Santon repeated the North Ridge and three Italians and one Czech climber reached the summit. It was Kurt Diemberger's first attempt on the mountain which he was filming with Julie Tullis. Both were captivated by K2 and the face that Diemberger had read about in Shipton's *Blank on the Map*. They reached 8000 metres before being stopped by a storm. Their desire for K2 became an obsession and they returned twice more, once unsuccessfully in 1984 after Julie Tullis climbed Broad Peak with Diemberger who had made the first ascent of the mountain in 1957, and again, tragically, in 1986.

Also in 1983 on the south side of K2, Doug Scott returned for his third attempt. It was an ambitious expedition with both K2 and Broad Peak booked, as well as a month acclimatising lower down the Baltoro Glacier on the Lobsang Spires. There were ten climbers, including Don Whillans who celebrated his fiftieth birthday on what would be his last expedition. They worked in pairs and had a very flexible approach to the whole expedition. Amongst its achievements Doug Scott, Jean Afanassieff, Roger Baxter-Jones, Andy Parkin, Steve Sustad and Alan Rouse climbed Broad Peak, but tragically Dr Peter Thexton died of cerebral/pulmonary oedema during his attempt with Greg Child. Several expedition members then returned home, but Doug Scott, Jean Afanassieff, Andy Parkin and Roger Baxter-Jones teamed up for an alpine-style attempt on the line to the left of the Abruzzi – the South-South-East Spur. This would be a substantial new route, leading to the foot of the Shoulder of K2 at about 7700 metres. Andy Parkin, Alan Rouse and Steve Sustad had already made a short foray on to the spur a few weeks before, retreating when a minor earthquake triggered off huge avalanches all over K2 and Broad Peak. Andy Parkin remembers how, before they set foot on the spur, Don Whillans had spent a couple of days intently studying the whole of the South Face before declaring that this line looked to be the best and safest way up the mountain. 'That's the route I want to do,' was his flat conclusion. But after the death of Pete Thexton, Don, disillusioned, returned home. He had spotted the route that, when finally completed twelve years later, was described as probably the 'easiest' way up K2. The legendary Whillans eye for a line had been exercised for the last time.

Scott's team made good progress and on the morning of the fifth day the four climbers were only some 150 metres below the junction with the Abruzzi Spur at the bottom of the Shoulder. Snow had fallen during the night and after some indecision they decided to press on in deep snow. After an hour Jean Afanassieff suddenly announced, 'I'm going blind.' He felt a pain around his kidneys and his face, arms and fingers were numb. 'Go down, must go down now,' he mumbled. With his team in trouble, Doug Scott had no hesitation in retreating and two long days later they efficiently shepherded Afanassieff down to the glacier, by now almost fully recovered. It had been a good effort, for they had virtually reached known ground before their enforced descent. Doug Scott was puzzled when three years later, Tomo Česen soloed the spur to the Shoulder of K2, claiming a new route. In fact the new climbing was only a few metres of snow slope, if anything at all, leading to the Shoulder. (Tomo Česen's claims on this will be discussed fully later on.)

After this attempt Scott and his team went home, except for Roger Baxter-Jones who stayed on with a Basque climber, Mari Abrego, who had previously climbed to 8200 metres on the West Ridge. Together they reached 8300 metres on the Abruzzi, above the Bottleneck and almost the foot of the summit snowfields, when deep avalanche-prone snow and threatening weather forced a retreat.

1984 was a quiet year. Stefan Wörner's international expedition to K2 and Broad Peak reached 7500 metres and, as already mentioned, Kurt Diemberger and Julie Tullis failed on the Abruzzi, having climbed Broad Peak. In 1985 four groups visited the Abruzzi Spur. Erhard Loretan's Swiss expedition put five climbers on the summit and Eric Escoffier's French team had three summiteers, one of whom (Daniel Lacroix) died during the descent. Three Japanese climbers from Kazuoh Tobita's party also climbed K2 via the Abruzzi. The final attempt was almost an afterthought. After their extraordinary ascent of the West Face of Gasherbrum IV, still one of the greatest ascents of all time in the Karakoram, Voytek Kurtyka and Robert Schauer reached 7000 metres on the Abruzzi.

And so at the end of 1985 K2 had received thirty-nine successful ascents and there had been twelve deaths. The mountain was seen by climbers as the hardest of the 8000-metre peaks, but by no means the most dangerous. Everest, with its Khumbu Icefall, and Nanga Parbat, with its grim pre-war history, had both exacted a far greater death toll. K2 was a mountain virtually unknown outside mountaineering circles, other than for its curious name. In 1986 all this would change for ever.

14

1986

It is tempting, with hindsight, to try to make neat packages of assumptions and conclusions about the worst year of K2's climbing history; to look for patterns where there are none, to find blame that does not exist and plots of Machiavellian intent that do not bear close examination. Alternatively, it would be easy to emulate the brief but succinct summary of the year made in a magazine: 'Numerous ascents by disjointed groups meeting in the wrong place at the wrong time . . .', and leave it at that.

Early in 1987 I set down the major events of the year in a book, *K2, Triumph and Tragedy*. In the Introduction I repeated the point made in *Mountain* magazine that a greater volume of words had been written about the events of 1986 on K2 than about any mountain event since the first ascent of Everest in 1953. Since then at least three more books have been published, including those by two of the climbers most involved in the final disastrous weeks on the mountain. As well as that, countless reviews, summaries and references have been made, some useful, some ill-informed and a few that would have been better left unwritten.

So it is with some trepidation that I approach the subject again. First I would like to describe the chronological sequence of the events of that year, as a reminder for those who already may be familiar with them, and as a crash course for those who are not.

In 1986 the Ministry of Tourism gave permission for no less than nine expeditions to attempt K2. Renato Casarotto was going to try and solo the Magic Line up the South-West Ridge, while two Basque members of his expedition would be on the Abruzzi Spur. A four-person French team led by Maurice Barrard was also attempting the Abruzzi. Alan Rouse led an eleven-man British team to the North-West Ridge, and an Italian-based team, 'Quota 8000' (but with

French, Austrian and British members), attempted first the South-West Ridge and then switched to the Abruzzi Spur. An American expedition led by John Smolich also had permission for the South-West Ridge. Another international expedition led by the controversial figure Karl Herrligkoffer was to try the unclimbed South Face, though most members ended up on the Abruzzi Spur. Alfred Imitzer from Austria had permission for the Abruzzi, as did a large Korean expedition led by Kim Byung Joon. Finally, Janusz Majer from Poland led an eight-person team, including three women, to the South-West Ridge. Over eighty climbers were involved, ranging from Casarotto's three-man team to the Koreans' nineteen members.

It is still a mystery as to why the Ministry allowed so many varied expeditions to so few routes. After all, there are eight obvious possibilities under Pakistani control – the North-West Ridge, West Ridge, West Face, South-West Ridge, South Face, South-South-East Spur, Abruzzi Spur and North-East Ridge – but the nine expeditions were concentrated on to only four of these routes and most were on either the Abruzzi or the South-West Ridge. It seemed to be a recipe for trouble and would call for immense co-operation and understanding if severe problems of overcrowding were to be avoided. By and large they were, but the seeds of disaster were sown by the very number of people involved. It was also quite incongruous to give permission for Casarotto to solo a route that had three other expeditions attempting it.

Of course the need for foreign currency was a large factor in the Ministry's decision, for K2 expeditions bring in large sums of money to the country. But it is still hard to see why each expedition should not have been allotted a different route and then forced to stick to it. Nobody was on the West Ridge or West Face or South-South-East Spur (except Tomo Česen, illegally) or the North-East Ridge. This would have made so much more sense, and certainly reduced some of the competitive feeling that undoubtedly developed during the summer, when comparatively unknown climbers summited via the fixed ropes of the Abruzzi while others watched them and were tempted to do the same. It put huge pressures on the luckless band of liaison officers at the foot of the mountain and, even at the time of writing after eight years have passed, some of the complexities of who had permission for what still remain unclear. But the first lesson of 1986 on K2 to be learnt must surely be to sort out permissions for different routes in a much more rational way. Since 1986 some steps *have* been taken to do this but the situation is still far from perfect. The most recent regulations for K2 and all other Karakoram mountains give permission for only six expeditions in any one year to each peak.

After a quiet start to the summer, with expeditions building up and stocking lower camps, the first disaster to strike was on 21 June when two Americans were hit by a huge avalanche from the slopes leading to the Negrotto Col and the start of the South-West Ridge. John Smolich and Alan Pennington were killed outright and Pennington's body recovered and buried at the Gilkey Memorial. The Americans abandoned the expedition and the Italians, 'Quota 8000', switched to the Abruzzi Spur.

On 23 June six people stood on the summit of K2. Wanda Rutkiewicz became the first woman to climb K2, followed shortly afterwards by Liliane Barrard, with her husband Maurice, and Michel Parmentier. It was perhaps Wanda's greatest achievement in her long career for she had climbed K2 in good style without oxygen. The two Basque climbers from Casarotto's expedition, Mari Abrego (who had come so close with Roger Baxter-Jones in 1983) and Josema Casimiro, also topped out via the Abruzzi. But the second tragedy of the year was soon to follow. The Barrards had been very slow on their ascent, and on their descent Maurice had insisted on stopping shortly below the summit at the spot where they had their last camp at 8300 metres above the Bottleneck. Next day the Barrards lagged behind and disappeared. They must have been avalanched, hit by a sérac fall or simply fallen off in their exhaustion. Wanda Rutkiewicz got down safely but Michel Parmentier, who had waited for the Barrards on the Shoulder in worsening weather, had a desperate epic, descending to the beginning of the fixed ropes in white-out conditions. He was in radio contact with Base Camp and late on a stormy afternoon an anxious crowd gathered in a big frame tent listening to his increasingly desperate calls as he tried to get instructions to guide him down. At last he announced that he had found urine stains in the snow, and to cheers of encouragement from everyone at Base Camp, he located marker wands and the ropes that would lead him to safety. A few weeks later the body of Liliane Barrard was found almost at the foot of the South Face, but there was no sign of Maurice, or how they died.

In variable weather the Italian 'Quota 8000' expedition made progress on the Abruzzi Spur and on 5 July brought off a major feat. Six climbers summited, including four Italians and the Czech, Jozef Rakoncaj, who had climbed K2 in 1983 and thus become the first person to climb the mountain twice. But the most amazing ascent was by the Frenchman Benoît Chamoux who, using the fixed ropes, camps and tracks already in place, climbed the Abruzzi in only *twenty-three hours*. Chamoux had already climbed Broad Peak in less than a day and was rapidly making a name for himself with a succession of speed ascents that left an older generation both impressed and baffled. On the same day, 5 July, two Swiss climbers from Herrligkoffer's expedition also reached the summit via the Abruzzi, but below them one of the most outstanding ascents of the summer was taking place.

Jerzy Kukuczka from Katowice in Poland was close on Reinhold Messner's heels in the race for the fourteen 8000-metre peaks. K2 would be his eleventh and with the exception of Lhotse all his ascents were either by new routes or first winter ascents. Kukuczka was described vividly by his one-time partner Voytek Kurtyka as 'the greatest psychological rhinoceros I've ever met amongst alpinists, unequalled in his ability to suffer and in his lack of responsiveness to danger'. He had teamed up with Tadeusz Piotrowski who in the 'sixties and early 'seventies was the outstanding Polish winter mountaineer with first ascents in the Polish Tatra, the Alps, Norway and also the first winter ascent of Noshaq in the Hindu Kush. This was the first time a 7000-metre peak had been climbed in winter.

The two were part of Herrligkoffer's international expedition. Kukuczka wanted to climb K2 by the South Face. After an initial foray to around 6000 metres it became all too obvious that the German and Swiss members of the expedition were unconvinced of the safety of the proposed line (which had been looked at previously by Messner and several other parties). After some uncomfortable discussions at Base Camp most opted for the Abruzzi Spur (for which, incidentally, they did not have permission) leaving Piotrowski and Kukuczka to fend for themselves on the South Face. Herrligkoffer objected to the change of plan and ordered the others to support the Poles, but shortly after celebrating his seventieth birthday the leader was whisked away in a helicopter suffering from suspected pulmonary oedema.

Supported only by the German climber Toni Freudig, Kukuczka and Piotrowski camped below the sérac barrier that Messner, Seigneur and others had baulked at. Kukuczka spotted a comparatively safe way through that was only exposed to danger for about fifteen minutes. Next day, minus Freudig, the two Poles ferried all their equipment and fixed rope up to just over 7000 metres. Then, in the knowledge that they had done everything possible to prepare the route for a summit attempt, they returned to Base Camp and sat out ten days of bad weather.

At the beginning of July they set off and in two days regained their high point. On the third they approached a long curving gully called the Hockey Stick, a prominent feature, particularly when seen head on from the slopes of Broad Peak. It led to a rock barrier a hundred metres high barring an exit on to the summit ridge. The exit is slightly higher than the point where Fritz Wiessner had almost gained the summit ridge. It is quite possible that if Kukuczka and Piotrowski had traversed diagonally right at the top of the Hockey Stick, instead of climbing straight up, they would have spared themselves the ordeal that was to follow. Two bivouacs in the gully led the Poles to the final obstacle. This took two days to overcome, the first day only yielding thirty metres of hard-won height, which Kukuczka described as being the hardest piece of climbing he had ever done at that altitude. Anvil clouds began to build on the horizon. Returning to their bivouac, they dropped the last spare gas cylinder and suffered the first torments of dehydration.

The following day Kukuczka found a candle stub and managed to melt a cup of snow. Then they set off abandoning all their bivouac equipment. In mid-afternoon of 10 July they emerged on to the summit slopes of the Abruzzi in thickening snowfall. Kukuczka led, as he had done throughout, and they forced themselves up through the murk. At one point they found some soup packet wrappers and for a depressing few moments Kukuczka thought they were still only at the Barrards' last campsite at 8300 metres. But they were actually just below the very last sérac under the summit and reached it in the gathering gloom. They managed to descend a couple of hundred metres and bivouacked. It was snowing heavily but there was no wind. Shivering with cold and fatigue the two huddled together and waited for dawn.

In the morning they could see nothing and in white-out conditions they felt their way down towards the Bottleneck on the Abruzzi route. It took them all day to reach a point high on the Shoulder and another wretched bivouac. Long out of food and drink, and with no sleeping-bags, Kukuczka and Piotrowski were stretched to their absolute limits. Even Kukuczka, the man Wanda Rutkiewicz said could survive by eating rocks, was running on empty.

Next morning Kukuczka led off down the Shoulder and at last spotted tents as the visibility improved. Piotrowski had nearly caught him up when first one, then the other, crampon fell off his boots. Turning round Kukuczka shouted a warning but Piotrowski had lost his grip on his ice-axe and shot down the slope, almost knocking Kukuczka off as well, and disappeared out of sight below. Mechanically, Kukuczka descended, picking up the crampons which had come to rest, and noticed that they were still done up. How had they fallen off?

Kukuczka descended slowly in a state of total exhaustion and at last reached the fixed ropes on the Abruzzi. Mildly frostbitten but otherwise uninjured he had made it safely down. The climb had been a *tour de force* but Piotrowski's death was surely the result of sheer exhaustion, pressing on for too long without food, drink, warmth and shelter. The 'psychological rhinoceros' had survived, and would do so three more times to become only the second man to achieve all fourteen of the 8000-metre peaks. Then in 1989 on the unclimbed South Face of Lhotse, the only mountain that Kukuczka had not previously climbed by a new route, he slipped and fell right at the top of the Face. The rope broke and one of Poland's greatest mountaineers was dead.

The deaths of Pennington and Smolich, the Barrards, and now Piotrowski, had a profoundly depressing effect on the international tented village at the foot of the mountain. The British team, to which I was attached as climbing cameraman, abandoned the North-West Ridge in favour of a strictly unauthorised ascent of the Abruzzi, sneaking round to the start of the route after a week of bad weather. But they were back the following evening, dispirited at the weather which had broken down yet again. Dave Wilkinson was the last back and mentioned he had heard that Renato Casarotto had fallen into a crevasse while descending from his last attempt to solo the Magic Line. Kurt Diemberger had apparently seen him on the Filippi Glacier on his way down: then he had disappeared. We went to bed puzzled but not too worried, for a rescue team had set out immediately. But at midnight we were awoken and asked to help. Two hours later we arrived at an eerie scene. The still form of Casarotto lay beside the crevasse he had been pulled out of; he had sustained massive internal injuries and had died shortly after his emergence. Kurt Diemberger and Gianni Calcagno were keeping a lonely vigil beside his body. At dawn he was lowered back into his icy tomb.

For many of us the death of Renato Casarotto was the last straw. His wife Goretta had been in radio contact with him at Base Camp and he had been able to call her from inside the crevasse, telling her he was dying and needed help urgently. The circumstances were so harrowing that I felt it was surprising that anyone had the willpower to stay on, yet even after six deaths some of us felt that there couldn't possibly be any more and that going home wouldn't change anything. And so, as July dragged on and the warm, wet monsoon-like weather kept everyone at Base Camp, the remnants of the nine expeditions re-formed and regrouped for one last big effort.

By now the only routes being attempted were the South-West Ridge, which six of Janusz Majer's Polish team were still committed to, and the Abruzzi Spur for which everyone else had opted. Everyone consisted of the large Korean expedition and the seven-man Austrian team, Kurt Diemberger and Julie Tullis from the 'Quota 8000' expedition, Alan Rouse, the British expedition co-leader, and Dobroslawa Wolf. Known universally as Mrufka (Ant), she was originally with the Polish South-West Ridge expedition but had decided to climb with Alan on the Abruzzi as she felt this gave her a better chance of the summit. Alan himself had taken the failure on the North-West Ridge hard and was reluctant to return to England without one more attempt on the mountain. It was curious that Al, who was originally so determined to climb a new route on K2, eventually committed himself to the Abruzzi Spur, where the most he could hope for was the dubious satisfaction of a first British ascent, but he would be only the sixty-fourth person to climb K2, which was really no big deal in Al's own highly competitive view of his place in the world of mountaineering.

At the end of July the weather improved significantly and it seemed that a really settled spell was on the way. The Koreans on their siege of the Abruzzi Spur had ropes fixed, camps in place and still occupied the lower ones. On 28 July Kurt Diemberger, Julie Tullis and four Austrians left Base Camp and set off for the Abruzzi. Al Rouse and Mrufka Wolf followed late in the evening of 29 July and at midnight the Poles left for their last attempts at the Magic Line. The stage was set for the final act of the drama.

With four different parties on the Abruzzi two things were needed if harmony and success were to prevail: co-operation and communication. Both existed to some extent but neither was perfect. During the days that followed, critical moments occurred in which one or the other was lacking, sometimes both. Situations evolved without the full knowledge of everyone involved and various game plans proved to be inadequate and inflexible. The need to modify tactics proved to be difficult for most to grasp and impossible for a few.

The first setback came with the discovery that the Austrian Camp III had been destroyed by a monster avalanche that had swept down to the Godwin-Austen Glacier. Kurt Diemberger had found possible evidence of this when he discovered a teapot and a sweater down on the glacier that should have been at the camp, but his warnings to the Austrians went unheeded. Now, just below the Shoulder, they were faced with a tent shortage and, in what came to be seen as one of the most controversial moments of the summer, they did a deal with the Korean expedition whereby they carried a Korean tent and some fixed rope up to the Shoulder and in exchange for fixing the rope above the Bottleneck they would be allowed to use the tent for their first summit push. The ramifications of this arrangement were to cause a critical day to be wasted.

Three Austrians, Alfred Imitzer, Hannes Wieser and Willi Bauer reached the Shoulder on the evening of 1 August and on the 2nd set off for their summit bid. During the day Diemberger and Tullis, three Koreans and Al Rouse and Mrufka Wolf all arrived on the Shoulder. Diemberger watched the Austrians as they slowly made progress across the traverse above the Bottleneck. At four p.m. in the afternoon at about 8400 metres they stopped and turned back. Diemberger realised that there would be serious overcrowding at Camp IV as ten people attempted to spend the night in three tents that were designed for a maximum of seven.

The Austrians arrived at seven p.m. and pleaded with everyone to be allowed to stay so that they could have another attempt and in the end Bauer and Wieser squeezed into the Korean tent and Imitzer did the same with Rouse and Wolf, camped a little way below. Only Diemberger and Tullis refused to accommodate anyone in their tiny two-man tent. On 3 August the three Koreans set off for the summit on oxygen but Rouse and Wolf, after a sleepless night, decided to have a rest day in perfect weather. Diemberger and Tullis, racked with indecision, also stayed in camp as did the three Austrians. This inactivity was apparently influenced by Tullis who wanted to climb with Al Rouse and possibly felt uneasy about summiting ahead of him.

In the light of the dramas to come, the Polish ascent of the South-West Pillar has not really had the accolades it deserved. First sieged by the French in 1979, most if not all the ground had been previously covered. (The Japanese 'West Ridge' line traverses on to the final section of this route.) But there is little doubt that the Pillar gives the most technical climbing so far undertaken on K2, with frequent hard sections of iced-up rock, some of it very steep indeed and all at altitudes between 6000 and 8000 metres. On their last attempt the Poles had split their team with Janusz Majer, Anna Czerwinska and Krystyna Palmowska a day behind the leaders. Eventually, these three would make a safe retreat. But on 3 August the three-man summit team could be seen from Base Camp almost imperceptibly moving up the last rocky ridge. The party consisted of Przemyslaw Piasecki, the Czech guest climber Peter Bozik, and Wojciech Wröz, about to be successful at last on his third attempt.

The three Koreans summited just before them in the afternoon. The Magic Line team decided to descend to the Shoulder, to the consternation of those in Camp IV. But coming down in the dark and desperately tired after leading most of the last days on the South-West Ridge, Wröz fell to his death, probably after abseiling off the end of a fixed rope that was not anchored at the bottom. The weary and distraught Piasecki and Bozik reached Alan Rouse and Mrufka Wolf's tent where Al made way for them by bivouacking half out of a tent, in a snow hole. Two of the Koreans made it back to Camp IV but a third had to bivouac tied to a piton above the Bottleneck. In the dawn of 4 August Al Rouse and Mrufka Wolf were first away, followed by Alfred Imitzer. Kurt Diemberger and Julie Tullis, Willi Bauer and Hannes Wieser brought up the rear but Wieser, suffering wet gloves and going very slowly, soon turned back. When Bozik and Piasecki started their descent from Camp IV they asked Wieser if he wanted to go with them, but he refused. Ahead, Al Rouse broke trail almost all day, but Imitzer and Willi Bauer slowly caught him up. Mrufka Wolf, pushed to her limit, was flagging and climbing erratically. Above the Bottleneck at 8400 metres Kurt and Julie found her actually asleep in the snow. She persisted in carrying on but Kurt was worried that she could fall off and take them with her.

Bauer and Imitzer overtook Rouse not far from the top. Al was grateful to have someone else to break the trail for the last section and the two Austrians stood on top at three fifteen p.m. Rouse met them just a few metres under the summit. Descending slowly the Austrians met Diemberger, Tullis and Wolf. Kurt and Julie were determined to press on but the weather had been slowly breaking all day and it was already four p.m. Later, as Alan Rouse descended, he managed to persuade Mrufka, by now climbing beyond her limits, to go down. The Austrians, Rouse and Wolf made a safe descent to Camp IV on the Shoulder, but Diemberger and Tullis, arriving at the summit late in the day (the time has become another subject of controversy), started descending in the grey twilight. Not far below the summit Julie fell, pulling Kurt off as well, and they both went about a hundred metres before coming to rest in soft snow directly above the huge séracs that would have killed them both. They had a grim bivouac at just under 8400 metres though the weather was overcast and not as cold as it would have been on a clear night.

The next morning they slowly descended in a white-out and reached the vicinity of Camp IV around midday where Willi Bauer heard their shouts and directed them down. Julie, exhausted and having trouble with her eyesight, was pulled on her backside to the tents where Imitzer, Bauer and Wieser took her into the biggest tent and tried to warm her up with hot drinks and a spare down jacket. Kurt slept in his tent and later Julie, seemingly recovering a bit, joined him.

Now it was the evening of 5 August and the storm, which had broken in earnest the day before lower on the mountain, hit the Shoulder with a vengeance. It was by far and away the worst storm of the summer and it was to rage until 10 August. Those at Base Camp had been made aware of the death of Wröz by radio, and also that of a high-altitude porter, Mohammed Ali, sirdar to the Korean expedition who was killed by a falling stone between Advance Base and Camp I. Morale and hope for survivors of the storm gradually faded over the following days.

Seven people were trapped on the Shoulder in three tents that on 6 August became two when Kurt and Julie's collapsed under the weight of snow. Julie returned to the Austrians' tent and Kurt was taken in by Alan and Mrufka and the three crammed into the tiny two-man tent. In the Austrians' tent Julie Tullis was sinking, her eyesight was fading and she was sleeping for longer and longer stretches. Either on the night of the 6/7 August, or possibly 7/8 August, she asked, 'Willi, get Kurt down safely,' before she died. Diemberger, who wasn't told of her death until the next morning, was devastated and Rouse did his best to comfort him.

Until the gas ran out on the 8th Al Rouse had been a dynamic force, digging out tents and doing everything possible to help them survive. But, increasingly dehydrated, he was the first to succumb to

Wiessner's 1939 expedition. *Left*, Pasang Lama
belaying Fritz Wiessner on their summit attempt when
they reached 8365m. *Above*, Durrance, the late
replacement (left) met Wiessner and Wolfe for the first
time on the voyage out. *Below*, the team: standing,
Sheldon, Cranmer, Durrance, Trench; seated,
Cromwell, Wiessner, Wolfe.

Above left, Pasang Lama, the strongest of Wiessner's Sherpas. *Above right*, looking up to the Bottleneck and the sérac band that overhangs it. (*Jim Wickwire*) *Below*, mixed ground on the lower reaches of the Abruzzi Spur. (*Julie-Ann Clyma*)

The American 1953 expedition. *Top l to r*: Houston, Bates, Schoening. *Centre right*, Molenaar's drawing of the route and camps on the Abruzzi Spur. *Above left*, his diagram to illustrate the multiple fall that Pete Schoening managed to arrest. *Above right*, Art Gilkey whose life the team vainly attempted to save.

Above left and right, Lino Lacedelli and Achille Compagnoni, the first men to reach the summit of K2 with the 1954 Italian expedition. (*both Museo Nazionale della Montagna, Turin*) *Below left*, Walter Bonatti, the greatest climber of his generation and the youngest in the team, whose support of the summit pair led to bitter recrimination for years after. (*Mario Fantin*) *Below right*, Ardito Desio, geographer with the Italian 1929 party and prime organiser of the successful 1954 expedition exhorts his troops from Base Camp. (*Museo Nazionale della Montagna, Turin*)

The British 1978 expedition. *Above left*, Nick Estcourt who was lost in an avalanche between Camps I and II. *Top right*, Peter Boardman (*Chris Bonington Picture Library*) and *above right*, Joe Tasker (*Mike Shrimpton*), a famous Himalayan partnership forged on Changabang. *Below*, Doug Scott (left) and Joe Tasker immediately after the avalanche. The fracture line is clearly visible below the rock ridge. (*Peter Boardman*)

Above, an aerial view of the Karakoram with the unmistakable pyramid of K2 dominating the skyline left, and Broad Peak, right.

Renato Casarotto
(Mountain Archives)

Peter Bozik
(Jim Curran)

Wojciech Wröz
(Josef Nyka)

Mrufka Wolf
(Jim Curran)

Al Rouse
(Mike Shrimpton)

Tadeusz Piotrowski
(Josef Nyka)

Below, some players in the catastrophic drama of 1986.

Wanda Rutkiewicz
(*Jim Curran*)

Julie Tullis
(*Jim Curran*)

Przemyslaw Piasecki
(*Jim Curran*)

Jerzy Kukuczka
(*Josef Nyka*)

Kurt Diemberger
(*Jim Curran*)

Willi Bauer
(*Janusz Majer*)

Above, left to right, Christophe Profit, Pierre Béghin and Benoît Chamoux, three of the French stars to make their mark on K2. (*all Mountain Archives*) *Below,* a view from the North-West Ridge at around 7000m, looking down on the American Towers with the Savoia Glacier below. (*Alan Rouse*)

the effects of staying too high too long. While the storm raged the six occupants of the two tents sank into apathy and torpor, trying to eat snow and constantly falling asleep. On the night of the 9th Rouse became delirious, begging for water and mumbling incoherently in his sleep.

On the morning of the 10th the wind and snow abated somewhat. In the Austrian tent Imitzer and Wieser were both in a bad way but Bauer was still able to get himself ready to descend. Urging the others to do the same, he cajoled the other Austrians into action. Diemberger and Mrufka Wolf also got ready, but Al Rouse was beyond help and Kurt had to make the dreadful decision to leave him. He made his farewell to Julie who had been placed in the wrecked tent, and, as a last gesture, found a dry sleeping-bag for Al. Then he left and followed the others down through the bottomless powder snow and driving spindrift. After only a hundred metres Imitzer and Wieser both collapsed. Wolf and Bauer did everything they could to keep them going but it was a hopeless task. They too were left.

When Diemberger caught Bauer and Wolf up the three made slow but steady progress downward through the murk. At last they crossed the bergschrund at the foot of the Shoulder and, finding the going a bit easier, descended the slopes to the remains of Camp III at the top of the Black Pyramid and the beginning of the fixed ropes. Mrufka Wolf was abseiling on a Sticht plate, a belaying device that was awkward and slow to use on the frozen ropes. She was going slowly but apparently in control. Willi Bauer, by far the strongest of the three, was out ahead clearing the ropes. Diemberger passed Wolf and joined Bauer in Camp II which was still standing. But Mrufka Wolf never arrived.

The next day Bauer drew ahead and, as the light faded at Base Camp, the remaining occupants, who had now given up all hope for the seven missing climbers, saw the ghastly sight of a lone figure staggering down the strip of moraine to the tents. Frostbitten, haggard with torn clothing, Bauer looked like a survivor from an air crash. Barely able to speak he at last indicated that Kurt Diemberger was on his way down and that Mrufka Wolf was missing. I was one of the small search party who went up the Godwin-Austen Glacier in the night and found Kurt on the very last slopes above Advance Base, downclimbing slowly and mechanically in the darkness. When we met he simply said, 'I have lost Julie.'

Piasecki and Bozik forced their tired bodies back up the Abruzzi Spur in the forlorn hope of finding Mrufka Wolf, but there was no sign of her. At the time her death was a mystery and both Bauer and Diemberger thought she must have made a mistake and fallen, probably while changing over ropes. They were wrong, but it would take a year before any more light was to be shed on the fate of the brave Polish woman.

After several frustrating days at Base Camp waiting for a rescue helicopter that never came, Kurt and Willi were at last flown to Skardu, then home to lengthy hospitalisation in Innsbruck, where both men lost finger ends and toes.

This was not quite the whole story, for on the north side of the mountain an American expedition led by Lance Owens reached just over 8000 metres on the North Ridge. A summit bid was foiled by the same storm that took such a toll on the Abruzzi Spur but mercifully everyone retreated safely. The expedition caused a minor sensation when it was revealed that an accompanying survey, using the most sophisticated satellite technology, suggested that K2 might be higher than Everest. A receiver at Base Camp picked up one signal from the passing satellite before its batteries failed. It was planned to receive and cross-check up to fifteen signals but, on the basis of this incomplete data, K2 was tentatively given the height of 29,064 feet, thirty-six feet higher than Everest (Americans still prefer feet to metres). George Wallerstein, an astronomy professor from the University of Washington, Seattle, who led the survey, was suitably circumspect about his findings, pointing out that using the same system could significantly alter Everest's height as well. But the media, not unnaturally, went to town and many newspapers announced the elevation of K2 as if this were already proven. The implications were, of course, fascinating, particularly in Italy and Britain. Could Compagnoni and Lacedelli be about to steal Hillary and Tensing's crown? Would Sir Edmund have to give up his knighthood? Would the other Karakoram peaks be similarly upgraded? If so, this could raise the fiendishly difficult Gasherbrum IV to the ranks of the 8000-metre peaks, which presumably would be something of a blow to Reinhold Messner and Jerzy Kukuczka, both on the point of completing their fourteen eight-thousanders. Would Skardu then become the new Kathmandu, as thousands of trekkers deserted the Everest walk-in? The whole economies of Pakistan and Nepal could change overnight!

Most climbers found the notion extremely far fetched, but it was the indefatigable veteran Ardito Desio who took up the challenge and quickly organised an expedition to the Rongbuk valley on the north side of Everest and to the Baltoro Glacier to resurvey both mountains. Desio, as the leader of the successful Italian expedition, could be thought to have a vested interest in a result favouring K2, but his conclusions appear beyond question. The expedition made multiple observations from four ground stations at each mountain base with repeated signals from four Navstar satellites, the most advanced components of the US Air Force Global Positioning System. The new results showed that K2 was 8616 metres (a gain of five metres) and Everest was 8846 metres (a loss of two). The 150-year-old Great Trigonometric Survey measurements were still remarkably accurate and it must now be safe to assume that whatever minor variations are recorded, caused by the gradual upthrust of the Himalaya or collapsing cornices or melting snowcaps, no significant changes in the relative positions of the two highest mountains in the world seem likely in the foreseeable future.

So ended the dreadful summer of 1986, when no less than twenty-seven people climbed K2 but thirteen died in the process. The events on the mountain were over, but around the world the aftermath of grief and bitterness and controversy had only just begun.

15

Settling Dust

So many of the stories of K2 seemed to be repeated like a speeded-up film in 1986. New routes were attempted, two were achieved, one failed, there were twenty-seven successes and the death toll doubled. A strong sense of *déjà vu* prevailed. But unlike the controversies surrounding, say, Crowley, Wiessner and Bonatti, the recriminations and post mortems took place on a worldwide scale. Within months misconceptions and far-fetched theories had taken hold and were difficult to dispel. Incidents were invented, like Casarotto's 'last speech' at the top of the crevasse before he died – a figment of someone's imagination that was repeated many times. Other, more unpleasant rumours abounded and for months after my return to England I, like Kurt Diemberger and Willi Bauer, both in hospital in Innsbruck, was bombarded by outlandish, sometimes ghoulish queries from journalists picking over the stories with an eye to exploit grief and misery.

My own book was written from the viewpoint of one of the very few people to hear the story for the first time and to deal evenhandedly with all the deaths. I was more concerned with getting the detail right than offering an in-depth analysis. Written four years after the events it described, Kurt Diemberger's, *The Endless Knot*, is a memorable and powerful account of a highly charged, painful and personal experience. As for Willi Bauer, he speaks very little English and is, at best, taciturn. His book (co-written with journalist Gertrude Reinisch) *Licht und Schatten am K2* (Light and Shadow on K2) has not yet been translated into English. It contains several factual errors, perpetuating the myth of the Casarotto crevasse speech being one of them, and key photographs are wrongly captioned (one is also printed back to front). It is written in the third person and it is not always clear who is speaking in the many passages of dialogue, and whether the conversations themselves are verbatim recollections or journalistic devices to keep the story flowing.

In talking again recently to Diemberger and in examining his and Bauer's books I must emphasise that about ninety per cent of their stories tally completely and were exactly the same as told to me (mainly by Diemberger) at Base Camp in the days immediately after their return from the mountain. It is stating the obvious to say that in terms of proof we have only their stories to assess, plus a few photographs that Willi brought down with him. (Kurt and Julie's camera was either lost in the fall or left at Camp IV.)

In trying to analyse why things were allowed to go so disastrously wrong there are various questions to address. The first and in many ways the biggest problem is the exact nature of the deal struck between the Austrians and the Koreans. The tent controversy was made public after the expedition and thoroughly investigated by Peter Gillman in a postscript to Julie Tullis's autobiography, *Clouds From Both Sides*. But at Base Camp, both during and after the final disasters, I never heard any comments about the Austrian–Korean deal from anyone, including Kurt whom I spoke with at length. I mention this only to put the matter in perspective. It may well be that it has assumed more importance after the event than it did at the time. There is no doubt, however, that the deal, to take a Korean tent and some ropes to fix above the Shoulder, was made. There is evidence to suppose that the Koreans expected the tent to be vacated by the evening of 2 August, and that there was a disagreement when the Austrians returned from their unsuccessful summit bid. What remains unclear is, as I pointed out in *K2, Triumph and Tragedy*, how much did each party really understand? Both sides were communicating in English and the Koreans' command of the language was at best eccentric and at worst unintelligible. Willi Bauer spoke little English and claims that he thought the Koreans would be bringing another tent up to the Shoulder with them. I see no reason to doubt that he *did* think this, but it does seem to me that the arrangement would almost inevitably produce misunderstandings on both sides. But to apportion sole blame to the Austrians, as Kurt Diemberger has done so publicly since, seems to me to be harsh. The Austrians assumed too much, the Koreans maybe were rather naive in not foreseeing what might occur. But surely it *is* valid to question the wisdom of the Austrians in deciding to rest at Camp IV and have another attempt at the summit, thus committing themselves to at least four nights at around 8000 metres? True, this had been done before (e.g. the Americans in 1978) and has been done since (e.g. Stephen Venables on Everest in 1988), but a cardinal rule of climbing at or above 8000 metres is to spend as little time at that altitude as possible. Even if they had brought their own tent the Austrians would have been significantly loading the dice against their survival if anything went wrong, which it did.

It has always seemed strange that, having refused to accommodate any of the Austrians in his and Julie's tiny tent on the Shoulder, Kurt then should blame them for the loss of a critical day when he and Julie sat in perfect weather at Camp IV while the Koreans went to the summit. For whatever reasons, Kurt and Julie *chose* not to go to the top on the 3rd, and in his book he describes clearly and power-fully how he weighed up the pros and cons. But it *was* a choice, and it was a choice based on what he saw as his best option for climbing K2. Though Kurt claims he had no wish to rely on anyone else, the passage analysing his chances of reaching the summit shows that he and Julie were depending on others to help break trail with them. 'Most of our climbing to date we have done on our own, just the two of us. However if the snow is as Alfred [Imitzer] reported – heavy and deep – two people on their own could not manage the trail-breaking to the summit. Ergo: we *have* to start *with* the Koreans. This means be ready in time.' In then deciding *not* to attempt the summit with the Koreans, they made what proved to be the wrong choice – to wait a day, and go with Alan Rouse and Mrufka Wolf, and it cost them dear.

As for Alan and Mrufka it is still hard to understand why Al broke his own strongly held maxim – one night only at 8000 metres before the summit and, if possible, get down even lower at the end of the summit day. Even after a terrible night's sleep, I can't help but feel Al should have either gone with the Koreans or given up. But Al, again self-sufficient in so many ways, could not have calculated the effects of Imitzer in his tiny tent. So, although the tent shortage exacerbated the problems at Camp IV, each climber had a clear choice about what to do next. They all decided to chance their arm by waiting with the Austrians. This, given their strong motivation, is understandable, but it was a mistake.

The next problem concerns the collective and individual judge-ments about the weather. From Base Camp it was painfully obvious that, as with every other good weather spell that summer, it was not going to last. No doubt, in my anxiety as an impotent watcher of events on the mountain, I read too much into any minor indication of weather change, but by the morning of 4 August it was absolutely self-evident that the weather was breaking down in a big way and that a major storm was imminent. I accept that, high on the mountain, the weather stayed clear for most of the day, but there are quite specific indications in Bauer's and Diemberger's accounts that they were well aware that it was breaking. It seems self-evident that all the climbers in Camp IV on the summit day took a chance in getting up and down before it broke, and all of them got it badly wrong. It is particularly poignant though that the Austrians just might have been able to extricate themselves if they had listened to Hannes Wieser. It will be remembered that he had already turned down the chance to descend with Piasecki and Bozik, which undoubtedly would have been the most sensible thing for him to have done, as it would have left more space, food and fuel at Camp IV. On the evening of the 4th Bauer and Imitzer returned to Camp IV at around six p.m. and Wieser suggested they go all the way to Camp III that evening. But Imitzer said his 'feet were like butter' and Hannes agreed that there was only an hour's daylight left. Better to rest for a few hours and go down at first light. But it wasn't better and the decision would cost him and Wieser their lives. Poor Hannes, twice on 4 August the door was opened for him to escape and twice it closed.

On the summit day most of both Diemberger's and Bauer's accounts tally. But there is one strangely unresolved question. On his return to Base Camp, I had the strong impression of Kurt telling me that he and Julie reached the summit at seven p.m. Only Kurt could have told me this (Willi Bauer, who spoke little English, was almost totally uncommunicative) and at the time I didn't think much about it. Many climbers have pushed on to the summit of K2, Everest and other high mountains late in the day. Kurt himself had twice climbed Broad Peak, with Hermann Buhl and Julie Tullis, and reached the top at nightfall. In the context of what befell them (Julie's fall, the bivouac, etc.) his story made sense and didn't seem to be an issue. Yet when Kurt visited England in the autumn of 1986 he told Dennis Kemp in an interview for *Climber* magazine that he and Julie had got to the top between five thirty and six p.m. and when my book was published he was quick to correct me. The following year in Kathmandu I had a chance meeting with an Australian doctor, Major Tony Delaney, who had led an Australian army expedition to Broad Peak in the summer of 1986. Delaney had organised the stretcher party which met Kurt and me about a mile from Base Camp and carried Kurt down. He told me that I was quite right about Kurt's original story. He himself had made a short video interview with Kurt during the time we had been waiting for a helicopter and he assured me that Kurt had told him also that he had got to the top at seven p.m. I awaited Kurt's own book with interest.

When it was published in English in 1991 I read it avidly, reliving the ghastly days in early August and shedding tears at the pity and horror of what happened. As a factual document it was sometimes hard to follow but one passage struck me as being very strange. It is the afternoon of 4 August. Kurt and Julie are on the long summit snow slopes.

It is four o'clock. This was to have been our limit for the summit but we are so near now, so near.

Suddenly Willi Bauer appears. He and Alfred are on their way down.

'Are you sure you still want to go up?' he asks me.

The question takes me by surprise. 'It shouldn't take us more than an hour at most,' I answer. What is he talking about?

'You're wrong,' says Willi. 'It took us four hours!'

'Come off it, Willi!' I object reproachfully and for a moment feel a sense of panic, wondering how such a thing could be possible, he must have misunderstood me.

'It took us four hours,' Willi continues, 'from down there.' And points in the direction of the ice traverse.

'Ah well. That's an entirely different thing!'

Nevertheless Kurt then asked Willi, 'Are there any crevasses where you can bivouac?'

Willi nods. 'Yes, sure – and of course you'll reach the summit.'

The curious thing about this passage is what Bauer was trying to say. Normally, if you meet someone going up a hill when you are on the way down you tell them how long you think it will take *from the point where you meet them*. It was a strange reply to tell Kurt how long it had taken them from some unspecific point lower down, possibly accounted for by Bauer and Imitzer's achievement at making the first Austrian ascent and not being over-keen that Kurt Diemberger should eclipse them.

In Bauer's book the encounter is recalled rather differently. On their way down they meet Kurt and Julie and tell them it's time to turn back. 'Don't bother about us, we know our capabilities, but Mrufka *should* turn round, if she slips she'll take us all with her.' Though there is no way of knowing for certain, it does seem that Kurt and Julie, whatever time they actually *did* reach the top, were further out on a limb than Kurt is prepared to admit. But, as he says, by the time he decided to carry on it probably would not have made any difference to their subsequent confinement in Camp IV. Unless of course *everyone* had returned to Camp IV by early evening and all had made one final effort to get down before the storm broke in earnest . . .

The next controversy concerns the state of Julie Tullis on the morning of 5 August on their return to Camp IV. Kurt is certain that her frostbite was superficial and that, after a good rest, she would be able to get down under her own steam. But Willi Bauer's book paints a much grimmer picture. Hearing cries for help, Bauer, in only his inner boots, emerges from the tents and finds Kurt standing next to Julie who is lying with her head downhill in the snow waving a gloveless hand:

> With horror Willi fights his way over to them. They seem to be at the end of their strength, Julie is in a dreadful condition . . . her nose and cheeks are quite black showing definite signs of first-degree frostbite, her . . . right hand is swollen badly and bits of flesh are hanging down . . . she's not bleeding which also points to severe frostbite.

Kurt's book bitterly refutes this version of events and says, 'The considerable discrepancies which occur again between our two accounts could, in my opinion, indicate that Willi was the victim of hallucinations, that he experienced visions and thoughts which have no relation to reality. Nobody who reaches 8000 metres can be sure of being immune against that.' The problem is that if this is the case, we can't be sure of Kurt's version either! Could it be that Willi Bauer, suddenly exposed to the sight of Julie in trouble, and realising the implications of this, could be over-reacting (but not much, as events would show) and Kurt, who has lived through the fall, the bivouac and descent, is now so relieved at reaching Camp IV that his reaction is to play down her plight?

Later that day, when a detailed discussion about a possible helicopter rescue takes place inside the Austrians' tent, Kurt almost laughs it off as ridiculous. 'Julie did not take the idea of rescue seriously, although she would not have turned her nose up at a helicopter flight – anywhere! She told Willi that General Mirza (the President of the Alpine Club of Pakistan) had promised her a ride in a helicopter if she reached the summit of K2.' In Bauer's book, however, the conversation is preceded by Wieser and Imitzer questioning whether Julie can be lowered in a bivouac bag to Camp II and picked off by a rescue helicopter, which sounds far from lighthearted. But both agree she *did* recover somewhat, though this proved to be only a temporary revival, and she joined Kurt in his tent.

When Kurt and Julie's tent collapsed, Bauer makes no secret that Kurt was not welcome to the Austrian tent. Imitzer had been bitterly incensed when he was refused admission to Kurt and Julie's tent on the evening of the 2nd. Imitzer kept the tent door closed and 'without a word Kurt went over to Alan and Mrufka's tent.' Julie, on the other hand, was pulled out of the buried tent and made as comfortable as possible and put into Willi's sleeping-bag. It is still not clear to me whether or not Julie died on the night of 6 or 7 August. At Base Camp later I had to make an accident report to submit to the Assistant District Commissioner in Skardu and I vividly remember Kurt and Willi gazing blankly at each other, trying to remember which night it was. I had the impression that it was the 6th and that this might have accounted for the lack of any attempt to set off down early on the morning of the 7th when Kurt was told of her death during a lull in the storm. It would also explain how, when Kurt left Alan on the 10th, he gave him Julie's dry sleeping-bag from the wrecked tent. It is hard to imagine Willi sitting all through the nights of the 6th and the 7th without retrieving the bag for Julie so that he could use his own. In Kurt's account, however, he describes how on the 7th Julie visits him in Al and Mrufka's tent and she says, 'Kurt, I am feeling rather strange.' It is a question that probably cannot ever be completely resolved and is yet another example of how, *in extremis*, at high altitude, it is possible to confuse even the most simple sequence of events.

The next bone of contention concerns the different perception of Mrufka Wolf's behaviour through the storm. In Kurt's view she went into a state of semi-hibernation and barely moved. But towards the end Mrufka was the only person still fighting, according to Willi Bauer: 'The little Polish woman keeps coming out of her tent and trying to free it from the mass of snow. Alan is lying in his sleeping-bag and Kurt isn't moving. "Kurt, problem," the Polish woman keeps saying in exasperation. Kurt, it seems, is taking up too much space in the cramped tent.'

Once on the descent Bauer's account of the demise of Alfred Imitzer and Hannes Wieser is rather different to Diemberger's. According to Bauer they both died and he 'lay the two friends close together with rucksacks under their heads'. Willi decided not to take anything from them although he 'perhaps should have fulfilled a wish to the families by bringing something back as a memento'. Mrufka starts to sob and Willi takes her by the hand and they continue the descent. In Kurt's book, however, he finds Alfred lying face down, but Hannes is sitting in the snow. 'Hannes moves his arms weakly rowing in the air in slow motion . . . His eyes, blank, stare into space. He does not see me. I shout his name but he does not even move his head. Only his arms keep rowing through the air . . .' A graphic description that is hard to put down to high-altitude hallucination.

On the descent it is quite clear from Willi's book that there was no love lost between Kurt, Mrufka and Willi. There was a heated argument over a last sweet that Mrufka was saving, and at one point she complained that Kurt wasn't pulling his weight. 'What on earth are these two going on about?' Willi wondered. At one point Kurt was so slow that Willi threatened to leave him behind. Once on the fixed ropes Mrufka, who was using a Sticht plate to abseil, slowed down badly. Kurt tried to persuade her just to clip a karabiner into the rope and not bother with her time-consuming belay method, but Mrufka was adamant. Feeding the frozen ropes through the Sticht plate would have been difficult and the change-overs from one rope to the next a real problem, yet, with badly frostbitten fingers and suffering the last throes of exhaustion, it must have felt highly insecure just to clip into the rope and use it as a handrail. It may well be that Mrufka, falling behind the others, simply ran out of the dogged strength and determination that had so nearly carried her through to safety. She was found the following year not far below where Kurt had last seen her still attached to the fixed ropes. Most likely she simply fell asleep. She was buried near Advance Base.

So, discrepancies between accounts certainly do exist but now, nine years on, most of them can be seen as being perhaps more to do with wounded pride, colossal stress and the confusion of altitude rather than anything more sinister. At the time, however, there were many people who felt that the whole story hadn't been told and who found the seeming abandonment of Al Rouse and Mrufka Wolf, and to a lesser extent Alfred Imitzer and Hannes Wieser, hard to accept. This was perhaps the most painful issue. It harked back to the fate of Dudley Wolfe in 1939, and the behaviour of those in Camp IV in 1986 was compared unfavourably with the unselfishness of Charlie Houston's team in their forlorn attempt to rescue Art Gilkey. Letters were even written to *The Times* voicing criticisms that were little more than ill-concealed accusations of irresponsibility and negligence. I felt then, and still do, that these were quite unjustified. Mistakes, errors of judgement, lack of concern *were* all present in the events leading up to the desperate siege in Camp IV, but once the storm had broken it was simply the survival of the fittest. There is all the difference in the world between the plights of Art Gilkey and Alan Rouse. Gilkey was being helped down by *six* tired but not totally exhausted climbers who still had some food and fuel to keep them going. There was absolutely no chance, despite their best efforts, that Kurt, Willi and Mrufka could have helped Imitzer and Wieser, let alone Alan who could not even leave the tent. It is possible that Kurt just *might* have been able to do more in encouraging Mrufka down the fixed ropes if he remained above her, but by then nobody was in a position to take on the problems of others. What may not be appreciated by those who have not taken part in a fixed-rope expedition is that when the umbilical cord of climbers roped together is absent, there is very little anyone can do to help anyone else, particularly if they are above. Once Kurt Diemberger overtook Mrufka it would have been *quite* impossible to reascend even a few metres. As in the case of the dreadful death of Harsh Bahaguna on the fixed ropes of the West Ridge of Everest in 1971, Mrufka really had to extricate herself through her own efforts.

Perhaps in the end, the worst charge that can be levelled against the two survivors is that neither seem able to accept any significant share of responsibility for their actions, and by seeking to blame or criticise each other for their all too human failings, they have failed to command all the sympathy they deserved in the aftermath of the tragedy.

Before the terrible events of 1986 are left behind, mention must be made of Tomo Česen's 'new route' on the spur to the left of the Abruzzi. At the time Česen was almost unknown outside his native Yugoslavia, as it then was. Using the same furtive approach as the British team had employed on switching to their illicit attempt on the Abruzzi, Česen, who was a member of a Broad Peak expedition and had already climbed that mountain, sneaked past the Base Camp tents and on 3 August made a rapid ascent of the line that Doug Scott had virtually completed to the Shoulder. Česen says he reached the Shoulder and on the morning of 4 August he climbed up for a little way (presumably not as far as Camp IV) before retreating in worsening weather down the fixed ropes of the Abruzzi. His claims for a new route are obviously extravagant – he covered little (possibly no) new ground and didn't reach the summit, but in the light of the much more serious controversies that have dogged him since his alleged ascents of the North Face of Jannu and the South Face of Lhotse (neither of which are subjects for discussion here), his K2 route must be given a closer scrutiny.

At the time his climb was totally overshadowed by the events at Camp IV but when his story emerged I felt that Česen's claim was probably true. Even now, despite a complete lack of published photographic evidence, I think on balance that he probably *did* do the route. He was apparently spotted by the leader of the Broad Peak expedition just below the Shoulder, but the most compelling argument in his favour is that he could not possibly have known that, on the way *down* the Abruzzi, he would not meet all sorts of climbers and porters in and between camps. Yet by a strange quirk there was a window before Piasecki, Bozik and the Koreans left Camp IV, when Česen could indeed have descended virtually the whole spur to the glacier without seeing a soul. It would be an incredibly naive story to concoct if Česen hadn't done it unless he was exceptionally well informed about the events on the mountain, which seems unlikely. If he hadn't done it, he would be much more likely to claim he descended the route of ascent, as Doug Scott's team had done, in which case there would be no chance of his being seen (or not seen). But it is sad that such an obviously talented climber has since been the source of so much bitter controversy. It is hard to see how he can ever refute the charges made against him without reclimbing at least one of his routes with witnesses or, even better, doing an even harder one.

For family, friends and participants, the scars from 1986 still remain and periodically reopen. The nadir of K2's history should have taught some harsh lessons but, incredibly, several of the survivors of that summer have since been killed in circumstances almost identical to the events they only just escaped. The first casualties occurred in 1988 when Michel Parmentier attempted Everest from the north and decided to sit out a storm on his own at above 8000 metres, despite the advice of his team, which included Benoît Chamoux who had talked him down from the Shoulder of K2 in 1986. This time Michel Parmentier, who had been so aware of the mistakes of the Barrards on K2, did exactly the same thing and paid the price. On the south side of Everest in the same year Peter Bozik was involved in the first alpine-style ascent of the South-West Face, with a Czech expedition. Travelling light with only a tent inner and sharing sleeping-bags, four climbers reached the South Summit and one carried on to the top. Suffering from blindness presumably caused by cerebral oedema, and worsening weather, all four failed to get down to the South Col. Peter Bozik had been one of the trio who forced the Magic Line in 1986 and descended with Piasecki to the 'safety' of Camp IV on the Shoulder when Wröz was lost. One has to say that Peter Bozik, like Michel Parmentier, should have known better.

In 1989 Jerzy Kukuczka, the 'psychological rhinoceros', died almost at the top of the South Face of Lhotse when he fell and a cheap secondhand rope purchased in Kathmandu broke. Then in 1992 Gianni Calcagno who had tried so hard to save Renato Casarotto was himself killed the same way, in a crevasse fall, on Denali in Alaska. Finally, with a feeling of tragic predestiny, in May 1992 the world heard that Wanda Rutkiewicz had bivouacked just below the summit of Kangchenjunga in a miserable snow hole with no sleeping-bag, stove, food or drink. A Mexican climber, Carlos Carsolio, tried to persuade her to descend but to no avail. That night a storm broke. She never came down. Earlier in the year she had given a moving lecture to a huge audience at a film festival in Katowice. I watched enthralled at a beautiful presentation of her 8000-metre peaks. Formally attired in a black dress, the small figure on the stage gave an emotional account of her long list of adventures. I was not the only member of the audience to imagine this to be her swansong. Later that evening at a party we talked quietly of the events of 1986. When she left I felt the same as I had done saying goodbye to Nick Estcourt all those years before. Wanda had climbed eight of the fourteen eight-thousanders and she had done much for the cause of women's climbing. Her death left the ranks of Polish mountaineers shattered.

At the end of 1986 the pall of sadness hanging over the climbing world was so pervasive it was hard to imagine how anyone would have the temerity to return to K2 in the immediate future.

16

The Golden Age of Himalayan Mountaineering?

During the next four years nobody reached the summit of K2 and several expeditions barely got started on the mountain before giving up in the face of prolonged bad weather. How much this had to do with the psychological impact of 1986 is impossible to assess. But one cannot help wondering whether, for a while at least, mountaineers were wary of pushing too hard on the Savage Mountain. Between 1987–90 no less than sixteen expeditions failed, and there was one death, the Japanese Akira Suzuki who fell high on the Abruzzi.

It would be tedious to describe every one of these expeditions in detail. Eleven of them were on the Abruzzi Spur. But all are listed in Appendix I. Brief mention must however be made of one or two of the more interesting attempts. Perhaps the most innovative was the first winter expedition to K2 via the Abruzzi Spur in 1987 by a strong Polish team led by the doyen of winter expeditions, Andrzej Zawada. Zawada had a long and impressive list of successes starting in 1971 with the first ascent of Kunyang Kish (7852m) and including the first winter ascent of Everest (1980) and Cho Oyu (1985). But K2 was obviously going to be in a different league of difficulty, not least due to its remoteness and long glacier approach. Zawada solved this last problem by carrying the bulk of his equipment to Base Camp in the autumn when porters were still willing and able to carry, and placing guards on the stores to stop the whole lot being spirited back to Askole. But on the mountain itself the expedition (which included English climbers Roger Mear and Mike Woolridge) could make little headway. Arctic conditions, with constant high winds, stopped the team reaching any higher than the Black Pyramid at 7350 metres and after a prolonged siege the expedition was abandoned. Roger Mear, whose experiences in the Antarctic caused him to know a thing or two about survival in low temperatures, was impressed at the Poles' persistence and discipline but it was an experiment that he personally does not wish to repeat.

Doubtless there will be other attempts on K2 in winter and one day it will probably be climbed. Whether or not it will be by the Abruzzi Spur is another matter. It may well be that the Abruzzi, forming the profile of K2 opposite Broad Peak, is just too windy in winter months, and that the West or South Faces might be slightly more sheltered. But even for the most hardbitten Himalayan climbers K2 in winter is a prospect that will only ever appeal to a tiny minority prepared to endure the suffering and extremely high risk of frostbite and worse that any attempts must entail. Winter climbing in the Himalaya is still in its infancy and its future popularity is not guaranteed.

During the barren years from 1987–90 two expeditions also attempted the unclimbed East Face. Neither Doug Scott's 1987 expedition, nor the Austrian one in 1989 led by Eduard Koblmüller made much headway on the vast snow spurs and hanging séracs between the Abruzzi and the North-East Ridges. This Face holds more snow and ice than any other side of K2, gets the sun early, and in my view is the least attractive aspect of the mountain. Like the Kukuczka–Piotrowski route on the South Face, any prospective line seems to be innately dangerous and threatened by sérac falls and avalanches. A successful ascent would need perfect conditions and to be done quickly, particularly in its lower reaches.

In 1990 an expedition to K2 was mounted unlike any other one. Its objective was not to climb, but to clean up K2. The international expedition, organised by Mountain Wilderness environmental group and led by an Italian, C. A. Pinelli, marked a sea change in Western attitudes to the Karakoram. Since the explosion of climbing and trekking in the late 'seventies and early 'eighties concern had been growing about the impact of expeditions on the fragile mountain environment – not just on K2 but right across the Himalaya, and indeed all the world's great ranges. Much hand-wringing was indulged in but little real attempt was made to address the fundamental problems posed by the sudden invasion of the mountains. Undoubtedly, Everest in particular, but also K2, have become symbols of all that is reprehensible in lack of mountain awareness. True, litter, excrement, abandoned gear, even bodies, are left lying on the mountains, but the politically correct media present a simplistic picture of the problems of mountain conservation and have frequently ignored the positive actions taken by local groups, climbers and trekkers themselves. Many of the problems of Himalayan pollution are cosmetic. Toilet rolls and turds are, after all, biodegradable and in the Karakoram it is mainly the campsites on the K2 walk-in that have become eyesores. These take up a very small part of the whole area. Far more serious are the problems of wholescale deforestation of the foothills and constant burning of ever-dwindling trees for fuel. Only legislation at a high level (and the will to enforce changes through education) can solve these problems. However, climbers and trekkers, of all people, should be the ones to set good examples, and in the past it is true they have frequently been appallingly remiss in their actions.

In 1990 the Mountain Wilderness expedition produced a film of their efforts, *Free K2* (Kailas Films). In many ways it highlighted the very contradictions they set out to tackle. The film opened with an own goal of monumental stupidity: a grotesque sequence of climbers placing bolts into a beautiful blank slab of granite on which to hang a plaque commemorating their clean-up achievements! Once on the mountain there are some impressive sequences of great bales of fixed rope and caving ladders being rolled down the lower slopes of the Abruzzi Spur and most, if not all, the fixed rope was removed as far as the Black Pyramid. Altogether they stripped twelve kilometres of fixed rope, fifty abandoned tents, ladders, stoves, oxygen cylinders and gas cartridges from the Abruzzi. But the expedition admitted that it could not stop its own porters cutting firewood from the fast-disappearing oasis at Paiju and by using less porters for the walk-out than the walk-in, one cannot help wondering what the net gain was for conservation. Interesting finds were later auctioned off in Italy, re-posing the old question of when does rubbish become archaeology? Scrap metal was returned to Skardu and compressed into recyclable lumps for resale. But does it actually get sold? Or is the refuse simply moved elsewhere?

Perhaps the expedition's main value was symbolic, an example, if not a perfect one, for expeditions to emulate, or preferably improve upon. There is really no excuse for any visible litter at all as far as Base Camp; it can be either removed, burnt or buried deeply without too much difficulty. The gear strewn on the mountain *is* a problem, though on K2 the effects of storms, avalanches and gravity ensure that most abandoned equipment finds its way to the bottom of the mountain sooner or later. Whereas in contrast, the completely flat South Col of Everest has become the highest junk yard in the world and until it is removed by man, will stay that way. Inevitably, it all boils down to the individual's responsibility for the environment. Even in the two decades I have been visiting the Himalaya I have noticed a huge change in attitude – for the better! But there are limits to the sheer volume of traffic any area can stand without fundamentally changing the very nature of the place. The Karakoram has not quite reached that stage, but some areas of Nepal are perilously close to existing solely for the benefit of tourism. It may well be that the harsh nature of the Karakoram in general and the K2 trek in particular, may prove to be a blessing in disguise by keeping the numbers down to manageable proportions and ensuring that those committed, determined and interested enough to go could be responsible as well. But I may be too optimistic.

At last in 1990 K2's summit was trodden again. A large Japanese expedition (twelve members and eight Chinese helpers) led by Tomaji Ueki completed the second route on the north side of the mountain. Using fixed ropes the expedition climbed new ground from the K2 Glacier up a diagonal line below the Savoia Saddle. This avoided the American Towers and joined the line of the Polish/British attempts on the North-West Ridge at the snow dome at around 7000 metres. From there on they followed the same line as the Poles to the junction with the North Ridge and then its original finish across the dangerous snow basin to the summit which was reached on 12 August by Hirotaka Imamura and Hideji Nazuka. Rather like the Poles on the Magic Line in 1986, who covered little or no new ground, the Japanese effort was difficult to get too exited about and consequently received little publicity in the climbing press. Interestingly, and more accurately, the authoritative Japanese magazine *Iwa To Yuki* refers to the route as the North-West Face.

Six days later on 18 August three out of a four-man American–Australian team also made the summit via the North Ridge. For Greg Child, an Australian climber living in the USA, it was the culmination of several major Karakoram expeditions that had very different outcomes. The first was a summit bid on Broad Peak that turned from near triumph to disaster when Dr Peter Thexton succumbed to what seemed to be cerebral, then pulmonary, oedema. This had been followed by a quite brilliant ascent (only the second) of Gasherbrum IV by the North-West Ridge. In 1989 he had an

epic retreat from a new route on the Trango Tower in a storm. He
had also failed on K2 in 1987.

Their expedition was only the third ascent of the North Ridge,
but it had been achieved by a far smaller team than either of the
others. Child, one of the best mountain writers in the world, wrote
a compelling account of their summit day ('A Margin of Luck' in
Climbing), in which he followed Steve Swenson and Greg Mortimer
to the summit. Below him Phil Ershler is having his doubts, having
crossed horribly dangerous snow slopes towards the summit couloir
that had threatened to avalanche at every step.

I look between my legs at Ershler outlined against the North
K2 Glacier below, frontpointing slowly toward me. He keeps
pausing to scan the skies, as if torn between his desire for the
summit and the inner voice of self-preservation warning that we
are getting ourselves into a borderline situation . . . As the clouds
close in around us, it looks very much like our luck is running
out.

Ershler gave up soon after and made a safe return to the top camp.

Overtaking Mortimer, Child relapsed into the same trancelike state
so often described by K2 and Everest summiteers: '. . . Icicles hanging
over cliffs transmute into fixed ropes; the squeaks of my axes and
crampons in the snow become sentences spoken by persons I've never
met.'

Swenson overtook him and below the top and following, Child's
mind wandered off again.

Diaphanous outlines of the Baltoro Glacier and Broad Peak
appear, then fade in a swirl of cloud. Perfect snowflakes float
on to my Gore-Tex suit. I pause to stare at these fellow travellers
to nowhere. They magnify before my eyes, occupying my entire
field of vision, each a little perfection of geometry. Time slips
away . . .

Yet Greg Child was all too aware of the danger of lingering too long
around the summit. Before he left home he had dreamt he was talking
to Al Rouse who had been on the 1983 expedition to Broad Peak with
Child and whom he had met again briefly in Islamabad in 1986 before
they had gone their separate ways to Gasherbrum IV and K2. In his

dream Al had warned him, '"Get down from the summit as fast and as far as you can . . ." I listened to Al's advice intently. He knew what he was talking about . . .'

Swenson passed him on his way down and at 8.05 p.m. (Chinese time) Child made the summit. He wandered around, bemused at 'the place . . . I dreamed of half my lifetime, a place I never really thought I'd reach.' Half an hour passed and Mortimer arrived. 'Until his arrival I'd been so outside myself I'd begun to doubt I was really on the summit. I'd even begun to doubt my own existence . . . up here in la-la land where brain cells are shorting out by the bucketload, anything is possible.'

Despite his worries about the weather and impending nightfall, the pair didn't leave the summit until nine p.m. and it took four gruelling hours to regain the tent at 8000 metres. Only a hundred metres away Child collapsed and Mortimer cajoled him into one last effort. Regaining the tents, Child plunged his hands into water heating on the stove and endured the exquisite agony of blood flowing into his fingers: 'We tear off our double boots and check for frostbite. Our feet are not frozen. We'll be taking home as many fingers and toes as we came with . . . lying there in that tent shoulder to shoulder with my companions, the fear drains out of me. I'm feeling lucky again.'

The following year, 1991, saw another fine ascent of the mountain, erroneously hailed by some of the climbing press as a major new route climbed alpine-style in a very fast time. Christophe Profit and Pierre Béghin completed the Polish route crossing the North-West Ridge and finishing via the North Ridge. As already pointed out, the route barely touches the North-West Ridge which, apart from the abortive 1975 American attempt on the Towers above the Savoia Saddle, has never really been attempted. The route climbed by Profit and Béghin probably covered no new ground at all (the Japanese having climbed the north side the year before) and actually took weeks of effort before the final very swift ascent. Though it was a two-man ascent it was scarcely alpine-style, as the pair used many of the fixed ropes left by the British and Polish teams. Nevertheless it was a memorable effort by two talented and bold climbers and deserved more detailed and accurate reporting than it initially received. It got this in one of the last issues of *Mountain* in an article by the forty-year-old Béghin, who had also been a member of the French South-South-West Ridge team back in 1979.

Accompanied by two doctors as far as Base Camp, reached on 30 June, the pair spent six weeks acclimatising and establishing the route as far as the crest of the North-West Ridge just below 7000 metres. (At a Christophe Profit slide show in Poland I was able to recognise many bits of fixed rope and gear on stances that we had left in 1986.)

On 8 August they left their tent at 6900 metres in the middle of the night, but they had hardly made fifty metres of progress before stopping to assess the weather. It was still and warm and their altimeter was climbing steadily, a sure sign of a big depression moving in. They retreated to the tent and before dawn were suddenly hit by a violent storm pinning them down for a day before forcing a retreat.

> The summit seems an impossible dream. After forty days on the desolate ridge, we haven't managed to climb halfway . . . During the descent I work out that since July, this is our sixth climb to 7000 metres. Each time the weather had prevented us from going any further. Result: a certain weariness and quite a few kilos lost. This adventure has turned into a fight to see who gives in first. We give ourselves to the end of August . . . because as Christophe says, 'We're not going to spend the winter up here.'

On 14 August in better weather they got above 7000 metres and launched out for the top. It took ten hours to climb 1000 metres to the intersection with the North Ridge and they arrived at the Eagle's Nest Ledge, an improbable, flat, rocky platform overlooking the huge drop down to the K2 Glacier, where at 7900 metres they pitched a tiny two-man tent. Next morning they were away by seven a.m. (Pakistan time) and faced the traverse across the hanging glacier towards the summit couloir. Like Greg Child and his party the previous years they took a calculated risk. 'I take the lead. Each step makes a big impression and adds another dot to my tracks. It's mentally exhausting; I'm terrified that I'll see the snow tearing apart along the "dotted line".'

They fell behind schedule and didn't reach the far side until midday. Then it took six long hours to climb the summit couloir and almost two more hours to reach the summit. In the last flickers of twilight they at last looked down towards Concordia and the Baltoro. Sitting astride the summit ridge, Profit was photographed by Béghin. Way below in Concordia, 'at that very moment a group of French trekkers are admiring K2 in the setting sun: suddenly from fifteen kilometres away they catch sight of a series of flashing lights. No! Not extraterrestrials but the flash of our cameras; a few days later it was they who inform the Pakistani authorities of our success!'

The descent was as harrowing as Greg Child's had been and it was just before midnight when the exhausted couple made it to the comparative safety of their tent.

> We've come full circle, sixteen hours without food and almost nothing to drink. What an incredible journey! . . . What a privilege to be able to tackle the most impressive faces around, alone or just with a friend. This is the Golden Age of Himalayan mountaineering like it was in the Alps during the great Bonatti era. During the ten years I have been organising expeditions I have never been successful unless I have been climbing alone or in a pair . . . If, one day, I happen to feel nostalgic for those powerful moments of my past, I'll never regret the way I did it nor the sacrifices I made to live my passion.

Sad last words these, for Pierre Béghin was killed just over twelve months later when an anchor failed while he was abseiling on the South Face of Annapurna.

While the Béghin/Profit route was not by any normal criterion a first ascent, it was the first time since 1986 that the summit of K2 had been reached from a base in Pakistan. Once again there were no successes on the Abruzzi Spur and now five years had passed since the dreadful events on the Shoulder. At last, in 1992, the drought ended.

That year four expeditions went to K2 including (for the second attempt) Wojciech Kurtyka and Erhard Loretan who were ambitiously trying the West Face in pure alpine-style, though again without success. A Swiss expedition led by Peter Switter abandoned the attempt on the Abruzzi at 7400 metres but one of its members, the talented French woman Chantal Mauduit, stayed on with a Russian–American team. On 1 August Vladimir Balyberdin and the Ukrainian Gennadi Kopieda reached the top, the first to summit via the Abruzzi since Kurt Diemberger and Julie Tullis. Like them, they were forced to bivouac at 8400 metres on the descent, but theirs was endured without mishap and the pair made a safe return. Two days later Aleksei Nikiforov and the American Thor Kieser left Camp IV at five thirty a.m. Chantal Mauduit started at seven thirty and caught up with the pair at the Bottleneck and impressively led for the rest of the way, reaching the top at five thirty p.m. Kieser gave up, but Nikiforov eventually summited at seven thirty. Descending he found Mauduit bivouacking without a headtorch, rather than attempting to descend in the dark. Helped by the Russian's light, they descended safely to Camp IV, though Mauduit suffered some snow blindness. Chantal Mauduit thus became the fourth woman to climb K2 and, at the time of writing, is the only living female K2 summiteer.

Later in the month Americans Ed Viesturs, Scott Fischer and Charley Mace also reached the top but on the descent had to help in the rescue of New Zealander Gary Ball who developed pulmonary oedema in the Bottleneck. The evacuation was successful and Ball was helicoptered out from Base Camp. Gary Ball, who with Rob Hall had become their country's top Himalayan performers, died suddenly the following year on Dhaulagiri from pulmonary oedema. This time the rescue did not work and one cannot help but question the wisdom of returning to high altitude after such a clear warning. Even if the evidence isn't conclusive there have been so many cases of oedemas recurring that it seems common sense not to tempt fate. There is, after all, still a wealth of satisfying mountaineering to achieve without the problems of high altitude. The 1992 season on K2 did suffer one death, that of the Mexican Adrián Benitez who fell when an anchor failed on an abseil.

In 1993 the number of expeditions grew again with ten active up both sides of the mountain. A mainly Slovenian party led by Tomaz Jamnik put four members on the summit via the Abruzzi, including the Mexican Carlo Carsolio who had climbed Kangchenjunga the previous year when Wanda Rutkiewicz disappeared. On the way down they met a couple of fellow members at Camp IV. One of them, Bostjan Kekec, showed signs of altitude sickness and died on the descent. Another summiteer of their party, the Swede Goran Kropp, had a desperate descent culminating in a bivouac on the glacier only five hundred metres from Base Camp.

At the beginning of July a joint American–Canadian expedition climbed the Abruzzi, three members reaching the summit, but one, the Canadian Dan Culver, was killed on the descent while using a video camera above the Bottleneck. There were two British expeditions. The first was the strong team of Roger Payne, Julie-Ann Clyma, Alan Hinkes and Victor Saunders. They were attempting the Abruzzi but also overseeing an aid project: micro hydro-electricity installations in the villages of Mango and Hoto in conjunction with the Aga Khan Rural Support Programme. Despite fast progress on the ridge bad weather soon slowed things down and it was not until 27 July that it improved enough to start moving again. From a snow cave at Camp III below the Shoulder, instead of a summit bid the team was involved in the rescue of an exhausted and frostbitten Rafael Jensen, a Swede who had summited the previous day and had had a grim struggle to descend with his partner Daniel Bidner who was suffering cerebral oedema from which he eventually died. Two German climbers had also failed to make it back to Camp IV. Victor Saunders and Alan Hinkes brought Jensen down to Camp III and gave up their own summit bid, as did Roger Payne and Julie-Ann Clyma who had an epic descent the following day with Jansen when he and Payne were simultaneously abseiling on an old fixed rope that broke. 'Fortunately some quick footwork meant a serious fall was just averted' must be one of the better understatements from Roger Payne's pen. The weather was never good enough to mount another serious bid and when on 19 August they regained the snow cave at Camp III, they found it had been buried under two metres of fresh snow and the expedition was abandoned. As if they needed any further reminder of human frailty on the Savage Mountain, it was they who discovered the remains of Art Gilkey and Pasang Kitar just above Base Camp.

The other British team at Base Camp was led by the then almost unknown Jonathan Pratt. Pratt had climbed Everest (with oxygen) in 1992 and in the same year with his American partner Dan Mazur he had tried and failed on the Abruzzi Spur with the Mexican team. This time his ambitions were higher – the second ascent of the West Ridge. It was a rather controversial expedition from the outset, as Pratt failed to get the support of either the Mount Everest Foundation or the British Mountaineering Council which could normally be relied on to give some financial help. The reasons seemed to be that Pratt hadn't been able to attend the interview and had sent along someone unprepared for the grilling of an expert panel. Also Pratt was himself unknown and from the outset his chances of success didn't seem high. Consequently, as Pratt wrote blandly in a later article, under the heading *Cost*: 'Expenditure: £44,000. Sponsorship and Grants: 0.' But the expedition did have some 'paying guests', an increasing trend in big Himalayan climbs where funding is raised by bringing trekkers to Base Camp, or actually guiding clients on the mountain.

It was greatly to his credit that Jonathan Pratt got it together to reach Base Camp only eleven days after arriving in Pakistan. Camped under the Gilkey Memorial as most British teams have done, the progress to the West Ridge and on to it was equally speedy and by 8 July Camp III at 7100 metres had been established. But it couldn't last and a long storm forced the team back to Base Camp and in Pratt's words, 'We elected for a change of strategy – we got organised.' Over the next month not much progress was made and the French climber Etienne Fine suffered two attacks of pulmonary oedema, the second involving a horrendous all-night rescue retreat. Miraculously, Fine was able to help himself down the worst parts (aided it must be said by a painful jab in his nether regions using an empty syringe) but he later lost all his toes through frostbite after a helicopter rescue to Skardu.

Their lack of progress called for another change of strategy: 'When the expedition was in chaos we had advanced 1700 metres in seven days. When we had organised siege tactics we advanced two hundred metres in thirty days. We voted for chaos.' After Fine's rescue, news of events on the Abruzzi Spur began to influence the team in very much the same way as the multiple deaths in 1986 had affected the British North-West Ridge team. Like us, Pratt's team was initially somewhat insulated from the tragedies through being physically removed from the Abruzzi area, but it was hard to ignore that virtually every summit bid had ended with a death. Dispirited, the team left one by one for home. In the end only Dan Mazur and Jonathan Pratt were left after a spirited bid had petered out in a storm at 8200 metres. When it cleared they were lured back for one last effort, before they had really recovered from their previous attempt. They decided to adopt 'continuous climbing' day and night until they reached the top. After thirty-six hours they reached Camp IV on 30 August and, deciding that 'continuous climbing' wasn't all that wonderful, they stopped for the night. The weather deteriorated over the next two days but not enough to stop climbing. At three in the morning of 2 September Pratt and Mazur started preparations for what would be a very long day. At seven a.m. they left in gentle snow and cloud and made reasonable progress to the junction with the Magic Line at 8300 metres, where they met a vicious wind.

All the way the team had found evidence of the first ascent by the Japanese in 1981 in the form of old ropes and wrecked tents. But now they were faced with a blank wall ten metres high leading to a narrow chimney. Mazur precariously aided his way to the chimney, which wasn't as hard as it looked, and the two progressed slowly up more broken rock and powdery snow. The summit occasionally appeared through drifting cloud still three hundred metres above. The unspoken decision was taken to climb through the night, using the dubious logic that as the weather was deteriorating it was safer to carry on than bivouac.

As night fell they stopped in the shelter of an overhanging boulder at 8550 metres for a rest. Totally committed, they pressed on, leaving their sacks, and gained the comparatively easy summit ridge through swirling clouds and in almost total darkness. They turned five or six false summits before realising at eleven p.m. that they could see ridges dropping away in all directions. Any elation at standing on the second highest spot on earth was dispelled by the wind and cold and the knowledge that Pratt had forgotten his camera! They made a rapid descent to the boulder and managed to brew tea and sleep for an hour – easily the highest 'bivouac', if it can be so described, suffered on K2. At two thirty they started down, regaining the top of the blank wall at six thirty and radioing their success to their patient liaison officer at Base Camp. It took them until three p.m. to regain their top camp – thirty-two hours since their departure! Shattered, but amazingly suffering no frostbite, it took another three days to reach Base Camp and for Jonathan Pratt to become the first Briton to complete a successful ascent of K2, Al Rouse and Julie Tullis having died on the descent. Indeed, the pair knew all too well that this year five people had already been killed descending K2. They reached their Base Camp to discover it had been virtually demolished by a sérac fall. In 1986 we too had had a narrow escape and considerable doubt must now be voiced as to the safety of the British Base Camp position below the Gilkey Memorial.

Sadly, what had been a major success by Jonathan Pratt and Daniel Mazur was greeted with some scepticism in England by people unconvinced that two comparative unknowns could pull off such a coup. However, their highest photographs, looking down to the Shoulder from high on the South-South-West Pillar, and from the top of the Pillar itself at 8300 metres, show beyond any doubt that they had overcome all the major difficulties of the route and only the most churlish sceptic could persist in doubting their story.

A postscript to 1993. Three Canadians, Barry Blanchard, Troy Kirwan and Peter Arbic climbed the Kukuczka–Piotrowski line on the South Face, exiting below and to the right of the original finish, quite possibly by the route Wiessner nearly completed. But the Canadians did not visit the summit and descended safely.

Which brings us to 1994, the fortieth anniversary of the first ascent by Compagnoni and Lacedelli. No less than twelve expeditions came to K2, nine to the Pakistan side and three from China. Once again the large numbers on the mountain would contribute to an ever-increasing death toll.

The year started with success and the completion of a route already attempted and claimed. The South-South-East Spur, first attempted by Doug Scott's team in 1983 and then climbed again by Tomo Česen and a Spanish expedition in 1987 (both as far as the Shoulder), was finally ascended to the top, via the Shoulder and Bottleneck. It was a Basque team led by Juan Oiarzabal who made a conventional fixed-rope ascent of the Spur (a retrograde step one must state, after the good style of Scott and Česen) and finally put six members on the top on 22 June. Using fixed rope, the Basques felt that their route was technically easier than the Abruzzi Spur. With no House's Chimney or Black Pyramid to contend with, they found the Bottleneck the hardest part of the climb. Eventually, it could possibly supersede the Abruzzi as the *voie normale* on K2, which would be a strange development. It might well reduce the sheer volume of traffic on the Abruzzi, but could simply make just another long line of old ropes and abandoned gear as far as the Shoulder.

Several other expeditions availed themselves of this route to the Shoulder and on 9 July a varied mixture of climbers left for the summit. New Zealander Rob Hall (who had retreated with Gary Ball from the Bottleneck two years earlier) was on oxygen (by now a rather unusual aid on K2) and was the only one to make the summit. Others, including the famous Pole Krzysztof Wielicki, gave up just below the summit, apparently not realising how near to the top they were. Their subsequent chagrin can only be imagined.

Two days later a Ukrainian expedition met with disaster. Dimitri Ibragimzade, Alexsei Kharaidin and Aleksandr Parkhomenko left the Shoulder and were not seen again. Two weeks later two bodies were found bivouacked at 8400 metres and part of a third body lower down. Whether or not any, or all three, reached the summit and perished on the descent is not known, though it seems most unlikely that they would bivouac on their way up and the probability must be that they were descending having reached the top.

On 23 July five more climbers stood on the summit of K2: Ralf Dujmovits, Veikka Gustafsson, Axel Schlonvogt, Michl Warthl and the Australian Michael Groom. On the descent Groom was low on the mountain and struggling. Steve Untsch, an experienced American climber, started descending from Camp II to assist him and met a Korean slowly ascending the fixed rope. Untsch changed to an old rope and started to abseil. The rope broke and Untsch was killed. None of the other Pakistan-based expeditions succeeded and there were mixed fortunes for the three expeditions based on the Chinese side.

The first, an Anglo–American expedition, featured the Burgess twins, Al and Aid, Alan Hinkes, Brad Johnson, Paul Moores and Mark Wilford. They were going for the North Ridge which in a normal year is a relatively safe route, at least up to 8000 metres. This year however there was that all too rare phenomenon, a long sustained spell of clear weather, which ironically makes the whole route extremely dangerous with stonefall and wet snow avalanches. Ropes were chopped and ice anchors melted. Alan Hinkes did make one abortive summit bid which was abandoned due to extreme avalanche danger in the traverse of the snow basin at 8100 metres. But it was a strange 'first' to claim – failure due to good weather! The one successful ascent was by a Basque team who put two members on the summit later on 4 August. Atxo Apellanitz and Juanjo San Sebastián bivouacked just below the top and next morning San Sebastián was avalanched four hundred metres, luckily stopping just above the point where a snowfield takes a huge plunge down the North Face. Unhurt, he could still communicate with Apellanitz high above, who was developing cerebral oedema. Both suffered a second bivouac but eventually Apellanitz regained Camp IV. At Camp III they were met by a two-man rescue party who brought them down to the comparative safety of Camp II at 6900 metres. But a storm kept them there for twenty-four hours and on 11 August Apellanitz died. San Sebastián later lost parts of seven fingers from frostbite.

Finally, and appropriately, an Italian expedition was trying to commemorate the fortieth anniversary of the first ascent by making a new direct finish to the North Ridge. Sadly, they failed only 150 metres from its summit. 1994 was the first year when the mountain was climbed from both sides and by the end of the season the total number of ascents stood at 113. The mountain has now claimed thirty-eight lives in the process, a figure that is worth pondering on by any future would-be ascensionists.

17

What Next?

Succeeding years on K2 will produce a fresh crop of stories of endeavour, success, failure and, I fear, yet more tragedy, if the volume of expeditions continues. There are signs, though, that only six expeditions a year are going to be allowed on K2 from Pakistan. Inevitably, the Abruzzi Spur will receive a high proportion of those seeking to climb the mountain to add to their tick list of 8000-metre peaks. I just hope that whatever routes are attempted they will be done in good style. I can accept that, for many climbers, fixed-rope ascents will still be the accepted way to tackle the mountain, and I have sympathy with the view that pure alpine-style ascents of K2 and other 8000-metre peaks are still terribly dangerous, but surely the days of the colossal caravans of six hundred plus porters and twenty or so climbers must be over? What possible value can there now be in using a sledgehammer to crack a nut? Though it is extremely unlikely to happen, given the financial interest at stake, it would be a major step in the right direction if the Himalayan authorities (not just the Pakistan Ministry of Tourism) could recommend a *maximum* number of climbers for each popular route or mountain, even if it could not be enforced. But I find it hard to understand why climbers themselves cannot see the pointlessness of such extravaganzas.

What is there left to do on K2? The mountain is still not at the evolutionary stage of Everest which has been climbed by almost every ridge, gully, buttress and face – and variations thereof. Most of the main ridges of K2 still await a direct ascent – the routes achieved on the West, North-West, and North-East Ridges all deviate significantly and straightening any one of these would be a major achievement. Though the mountain has been ascended by one ridge and descended by another (the South-South-West and the Abruzzi in 1976), nobody has attempted a genuine traverse. Though the most obvious, the North Ridge and the Abruzzi, would seem to be politically impossible, the future challenge of, for instance, climbing up the North-East Ridge and down the West Ridge, is not so outrageous as it might have seemed only a few years ago. As well as the 'direct' ridges, neither the West, nor the North, nor the East Faces have been climbed and between the North-West and West Ridges is the huge black Barrel Buttress that throws out a challenge to a future generation. So there is no shortage of objectives and some, maybe most, will undoubtedly succumb in the next few years, as long as the mountain remains open from both sides.

After that one can only guess. Smaller teams and less environmental impact are desirable, but surely a criterion of success should now be the safe return of all team members. However you analyse the statistics, thirty-eight deaths set against 113 ascents makes grim reading. Is it inevitable – a simple statistical probability – or can climbers do something about it? Is there now so much commercial gain and self-interest around the climbing world that mountaineers value their lives less highly than they did, say, in Charlie Houston's day? I do not know the answers to these questions but I can only repeat my plea that the lessons of the past are taken on board. Too many people still go to very high altitude without fully understanding the risk they are taking, or by persuading themselves that they are somehow immune from them. Talking recently to a small team attempting a peak in Karakoram, they told me with some pride that words like 'failure' and 'retreat' were not part of their vocabulary; to which I replied that words like 'corpse' and 'memorial service' might not be part of their friends' and relatives' vocabularies, but could soon be. The greatest climbers such as Houston, Messner, Bonatti, Bonington and Scott have all known when to back off and are still around to prove it.

Recently, peaks like Broad Peak, Gasherbrum II, Shishapangma, Cho Oyu and even Everest, have had guided ascents. These are out of reach to all but very wealthy clients but the numbers are increasing. Though I see nothing intrinsically wrong with this (the tradition of guided climbing being as old as Alpinism itself), I have doubts about the wisdom of doing this on the highest and hardest peaks. For if anything goes wrong you have to be able to extricate yourself without relying on others. On K2, of all mountains, there is no way a guide could fulfil his traditional role of assuming responsibility for his client. I sincerely hope that the trend does not get out of hand, and I would have little sympathy if it happens on K2.

Curiously, a speed ascent of K2 like that by Benoît Chamoux in 1986 has not been repeated. Chamoux climbed Nanga Parbat by the Diamir Face in a day the following year, a feat he considered much harder and more committing than his K2 climb. Apart from a few speed ascents of Everest it seems to be a trend that has not led anywhere, beyond underlining the general desirability of climbing quickly and efficiently at high altitude. But in the Alps, climbing times *have* become an important, overtly competitive part of the scene and it may be that the achievements of Benoît Chamoux on K2 or Marc Batard on Everest are simply the precursors of things to come.

Without doubt the most remarkable effort on K2 in 1986 was the near solo of the Magic Line by Renato Casarotto. If he had succeeded it would have been the first genuine solo of K2 and by a new route as well. (Benoît Chamoux's twenty-three-hour ascent was a solo of sorts but it was done with such heavy and systematic back-up from his quite large team that I don't think it can count – nor do I think that Chamoux himself saw it as such.) So the possibility of the first genuine solo ascent remains. It would be an impressive achievement by any route.

K2 has already been jumped off by Jean-Marc Boivin and a parapente descent from or near the summit will surely happen. A ski descent will doubtless be contrived, though it is hard to see how the mixed rock, ice and snow that makes up so much of K2 could ever really offer a desirable, let alone enjoyable, experience. But, mercifully, K2 has always been free of gimmicks and stunts, unlike Everest, and I hope it stays that way.

It is now 138 years since Montgomerie first gave the surveyor's mark to the distant sky-piercing triangle. Ninety-eight years passed before it was climbed and now it is forty years since Compagnoni and Lacedelli gasped the last few metres to the summit. Since then interest in the mountain has steadily increased and the Mountain of Mountains, the Savage Mountain, has become a household name along with Everest, the Matterhorn, and the Eiger. Its story is far from over and as long as climbers arrive at Concordia or the K2 Glacier and see that giant crystal form with its plume of driven snow blasting into the dark vault of sky on the edge of space, the legends will continue to unfold with all their attendant human strengths and weaknesses. May all who challenge the Savage Mountain return safely to tell their tales.

Appendix I

A Complete List of Expeditions to K2 down to 1994

(expanded from *The Endless Knot* by courtesy of Kurt Diemberger)

YEAR	EXPEDITION	LEADER	ROUTE (SE = Abruzzi Spur)	REMARKS
1272–4	Italian			Marco Polo's journey to China brought him into the vicinity of the Karakoram.
1835–8	British			G. T. Vigne visited Kashmir, Ladakh and Baltistan; in 1835 from Skardu he reached the snout of the Chogo Lungma Glacier.
1856	German	Adolf Schlagintweit		Schlagintweit was probably the first non-local to get close to the Baltoro area and to reach one – the western – of the Mustagh Passes (Panmah Pass).
1856	British	T. G. Montgomerie		In the course of mapping the Karakoram, Montgomerie was the first to employ the name 'K2'; from Haramukh (5142m) in Kashmir (about 200km from K2) he numbered the Karakoram summits on a sketch in his survey-log: K1, K2, K3, etc., and remarked that K2 seemed to be the highest. During the next two years the surveyor G. Shelverton, from observations from Kashmir, computed the height of K2 and announced it as the second highest peak in the world. It was later fixed at 28,250ft (8611m).

YEAR	EXPEDITION	LEADER	ROUTE (SE = Abruzzi Spur)	REMARKS
1861	British	H. H. Godwin-Austen		Godwin-Austen saw the summit pyramid of K2, 27km distant, from a point 600m above Urdokas on the Baltoro Glacier, and made what has become a celebrated sketch; previously he had been within 15km of Concordia. It was proposed that K2 be named after him. He made the first (1:500,000) map of the Karakoram.
1887	British	Francis Younghusband		Younghusband crossed the Karakoram mountains from China with a small group of porters; he discovered the Shaksgam valley and passed close to K2 (he was the first European to see it from the north), crossing the Old Mustagh Pass to reach the Baltoro Glacier.
1885-9	Polish	Captain B. Grombczewski		Younghusband's opposite number in the Great Game, a Pole in the service of the Tsar, travelled widely in the Kashgar mountains and, independently of the British, discovered K2 from the Shaksgam side.
1890	Italian	Roberto Lerco		He made the first reconnaissance of K2 (between May and October); also explorations around the Hunza valley (see *Rivista Mensile* 1954). He might just have been the first person to set foot on K2.
1892	British	William Martin Conway		An expedition with scientific and mountaineering objectives, and the first to penetrate the full length of the Baltoro Glacier. (Conway gave the enormous glacier junction its name Concordia, being reminded of the Place de la Concorde in Paris.) First ascent of Pioneer Peak (6890m) on Baltoro Kangri – a world altitude record at the time; valuable topographical work (Baltoro map), six

YEAR	EXPEDITION	LEADER	ROUTE (SE = Abruzzi Spur)	REMARKS
				'explorers' (climber/scientists), an ornithologist, four Gurkha soldiers.
1902	International	Oscar Eckenstein	NE Ridge	Climbing attempt on North-East Ridge to 6525m; six climbers – amongst them the notorious Aleister Crowley and the Austrian mountaineers Heinrich Pfannl and Victor Wesseley.
1909	Italian	Luigi Amedeo di Savoia, Duke of the Abruzzi	SE	Exploration and attempt on K2's 'feasible' route, the Abruzzi Ridge or Spur to a height of 6250m; twelve climbers.
1929	Italian	Prince Aimone di Savoia, Duke of Spoleto	(S; N)	Mountaineering attempt renounced in favour of important geographic and geological studies. Professor Ardito Desio took part as a geologist, exploring the Shaksgam valley with three other members; on the Baltoro side his explorations included reaching the 'Possible Saddle' described by Conway, between the Baltoro and the Siachen Glaciers (he named it after its discoverer).
1937	British	Eric Shipton	(N)	Exploration, scientific and topographical survey work, as well as climbs to the north of K2 in the region of several large glaciers and in the Shaksgam (E. Shipton, H. W. Tilman, J. Auden, M. Spender and seven Sherpas).
1938	American	Charles S. Houston	SE	First concerted attempt to climb the Abruzzi Spur; seven high camps erected and an altitude of 7925m attained (six climbers).
1939	American	Fritz Wiessner	SE	A push to 8382m – without artificial oxygen. Nine high camps. During the final retreat, despite a rescue attempt,

YEAR	EXPEDITION	LEADER	ROUTE (SE = Abruzzi Spur)	REMARKS
				the American, Dudley Wolfe, and three Sherpas perished. (Members: six climbers.)
1953	American	Charles S. Houston	SE	Eight high camps erected and a height of 7900m reached. A desperate bid to save the sick Art Gilkey failed and he was lost in an avalanche shortly after Pete Schoening astonishingly checked a mass fall. The Gilkey Memorial was erected below Base Camp. (Eight climbers.)
1953	Italian	Riccardo Cassin	SE	Reconnaissance expedition prior to 1954 attempt; Cassin and Desio went to the foot of the Abruzzi Spur (September).
1954	Italian	Ardito Desio	SE	*First ascent of K2.* Nine high camps. Fixed ropes and oxygen apparatus employed. On 31 July at about 18.00 hours Lino Lacedelli and Achille Compagnoni reached the summit, although their oxygen had run out a short while before. Eleven climbers; Mario Puchoz died of pneumonia.
1960	German/American	W. D. Hackett	SE	Bad weather made it impossible to surmount the 'Black Pyramid', a difficult and steep section of the Abruzzi Spur. (Seven climbers.)
1975	American	James Whittaker	NW	A new route, attempted from the Savoia Saddle; highest point reached – 6700m. Dianne Roberts became the first female mountaineer on K2. (Ten members.)
1976	Polish	Janusz Kurczab	NE	The Poles surmounted the difficult North-East Ridge; an attempt on the summit pyramid by Chrobak and Wróz reached 8400m before insufficient oxygen reserves forced a

YEAR	EXPEDITION	LEADER	ROUTE (SE = Abruzzi Spur)	REMARKS
				retreat. This route had originally been attempted in 1902. (Nineteen members.)
1976	Japanese	Takayoshi Takatsuka	SE	Reconnaissance. On 7 August three climbers attained 7160m on the Abruzzi Spur. (Six members.)
1977	Japanese	Ichiro Yoshizawa	SE	*Second ascent of K2.* Mammoth expedition: fifty-two members, 1,500 porters. Six Japanese and a Pakistani reached the summit on 8 and 9 August. A 35mm expedition film was made. Oxygen used. At seventy-three years of age, I. Yoshizawa was the oldest person to reach the foot of K2.
1978	British	Chris Bonington	W	First attempt on West Ridge (to 6700m) abandoned on the death of Nick Estcourt in an avalanche. (Eight members.)
1978	American	James Whittaker	NE/SE	*Third ascent of K2.* The Polish NE Ridge route was followed to a height of 7700m, then an oblique traverse made to the normal route. Four climbers reached the summit on 6 and 7 September – with little or no use of oxygen. (Fourteen members, amongst them three women.)
1979	French	Bernard Mellet	SSW	South-South-West Ridge attempted by massive expedition with 30 tons of equipment. One of the steepest and most difficult ridges on the mountain: five summit thrusts were made. Succeeded in reaching 8400m. (Fourteen climbers; death of one high-altitude porter.)
1979	International	Reinhold Messner	ML/SE	*Fourth ascent of K2.* Reinhold Messner and Michl Dacher gained the summit without using bottled oxygen on 12 July via the Abruzzi Spur. Four high camps. An attempt on

YEAR	EXPEDITION	LEADER	ROUTE (SE = Abruzzi Spur)	REMARKS
1980	British	Peter Boardman	W/SE	Reinhold Messner's projected 'Magic Line', the original objective of this expedition, was earlier abandoned. (Seven members; one porter killed falling into a crevasse.) After an attempt on the West Ridge to 7000m, 7900m was reached on the Abruzzi. (Four climbers.)
1981	Japanese	Teruoh Matsuura	W	*Fifth ascent of K2* (and first via the West Ridge). On 7 August one Japanese and one Pakistani stood on the summit. Oxygen employed.
1981	French/German	Yannick Seigneur	S	Attempt on a new route (on the South Face); 7400m reached. (Four climbers.)
1982	Polish	Janusz Kurczab	NW	Attempt to force a new route without touching the Savoia Saddle; 8200m finally gained on the Chinese side, where they were observed and ordered back! 3500m of fixed rope employed. (Twenty-one climbers: fifteen Poles and six Mexicans.)
1982	Japanese	Isaoh Shinkai	N	*Sixth ascent of K2*, and first from the Chinese side via North Ridge. Seven climbers reached summit on 14 and 15 August (a fatal fall during descent). No oxygen. (Fourteen climbers.)
1982	Austrian	(Hans Schell) Georg Bachler	SE	7500m reached, and further attempts abandoned to help in the evacuation of dead Polish woman climber. Bachler was the effective leader since Schell remained in Austria! (Four members.)
1982	Polish	Wanda Rutkiewicz	SE	Polish women's expedition: death of Halina Krüger; they

YEAR	EXPEDITION	LEADER	ROUTE (SE = Abruzzi Spur)	REMARKS
1983	Spanish	Antonio Trabado		reached 7100m. (Eleven women climbers, including one French, Christine de Colombel.)
1983	International	Doug Scott	W	A height of 8200m reached via West Ridge and West Face. (Juanjo San Sebastián and A. Trabado.)
1983	Spanish (Navarre)	Gregorio Ariz	S	An attempt on a rib to the left of the Abruzzi reached 7500m. (Three Britons, including R. Baxter-Jones, and one Frenchman, J. Afanassieff.)
1983	Italian	Francesco Santon	SE	Mari Abrego and Roger Baxter-Jones – after their respective expeditions had given up – reached a height of 8300m before bad weather turned them back. (Earlier the nine-person Navarre team had been to 7700m.)
1984	International	Stefan Wörner	N	*Seventh ascent of K2* (and second via the North Ridge). Summit reached by four members (three Italians, one Czech) on 31 July and 4 August, climbing without oxygen. Julie Tullis became the 'highest woman' on K2. (Twenty-three members in all.)
1985	Swiss	Erhard Loretan	SE	7500m reached.
1985	French	Eric Escoffier	SE	Five climbers reached the summit on two separate days. No oxygen.
1985	Japanese	Kazuoh Tobita	SE	Three climbers reached summit. Daniel Lacroix lost during the descent. No oxygen.
			SE	Three Japanese reached summit – probably without oxygen.

YEAR	EXPEDITION	LEADER	ROUTE (SE = Abruzzi Spur)	REMARKS
1985	International	Voytek Kurtyka	SE	Attempt foundered at 7000m. (With R. Schauer after climbing West Face of Gasherbrum IV.)
1986	Italian/Basque	Renato Casarotto	SE/SSW	Mari Abrego and Josema Casimiro: summit reached by Abruzzi Spur. Renato Casarotto died in a fall into a crevasse after attempting the SSW Ridge.
1986	French	Maurice Barrard	SE	Summit reached by all four members, Wanda Rutkiewicz and Liliane Barrard becoming the first women to climb K2. The Barrards, husband and wife, were lost during the descent.
1986	British	Alan Rouse/John Barry	NW/SE	Attempted NW Ridge to 7400m; Alan Rouse died after reaching summit via Abruzzi Spur. (Eleven members.)
1986	American	John Smolich	SSW	After Smolich and Pennington killed by avalanche, attempt abandoned. (Eight climbers.)
1986	Italian/ International	Agostino Da Polenza	SSW/SE	Eight members reached summit by Abruzzi Spur. Julie Tullis died during the descent. The attempt on the SSW Ridge was given up because of avalanche danger.
1986	International	Karl Herrligkoffer	S/SE	Two Swiss reached summit by Abruzzi Spur; two Poles made first ascent of South Face (Kukuczka route); death of Piotrowski during descent. (Sixteen members in all.)
1986	Austrian	Alfred Imitzer	SE	Two climbers to the summit, two deaths during the descent (Imitzer and H. Wieser); seven climbers altogether.
1986	South Korean	Kim Byung-Joon	SE	Three climbers to summit, using oxygen. Death of sirdar in stonefall. (Nineteen members in all.)
1986	Polish	Janusz Majer	SSW/SE	First ascent of SSW Ridge; death of W. Wróz during

YEAR	EXPEDITION	LEADER	ROUTE (SE = Abruzzi Spur)	REMARKS
				descent. 'Mrufka' Dobroslawa Wolf died during descent after attempt on Abruzzi. (Eight members, including three women.)
1986	American	Lance Owens	N	Attempt on N Ridge to a height of 8100m (eight climbers).
1986	Yugoslav	Viki Grošelj	S	Tomo Česen soloed new route to left of Abruzzi Spur, as far as the Shoulder, 7800m.
1987	International	Doug Scott	E	Attempts on East Face abandoned due to constant bad weather.
1987	French	Martine Rolland	SE	Attempt to 7000m. (Six members.)
1987	Polish/Swiss	Voytek Kurtyka	W	Attempt on West Face with Jean Troillet to 6400m.
1987	Japanese	Haruyuki Endo	SE	Attempt to 7400m.
1987	Japanese/Pakistani	Kenshiro Otaki	SE	Attempt to 8300m; one Japanese killed in a fall. (Fourteen members.)
1987	Spanish (Basque)	Juanjo San Sebastián	S	Climbed the rib to the left of the Abruzzi as far as the Shoulder, then the normal route to 8300m. (Seven climbers, plus a sirdar.)
1987–8	Polish/International	Andrzej Zawada	SE	Winter attempt on Abruzzi Spur to 7350m. (Twenty climbers.)
1988	Yugoslav	Tomaz Jamnik	SSW	Attempt to 8100m, then Abruzzi Spur to 7400m. (Fifteen members.)
1988	American	Peter Athans	SE	Attempt to 7400m. (Five members.)
1988	New Zealand	Rob Hall	SE	Attempt to 7400m. (Four members.)

YEAR	EXPEDITION	LEADER	ROUTE (SE = Abruzzi Spur)	REMARKS
1988	Spanish (Catalan)	Jordi Magriñá	SE	Attempt to 8100m. (Twelve members.)
1988	French	Pierre Béghin	N	Attempt on North Spur to 8000m. (Six members and a doctor.)
1989	Polish/Swiss	Voytek Kurtyka	NW	An attempt to open new route on NW Face couldn't get started on account of bad weather (with Jean Troillet and Erhard Loretan).
1989	Austrian	Eduard Koblmüller	E/SE	An attempt on the hitherto unclimbed East Face reached 7200m. Death of one member. An attempt on the Abruzzi Spur ended at 7000m. (Seven members.)
1989	Spanish (Basque)	Juanjo San Sebastián	SE	Attempt to 7400m. (Eleven members.)
1990	American	Doug Dalquist	SE	Reached 7600m on the Abruzzi Spur. At the end of July, they gave up further attempts due to excessive soft snow.
1990	International	C. A. Pinelli	SE	'Free K2' international cleaning expedition organized by Mountain Wilderness. No summit attempts were contemplated since they gave a specific commitment to the Pakistani authorities not to proceed beyond the Shoulder. (Nine members.)
1990	Australian/ American	Steve Swenson	N	A small expedition of four attempted the North Spur. Three climbers reached the summit on 20 August at eight p.m.
1990	Japanese	Tomoji Ueki	N	Attempt of a new route (NW Face and N Spur). Two climbers reached the summit on 9 August from the Chinese side. (Twelve members and eight Chinese helpers.)

YEAR	EXPEDITION	LEADER	ROUTE (SE = Abruzzi Spur)	REMARKS
1991	French	Pierre Béghin/ Christophe Profit	NW/N	Two-man ascent crossing NW Spur to N Face (a completion of Polish route).
1991	German	Sigi Hupfauer	SE	Attempt on Abruzzi Spur turned back at the Shoulder. (Seven members.)
1991	New Zealand	Robert Hall/Gary Ball	SE	Two-man attempt on Abruzzi Spur reached edge of Shoulder at 7600m.
1991	Italian	Fabio Agnostinis	N	Six-man team attained bivouac at 8200m on N Ridge before being beaten back by storms.
1992	Swiss	Peter Schwitter	SE	Four men and a Frenchwoman, Chantal Mauduit, failed at 7400m on Abruzzi Spur.
1992	Russian/American	Vladimir Balyberdin	SE	Expedition of sixteen put six members and 'one other' on summit via Abruzzi Spur. The other was Chantal Mauduit (French, see above.)
1992	International	Ricardo Torres	SE	Ten members (Mexican, Swedish, New Zealand) laid lengthy siege to the Abruzzi Spur in co-operation with Russian/American team (above); high point was 8300m in Bottleneck, where Gary Ball was taken sick. Earlier, Adrian Benitez had been killed in rapel fall.
1992	Swiss/Polish	Erhard Loretan/ Voytek Kurtyka	W	Two-man W Face attempt alpine-style abandoned on account avalanche danger.
1993	Slovenian/ International	Tomaz Jamnik	SE	Eight Slovenes and one each Croat, Mexican, Swede and Briton put five on summit, but Bostjan Kekec died during epic descent.
1993	American/Canadian	Stacy Allison	SE	Seven-person team saw Philip Powers, then Jim Haberl

YEAR	EXPEDITION	LEADER	ROUTE (SE = Abruzzi Spur)	REMARKS
				and Dan Culver on summit, on 7 July. Culver was lost in fall during descent.
1993	International	Reinmar Joswig	SE	Five-man (German/Kirgiz/Australian) team was joined on mountain by two Swedes. Six reached summit on 30 July, but three were killed during night descent in separate falls (Mezger, Joswig, Bidner.) The survivors were assisted down by other teams.
1993	Swedish	Magnus Nilsson	SE	Rafael Jensen and Daniel Bidner attached themselves to Joswig's team (above) for summit climb. Bidner was one of those killed.
1993	British	Roger Payne	SE	Five-person team reached Shoulder, then helped the frostbitten Jensen of Swedish expedition (above). Grim relics were found of Art Gilkey (lost 1953) and Pasang Kitar Sherpa (who disappeared in 1939.)
1993	Canadian	Barry Blanchard	SSW, S	Three-man team climbed to above Negrotto Col, then switched to S Face route before traversng to join Abruzzi. The Shoulder reached before joining in rescue of Jensen (see above.)
1993	Spanish	Josep Aced	SSE	Eight climbers of this twelve-man team turned back at 7200m, below the Shoulder.
1993	International	Wim Van Harskamp	SE?	Six-man team was stopped at 7400m by poor weather.
1993	International	Jonathan Pratt/ Daniel Mazur	W	Second ascent of the W Ridge by the two leaders of this twelve-man team. (Summit reached 2 September.)

YEAR	EXPEDITION	LEADER	ROUTE (SE = Abruzzi Spur)	REMARKS
1993	Spanish (Basque)	Joseba Urkia	N	Summit bid foundered in deep snow around 8000m. (Six-man team.)
1993	International	Vladimir Balyberdin	N	Seven-person team attempted N Ridge to reach high point of 6800m.
1994	American/British	Adrian Burgess	N	Summit attempt by A. Hinkes (climbing with two Basques, above) foundered in deep snow around 8100m.
1994	Spanish (Basque)	José Carlos Tamayo	N	After their attempt on N Ridge with Hinkes (above), Basques returned to the attack and successfully got two pairs to summit (30 July, 4 August).
1994	Italian	Arturo Bergamaschi	N	Attempt on direct finish to Japanese route beaten by technical difficulties at nearly 8500m.
1994	Spanish (Basque)	Juanito Oiarzabal	SSE/SE	Five of six members made (fixed rope) ascent, reaching summit on 22 June. They claim it an easier option than following Abruzzi all the way.
1994	International	Dave Bridges	NW/SSE	Original objective quickly abandoned in favour of SSE Spur. M. Groom reached summit; S. Untsch killed when fixed rope broke.
1994	American/Polish	Carlos Buhler/ V. Kurtyka/ K. Wielicki	W/SSE	Three-man team attempting W Face from the south turned attention to SSE Spur, along with other climbers. Wielicki reached summit ridge before turning back.
1994	International	Ralf Dujmovits	SE	Commercially organised ten-man expedition: Rob Hall to summit on 9 July (using oxygen); followed by four more on 23 July (accompanied by Groom, see above.)

YEAR	EXPEDITION	LEADER	ROUTE (SE = Abruzzi Spur)	REMARKS
1994	Ukrainian	Vadim Sviridenko	SE	First summit party of three failed to return, 10 July. Bodies were later discovered at or near bivouac site around 8400m. Two others reached summit fortnight later.
1994	Spanish (Catalan)	Angel Rifa	SE	Unsuccessful.
1994	Korean	Kin In-Tae	SE	Unsuccessful.
1994	Japanese	Yurifumi Konishi	SE	Unsuccessful.

Appendix II

A Complete List of Ascents of K2 down to 1994

(originally compiled by Xavier Eguskitza for *The Endless Knot* by Kurt Diemberger)

No.	Name	Nationality	Date	Route	Expedition	Leader
1	Achille Compagnoni	Italian	31.7.54	Abruzzi Spur	Italian	Ardito Desio
2	Lino Lacedelli	Italian	31.7.54	Abruzzi Spur	Italian	Ardito Desio
3	Shoji Nakamura	Japanese	8.8.77	Abruzzi Spur	Japanese	Ichiro Yoshizawa
4	Tsuneoh Shigehiro	Japanese	8.8.77	Abruzzi Spur	Japanese	Ichiro Yoshizawa
5	Takeyoshi Takatsuka	Japanese	8.8.77	Abruzzi Spur	Japanese	Ichiro Yoshizawa
6	Mitsuo Hiroshima	Japanese	9.8.77	Abruzzi Spur	Japanese	Ichiro Yoshizawa
7	Masahide Onodera	Japanese	9.8.77	Abruzzi Spur	Japanese	Ichiro Yoshizawa
8	Hideo Yamamoto	Japanese	9.8.77	Abruzzi Spur	Japanese	Ichiro Yoshizawa
9	Ashraf Aman	Pakistani	9.8.77	Abruzzi Spur	Japanese	Ichiro Yoshizawa
10	James Wickwire	American	6.9.78	NE Ridge/Abruzzi Spur	American	James Whittaker
11	Louis Reichardt	American	6.9.78	NE Ridge/Abruzzi Spur	American	James Whittaker
12	John Roskelley	American	7.9.78	NE Ridge/Abruzzi Spur	American	James Whittaker
13	Rick Ridgeway	American	7.9.78	NE Ridge/Abruzzi Spur	American	James Whittaker
14	Reinhold Messner	Italian	12.7.79	Abruzzi Spur	European	Reinhold Messner

No.	Name	Nationality	Date	Route	Expedition	Leader
15	Michl Dacher	W. German	12.7.79	Abruzzi Spur	European	Reinhold Messner
16	Eiho Ohtani	Japanese	7.8.81	West Ridge/SW side	Japanese	Teruoh Matsuura
17	Nazir Sabir	Pakistani	7.8.81	West Ridge/SW side	Japanese	Teruoh Matsuura
18	Naoé Sakashita	Japanese	14.8.82	North Ridge	Japanese	Isao Shinkai
19	Yukihiro Yanagisawa	Japanese	14.8.82	North Ridge	Japanese	Isao Shinkai
20	Hiroshi Yoshino	Japanese	14.8.82	North Ridge	Japanese	Isao Shinkai
21	Kazushige Takami	Japanese	15.8.82	North Ridge	Japanese	Isao Shinkai
22	Haruichi Kawamura	Japanese	15.8.82	North Ridge	Japanese	Isao Shinkai
23	Tatsuji Shigeno	Japanese	15.8.82	North Ridge	Japanese	Isao Shinkai
24	Hironobu Kamuro	Japanese	15.8.82	North Ridge	Japanese	Isao Shinkai
25	Agostino Da Polenza	Italian	31.7.83	North Ridge	Italian	Francesco Santon
26	Josef Rakoncaj	Czechoslovak	31.7.83	North Ridge	Italian	Francesco Santon
27	Sergio Martini	Italian	4.8.83	North Ridge	Italian	Francesco Santon
28	Fausto De Stefani	Italian	4.8.83	North Ridge	Italian	Francesco Santon
29	Marcel Ruedi	Swiss	19.6.85	Abruzzi Spur	Swiss	Erhard Loretan
30	Norbert Joos	Swiss	19.6.85	Abruzzi Spur	Swiss	Erhard Loretan
31	Erhard Loretan	Swiss	6.7.85	Abruzzi Spur	Swiss	Erhard Loretan
32	Pierre Morand	Swiss	6.7.85	Abruzzi Spur	Swiss	Erhard Loretan
33	Jean Troillet	Swiss	6.7.85	Abruzzi Spur	Swiss	Erhard Loretan

No.	Name	Nationality	Date	Route	Expedition	Leader
34	Eric Escoffier	French	6.7.85	Abruzzi Spur	French	—
35	Daniel Lacroix	French	7.7.85	Abruzzi Spur	French	—
36	Stéphane Schaffter	Swiss	7.7.85	Abruzzi Spur	French	—
37	Noboru Yamada	Japanese	24.7.85	Abruzzi Spur	Japanese	Kazuoh Tobita
38	Kenji Yoshida	Japanese	24.7.85	Abruzzi Spur	Japanese	Kazuoh Tobita
39	Kazunari Murakami	Japanese	24.7.85	Abruzzi Spur	Japanese	Kazuoh Tobita
40	Wanda Rutkiewicz	Polish	23.6.86	Abruzzi Spur	French	Maurice Barrard
41	Michel Parmentier	French	23.6.86	Abruzzi Spur	French	Maurice Barrard
42	Maurice Barrard	French	23.6.86	Abruzzi Spur	French	Maurice Barrard
43	Liliane Barrard	French	23.6.86	Abruzzi Spur	French	Maurice Barrard
44	Mari Abrego	Spanish (Basque)	23.6.86	Abruzzi Spur	Basque	(Renato Casarotto)
45	Josema Casimiro	Spanish (Basque)	23.6.86	Abruzzi Spur	Basque	(Renato Casarotto)
46	Gianni Calcagno	Italian	5.7.86	Abruzzi Spur	Italian	Agostino Da Polenza
47	Tullio Vidoni	Italian	5.7.86	Abruzzi Spur	Italian	Agostino Da Polenza
48	Soro Dorotei	Italian	5.7.86	Abruzzi Spur	Italian	Agostino Da Polenza
49	Martino Moretti	Italian	5.7.86	Abruzzi Spur	Italian	Agostino Da Polenza
50	Josef Rakoncaj	Czechoslovak	5.7.86	Abruzzi Spur	Italian	Agostino Da Polenza
51	Benoît Chamoux	French	5.7.86	Abruzzi Spur	Italian	Agostino Da Polenza
52	Beda Fuster	Swiss	5.7.86	Abruzzi Spur	International	Karl Herrligkoffer
53	Rolf Zemp	Swiss	5.7.86	Abruzzi Spur	International	Karl Herrligkoffer
54	Jerzy Kukuczka	Polish	8.7.86	South Face	International	Karl Herrligkoffer

No.	Name	Nationality	Date	Route	Expedition	Leader
55	Tadeusz Piotrowski	Polish	8.7.86	South Face	International	Karl Herrligkoffer
56	Chang Bong-Wan	S. Korean	3.8.86	Abruzzi Spur	S. Korean	Kim Byung-Joon
57	Kim Chang-Sun	S. Korean	3.8.86	Abruzzi Spur	S. Korean	Kim Byung-Joon
58	Chang Byong-Ho	S. Korean	3.8.86	Abruzzi Spur	S. Korean	Kim Byung-Joon
59	Wojciech Wröz	Polish	3.8.86	SSW Ridge	Polish	Janusz Majer
60	Przemyslaw Piasecki	Polish	3.8.86	SSW Ridge	Polish	Janusz Majer
61	Peter Bozik	Czechoslovak	3.8.86	SSW Ridge	Polish	Janusz Majer
62	Willi Bauer	Austrian	4.8.86	Abruzzi Spur	Austrian	Alfred Imitzer
63	Alfred Imitzer	Austrian	4.8.86	Abruzzi Spur	Austrian	Alfred Imitzer
64	Alan Rouse	British	4.8.86	Abruzzi Spur	British	Alan Rouse
65	Kurt Diemberger	Austrian	4.8.86	Abruzzi Spur	Italian	Agostino Da Polenza
66	Julie Tullis	British	4.8.86	Abruzzi Spur	Italian	Agostino Da Polenza
67	Hideji Nazuka	Japanese	9.8.90	North Side	Japanese	Tomoji Ueki
68	Hirotaka Imamura	Japanese	9.8.90	North Side	Japanese	Tomoji Ueki
69	Steve Swenson	American	20.8.90	North Spur	American	Steve Swenson
70	Greg Child	Australian	20.8.90	North Spur	American	Steve Swenson
71	Greg Mortimer	Australian	20.8.90	North Spur	American	Steve Swenson
72	Pierre Béghin	French	15.8.91	NW Ridge + N Spur	French	Pierre Béghin
73	Christophe Profit	French	15.8.91	NW Ridge + N Spur	French	Pierre Béghin
74	Vladimir Balyberdin	Russian	1.8.92	Abruzzi Spur	International	Vladimir Balyberdin
75	Gennady Kopieka	Ukranian	1.8.92	Abruzzi Spur	International	Vladimir Balyberdin

No.	Name	Nationality	Date	Route	Expedition	Leader
76	Chantal Mauduit	French	3.8.92	Abruzzi Spur	International	Vladimir Balyberdin
77	Aleksei Nikiforov	Russian	3.8.92	Abruzzi Spur	International	Vladimir Balyberdin
78	Ed Viesturs	American	16.8.92	Abruzzi Spur	International	Vladimir Balyberdin
79	Scott Fischer	American	16.8.92	Abruzzi Spur	International	Vladimir Balyberdin
80	Charley Mace	American	16.8.92	Abruzzi Spur	International	Vladimir Balyberdin
81	Zvenko Pozgaj	Slovenian	13.6.93	Abruzzi Spur	Slovenian	Tomaz Jamnik
82	Carlos Carsolio	Mexican	13.6.93	Abruzzi Spur	Slovenian	Tomaz Jamnik
83	Viki Groselj	Slovenian	13.6.93	Abruzzi Spur	Slovenian	Tomaz Jamnik
84	Stipe Bozic	Croatian	13.6.93	Abruzzi Spur	Slovenian	Tomaz Jamnik
85	Göran Kropp	Swedish	23.6.93	Abruzzi Spur	Slovenian	Tomaz Jamnik
86	Phil Powers	American	7.7.93	Abruzzi Spur	American	Stacy Allison
87	Jim Haberl	Canadian	7.7.93	Abruzzi Spur	American	Stacy Allison
88	Dan Culver	Canadian	7.7.93	Abruzzi Spur	American	Stacy Allison
89	Anatoli Bukreev	Kazakhi	30.7.93	Abruzzi Spur	International	Peter Mezger
90	Peter Mezger	German	30.7.93	Abruzzi Spur	International	Peter Mezger
91	Andrew Lock	Australian	30.7.93	Abruzzi Spur	International	Peter Mezger
92	Rafael Jensen	Danish	30.9.93	Abruzzi Spur	Swedish	Magnus Nilsson
93	Daniel Bidner	Swedish	30.9.93	Abruzzi Spur	Swedish	Magnus Nilsson
94	Reinmar Joswig	German	30.9.93	Abruzzi Spur	International	Peter Mezger
95	Dan Mazur	American	2.9.93	Abruzzi Spur	International	Dan Mazur
96	Jonathan Pratt	British	2.9.93	Abruzzi Spur	International	Dan Mazur

No.	Name	Nationality	Date	Route	Expedition	Leader
97	Juanito Oiarzabal	Basque	23.6.94	SSE Ridge variation	Basque	Juanito Oiarzabal
98	Juan Tomás	Catalan	23.6.94	SSE Ridge variation	Basque	Juanito Oiarzabal
99	Alberto Iñurrategi	Basque	23.6.94	SSE Ridge variation	Basque	Juanito Oiarzabal
100	Félix Iñurrategi	Basque	23.6.94	SSE Ridge variation	Basque	Juanito Oiarzabal
101	Enrique de Pablo	Basque	23.6.94	SSE Ridge variation	Basque	Juanito Oiarzabal
102	Rob Hall	New Zealand	9.7.94	Abruzzi Spur	German	Ralf Dujmovits
103	Mike Groom	Australian	23.7.94	Abruzzi Spur	American	David Bridges
104	Ralf Dujmovits	German	23.7.94	Abruzzi Spur	German	Ralf Dujmovits
105	Veikka Gustafsson	Finnish	23.7.94	Abruzzi Spur	German	Ralf Dujmovits
106	Axel Schlönvogt	German	23.7.94	Abruzzi Spur	German	Ralf Dujmovits
107	Michael Wärthl	German	23.7.94	Abruzzi Spur	German	Ralf Dujmovits
108	Benko Mstislev	Ukranian	23.7.94	Abruzzi Spur	Ukranian	Vadim Sviridenko
109	Vladislav Terzeoul	Ukranian	23.7.94	Abruzzi Spur	Ukranian	Vadim Sviridenko
110	José Carlos Tamayo	Basque	30.7.94	North Spur	Spanish TV	José Carlos Tamayo
111	Sebastián de la Cruz	Argentinian	30.7.94	North Spur	Spanish TV	José Carlos Tamayo
112	Juanjo San Sebastián	Basque	4.8.94	North Spur	Spanish TV	José Carlos Tamayo
113	Atxo Apelllániz	Basque	4.8.94	North Spur	Spanish TV	José Carlos Tamayo

Appendix III

A Complete List of Fatalities on K2 down to 1994

(originally compiled by Xavier Eguskitza for *The Endless Knot* by Kurt Diemberger)

Name	Nationality	Date	Cause	Route
Dudley Wolfe	American	30.7.39	Probably high altitude sickness, exhaustion: in Camp 7 (7550m).	Abruzzi Spur
Pasang Kikuli	Sherpa	31.7.39	Disappeared between Camps 6 and 7.	Abruzzi Spur
Pasang Kitar	Sherpa	31.7.39	Disappeared between Camps 6 and 7.	Abruzzi Spur
Phinsoo	Sherpa	31.7.39	Disappeared between Camps 6 and 7.	Abruzzi Spur
Art Gilkey	American	10.8.53	Avalanche near Camp 7 (7450m)	Abruzzi Spur
Mario Puchoz	Italian	21.6.54	Pneumonia at Camp 2 (5900m).	Abruzzi Spur
Nick Estcourt	British	12.6.78	Avalanche near Camp 2 (6500m).	West Ridge
Ali, son of Kazim	Pakistani	9.6.79	Fall into crevasse.	Savoia Glacier
Laskhar Khan	Pakistani	19.8.79	Heart attack between Camps 3 and 4.	SSW Ridge
Halina Krüger	Polish	30.7.82	Heart attack at Camp 2 (6700m).	Abruzzi Spur
Yukihiro Yanagisawa	Japanese	15.8.82	Fell during descent.	North Ridge
Daniel Lacroix	French	7.7.85	Lost during descent.	Abruzzi Spur
John Smolich	American	21.6.86	Avalanche death at 6000m.	SSW Ridge
Alan Pennington	American	21.6.86	Avalanche death at 6000m.	SSW Ridge

Name	Nationality	Date	Cause	Route
Liliane Barrard	French	24.6.86	Fall during descent.	Abruzzi Spur
Maurice Barrard	French	24.6.86	Fall during descent.	Abruzzi Spur
Tadeusz Piotrowski	Polish	10.7.86	Fall during descent.	Abruzzi Spur
Renato Casarotto	Italian	16.7.86	Fall into crevasse at 5100m.	SSW Ridge
Wojciech Wróz	Polish	3.8.86	Fall during descent.	Abruzzi Spur
Mohammed Ali	Pakistani	4.8.86	Stonefall below Camp 1.	Abruzzi Spur
Julie Tullis	British	7.8.86	Complex of causes, after fall, in Camp 4 (8000m)	Abruzzi Spur
Alan Rouse	British	10.8.86	Probably high altitude sickness and exhaustion, in Camp 4 (8000m).	Abruzzi Spur
Alfred Imitzer	Austrian	10.8.86	Probably high altitude sickness and exhaustion, below Camp 4 (8000m).	Abruzzi Spur
Hannes Wieser	Austrian	10.8.86	Probably high altitude sickness and exhaustion, below Camp 4 (8000m).	Abruzzi Spur
Dobroslawa Wolf	Polish	10.8.86	Unknown (embolism?) between Camps 3 and 2.	Abruzzi Spur
Akira Suzuki	Japanese	24.8.87	Fall from c.8200m.	Abruzzi Spur
Adrián Benítez	Mexican	14.8.92	Rapelling accident.	Abruzzi Spur
Bostjan Kekec	Slovenian	17.6.93	High-altitude sickness.	Abruzzi Spur
Dan Culver	Canadian	7.7.93	Fall.	Abruzzi Spur
Peter Mezger	German	30.7.93	Disappeared during descent from summit.	Abruzzi Spur
Reinmar Joswig	German	30.7.93	Fall.	Abruzzi Spur
Daniel Bidner	Swedish	31.7.93	Cerebral oedema and fall.	Abruzzi Spur
Dmitri Ibragimzade	Ukranian	11.7.94	High-altitude sickness & exhaustion at 8400m.	Abruzzi Spur

Name	Nationality	Date	Cause	Route
Aleksandr Parkhomenko	Ukranian	11.7.94	High-altitude sickness & exhaustion at 8400m.	Abruzzi Spur
Alexei Kharaldin	Ukranian	11.7.94	Fall in Bottleneck.	Abruzzi Spur
Steve Untch	American	26.7.94	Fall when fixed rope broke.	Abruzzi Spur
Atxo Apellániz	Basque	11.8.94	Exhaustion at Camp 2.	North Spur

Note by Xavier Eguskitza: Of the twenty-seven mountaineers who reached the summit of K2 during 1986, seven died on the descent (as well as six others). Since then five more have also died: Michel Parmentier and Petr Bozik on Everest in the autumn of 1988, Jerzy Kukuczka on the South Face of Lhotse in October 1989, Gianni Calcagno on Denali and Wanda Rutkiewicz on Kangchenjunga in 1992.

Appendix IV

A review by Jim Curran of *The Endless Knot: K2 Mountain of Dreams and Destiny* by Kurt Diemberger published in *High* 104, July 1991.

It is now five years since the grim summer of 1986 when thirteen people died on K2. Since then a plethora of books and articles have been written, analysing, criticising and disagreeing over a lot of what happened. Recriminations, bitterness and controversy have abounded. It has become public knowledge that Kurt Diemberger and I have had our differences of opinion, since the shared days at Base Camp immediately after the final tragedies. Why, then, am I reviewing this book? I am certainly not a disinterested observer; some might feel that my motives are suspect. What is Jim Curran, of all people, doing reviewing the book of the man who has so frequently criticised his own?

The answer is simple. The book *The Endless Knot* is an outstanding work and I want to pay full tribute to it and its author. It is a book of many elements, a monumental epic, a tale of human frailty, a highly emotional and romantic view of people and places, an invaluable reference book and above all a moving and lasting tribute to Julie Tullis in particular, but also to Al Rouse and all those who died on the mountain. The book sets out to tell the story of Kurt and Julie's obsession with K2, the Crystal Mountain, and their three attempts to climb their Mountain of Mountains. In the telling of the story many other issues are touched on. Sometimes the book takes on a dreamlike quality: events are juxtaposed, overlaid and interrelated in a way that I found compulsive reading, if occasionally slightly fragmentary and confusing. Throughout the book a constant question is posed though the answer is never given. Are Kurt and Julie victims or masters of their own destiny and, it follows, are any of us? If we choose to climb, life and death decisions frequently have to be made. Most, as in 'ordinary' life, are common sense, some, like those made on K2 in 1986, have far-reaching effects, and very few can be compared to the throw of the dice.

Throughout Kurt's book destiny versus rational calculation is revealed as a constant struggle. Premonitions, feelings, 'inner voices' and intuition are listened to, and contrasted with cold logic and reason. Sometimes one side holds sway, sometimes the other. But above all, there is the raw emotional conviction that he and Julie have a pre-ordained path that will lead them eventually to the summit of K2. Their tryst with destiny is fulfilled, but at what cost?

Throughout his almost spiritual journey, Kurt tells the stories of their first two attempts on the mountain as well as his two successes on Broad Peak with Herman Bull and, twenty-seven years later, with Julie herself. These are comprehensive and detailed accounts giving another perspective to the ground covered by Julie Tullis in *Clouds From Both Sides*, her posthumously published autobiography. All this is preparation for the bulk of the book – the events of 1986 and in particular the final days when six of the thirteen deaths occurred on the upper slopes of the Abruzzi Spur. Firsthand we read in awful and compelling detail the events surrounding the storm on the Shoulder of K2, the nightmare decline into apathy and exhaustion of the trapped climbers and the heartbreaking farewells that Kurt has to make, first to Julie, dead in her wrecked tent, and then the agonising decision to leave Al Rouse, sinking into coma in the squalid remains of the tent that Kurt and the Polish woman climber, Mrufka Wolf, have survived in for six nights. It goes without saying that these pages are harrowing in the extreme. Few will finish these final chapters without shedding tears of sorrow and of pity for everyone involved in the whole ghastly saga.

One of the main values of the book must be to question the contemporary state of Himalayan mountaineering. While controversy rages on the home front over the use, or misuse, of bolts and hold chipping, environmental concerns and climbing competitions, the vastly experienced Kurt Diemberger poses similar hard questions about tactics and ethics in the greater ranges. Alpine-style versus expedition-style? Safety in numbers? Should teams use 'easy' routes for descent having completed hard ones? What obligations do climbers from different expeditions have to each other? How can the various authorities in Pakistan, China, India and Nepal regulate the increasing masses? These are questions that need to be addressed and more conclusions drawn pretty quickly in order, as Kurt says, that climbers 'can drink tea together in their overcrowded Base Camps as real companions and not as victims of an illusion'.

It was, in the broadest sense, a multiple failure of communications that led to the desperate situation on the Shoulder of K2 in the first two weeks of August. Selfishness, misplaced ambition, unspoken assumptions and broken promises all played their part. Five years later many of the subtle threads that wove the complex tapestry seem to have become rather less important, other factors now seem much clearer. And of course there are some poignant 'if onlys . . .' that remain. If only the overcrowded personnel at Camp IV had had the individual or collective will to dig a snowhole then the Austrians would not have needed to crowd into Al Rouse's and the Korean tents on the fateful night of 2/3 August. Then Kurt, Julie, Al and Mrufka could have gone to the summit on 3 August instead of wasting the extra day which proved so costly . . . If only just Kurt and Julie had followed Kurt's deepest instincts and gone with the Koreans on the 3rd then the subsequent overcrowding in the storms would have been alleviated somewhat and Julie in all probability would have got down alive . . . If only Hannes Wieser had taken up the offer on 4 August to descend with the two Polish climbers instead of waiting for his two Austrian summiteers . . . If only Mrufka had taken a figure-of-eight descendeur with her . . . If only . . . If only . . .

But none of these things happened. Which brings me to the only difficulty with the book. In his analysis Kurt has not minced his words about some of the decisions that were made and is highly critical of any accounts that differ from his own. Thus the Austrians and in particular Willi Bauer are frequently portrayed as the villains of the piece and no doubt Bauer must take some share of responsibility. But some of Kurt's own obsessive nitpicking, while understandable at the time, now seems irrelevant. Was Julie pulled into Camp IV, or did she crawl? Did Kurt and Julie get to the summit at five thirty or seven p.m.? No one except Kurt or Willi will ever really know, and even Kurt admits to having confused recollections of some of the events. Does it really matter? Kurt does tend to set himself up as the sole repository of the truth but even he can make the odd factual mistake. For example at Advance Base his own and Julie's tent was left standing, equipped with cooker, water and matches until the very day Kurt descended, when it was stolen by a Balti porter (who had undertaken to me not to touch it). In Kurt's account he states flatly that the site was cleared a week after they were last seen ascending. 'We had been left for dead.' Not, in the event, an important point, as we realised what had happened in time, but it does show how easy it is to get things slightly wrong and how out of proportion errors can seem when they affect you. But now perhaps I am falling into the same trap . . .

What does matter though is the bigger picture. In 1986 too many people spent too long too high with too little food and fuel. Circumstances led them into decisions that allowed too little margin for error and the subsequent price paid was (obviously) far too great. Kurt Diemberger's book will, I hope, stand both as a monument to the event, as a warning to all who challenge high mountains and, hopefully, as a spur to climbers everywhere to ask themselves some awkward questions. On the last count I am not very optimistic. I have just read an intriguing (as yet unpublished) new account of the 1939 expedition to K2 when Dudley Wolfe and three Sherpas were lost on the Shoulder of K2. Fifty-two years ago the complex sequence of events leading to the disaster were of course different from 1986 but there were also uncanny parallels. Will we ever learn? '*Plus ça change, plus c'est la même chose!*'

Last but not least I would like to record my personal appreciation of the generous and moving words Kurt has written of Al Rouse. In the aftermath of the tragedy I did not quite appreciate just how much Al had contributed in trying his utmost to help out in a whole variety of ways. Kurt pays fulsome tribute to Al's 'fairness and helpfulness . . . his endless energy', to 'good kind Alan who took my arm and tried to comfort me when Julie died . . .' These words and more like them will also bring some comfort to us in knowing that in his last days Al behaved as we would have expected him, with care and compassion to his fellow men.

A Select Bibliography

John Barry, *K2 Savage Mountain, Savage Summer* (Oxford Illustrated Press, 1987)
A personal account of the British expedition to the North-West Face in 1986.

Robert Bates, *Five Miles High* (Dodd, Mead, 1939)
A classic account of the 1938 American expedition.

Louis Baume, *Sivalaya* (West Col, 1978)
Standard reference for the 8000-metre peaks.

Cherie Bech, *Living on the Edge* (David & Charles, 1987)
Contains a personal account of the 1978 American expedition.

Walter Bonatti, *On the Heights* (Hart-Davis, 1964; Diadem, 1979)
Chapter on author's bivouac on the Abruzzi Shoulder in 1954.

Chris Bonington, *The Everest Years* (Hodder & Stoughton, 1986)
Chapter on 1978 West Ridge expedition and death of Nick Estcourt.

Chris Bonington, *The Climbers* (Hodder & Stoughton/BBC Books, 1992)
Contains several K2 accounts, including Wiessner's 1939 attempt.

Riccardo Cassin, *50 Years of Alpinism* (Diadem/Mountaineers, 1981)
Chapter on K2 reconnaissances with Desio in 1953.

Benoît Chamoux, *Le Vertige de l'Infinie* (Albin Michel, 1988)
Chapter on author's twenty-three-hour ascent of the Abruzzi Spur in 1986.

Greg Child, *Mixed Emotions* (Mountaineers, 1993)
Three chapters on K2, including author's ascent of North Ridge.

Martin Conway, *Climbing and Exploration in the Karakoram-Himalayas* (Fisher Unwin, 1894)
His exploration around the Karakoram and ascent of Pioneer Peak in 1892.

Aleister Crowley, *The Confessions of Aleister Crowley* (Bantam, 1971)
His autobiography, containing a first-hand account of the Eckenstein expedition.

Jim Curran, *K2: Triumph and Tragedy* (Hodder & Stoughton, 1987)
The events of 1986, when thirteen climbers died on K2.

Ardito Desio, *Ascent of K2* (Elek Books, 1955)
The Italian first ascent by Compagnoni and Lacedelli.

Kurt Diemberger, *The Endless Knot: K2, Mountain of Dreams and Destiny* (Grafton Books, 1981)
A personal account of author's attempts on K2 and the 1986 tragedies.

Gunter Dyhrenfurth, *To the Third Pole* (Laurie, 1955)
A history of the high Himalayan peaks.

Oscar Eckenstein, *The Karakorams and Kashmir* (Fisher Unwin, 1896)
An account of Conway's 1892 expedition.

Filippo de Filippi, *Karakoram and the Western Himalaya* (Constable, 1912)
The authorised account of the Duke of the Abruzzi's 1909 expedition.

Peter Fleming, *Bayonets to Lhasa* (Hart-Davis, 1961)
Contains much information about Sir Francis Younghusband.

Peter Gillman, *In Balance* (Hodder & Stoughton, 1989)
Includes reports on the death of Nick Estcourt and the 1986 tragedies.

Charles Houston and Robert Bates, *K2: The Savage Mountain* (Collins, 1955, Diadem/Mountaineers, 1979; and to mark the fortieth anniversary of the ascent, Edward Burlingame, Adventure Library series, 1995).
Classic account of the American 1953 expedition.

Robert Julyan, *Mountain Names* (Mountaineers, 1984)
Sources and derivations of the names of many of the world's most famous peaks.

Andrew J. Kauffman and William L. Putnam, *K2: The 1939 Tragedy* (Mountaineers/Diadem 1992)
An exhaustive analysis of the 1939 disaster.

John Keay, *When Men and Mountains Meet* (Murray, 1977)
Scholarly account of early explorations of the Karakoram and Western Himalaya.

Zbigniew Kowaleski and Andrej Packowski, *Karakoram, Polskie Wyprawj Alpinistyczne* (Wydawnictwo Sport 1 Turystyka, Warsaw, 1986)
An extensive account of Polish mountaineering in the Karakoram.

Jerzy Kukuczka, *My Vertical World* (Hodder & Stoughton, 1992)
His autobiography, containing a chapter on his new route on the South Face of K2 in 1986.

Fosco Maraini, *Karakoram: the ascent of Gasherbrum IV* (Hutchinson, 1961)
Informative classic of Karakoram history.

Kenneth Mason, *Abode of Snow* (Diadem/Mountaineers Reprint, 1983)
History of Himalayan exploration with several K2 sections.

Teruo Matsuura, *K2 West Face* (Waseda University, 1982)
Contains an English precis of the Japanese first ascent of the West Face/Ridge.

Museo Nazionale della Montagna, *Alpinismo Italiano in Karakoram*, 1991.
Contains a useful section on early Italian exploration on K2 with an English precis.

Museo Nazionale della Montagna, *K2 Millenovecontrocinquantaquattro* 1994
Marking the fortieth anniversary of the first ascent in 1954.

Gertrude Reinisch and Willi Bauer, *Licht und Schatten am K2* (Pinguin-Verlag, Innsbruck, 1988)
Willi Bauer's ghosted account of the events of 1986.

Rick Ridgeway, *The Last Step: The American Ascent of K2* (Mountaineers, 1980)
First ascent of the North-East Ridge and first oxygenless ascent of K2 by Lou Reichardt.

Galen Rowell, *In the Throne Room of the Mountain Gods* (Sierra Club/Allen & Unwin, 1977)
Story of the ill-fated 1975 American expedition and history of K2.

Doug Scott, *Himalayan Climber* (Diadem/Mountaineers, 1992)
Accounts of 1978 and 1980 expeditions and attempt on a new route to the left of the Abruzzi Spur.

Eric Shipton, *Blank on the Map* (Hodder & Stoughton, 1936), reissued in *The Six Mountain Travel Books* (Diadem/Mountaineers, 1985).
Shipton's inspirational account of exploration north of K2 in 1937.

Joe Tasker, *Savage Arena* (Eyre Methuen, 1982) reissued in *The Boardman Tasker Omnibus* (Hodder & Stoughton, 1995)
Contains chapters with graphic details on K2 expedition in 1978 and 1980.

Julie Tullis, *Clouds From Both Sides* (Grafton, 1986)
Autobiography with two K2 chapters; the paperback edition (Grafton, 1987) has a 1986 K2 postscript by Peter Gillman.

Walt Unsworth, *Because It Is There* (Gollancz, 1968)
Chapter on Oscar Eckenstein.

Walt Unsworth, *Encyclopaedia of Mountaineering*, updated version (Hodder & Stoughton, 1992)

Walt Unsworth, *Hold the Heights: The Foundations of Mountaineering* (Hodder & Stoughton, 1994)
Contains some early history of K2.

Fanny Bullock Workman, *In the Ice World of the Himalaya* (Fisher Unwin, 1900)
Accounts of travels in the Karakoram.

Arata Yamada, *The Way to Chogori* (Asahi and Shimbun, 1982)
Account of the first ascent of the North Ridge.

Sir Francis Younghusband, *The Heart of a Continent* (Murray, 1986)
Contains the story of crossing the Mustagh Pass and journey around the Karakoram and Kashmir.

Index

Page-numbers in *italics* refer to the Appendices

Continued overleaf

Continued overleaf